Mobilising China's One-Child Generation

Series Editors: Victoria M. Basham and Sarah Bulmer

The Critical Military Studies series welcomes original thinking on the ways in which military power works within different societies and geopolitical arenas.

Militaries are central to the production and dissemination of force globally but the enduring legacies of military intervention are increasingly apparent at the societal and personal bodily levels as well, demonstrating that violence and war-making function on multiple scales. At the same time, the notion that violence is as an appropriate response to wider social and political problems transcends militaries: from private security, to seemingly 'non-military' settings such as fitness training and schooling, the legitimisation and normalisation of authoritarianism and military power occurs in various sites. This series seeks original, high-quality manuscripts and edited volumes that engage with such questions of how militaries, militarism and militarisation assemble and disassemble worlds touched and shaped by violence in these multiple ways. It will showcase innovative and interdisciplinary work that engages critically with the operation and effects of military power and provokes original questions for researchers and students alike.

Available Titles:

Resisting Militarism: Direct Action and the Politics of Subversion
Chris Rossdale
Making War on Bodies: Militarisation, Aesthetics and Embodiment in International Politics
Catherine Baker
Disordered Violence: How Gender, Race and Heteronormativity Structure Terrorism
Caron Gentry
Sex and the Nazi Soldier: Violent, Commercial and Consensual Contacts during the War in the Soviet Union, 1941–1945
Regina Mühlhäuser (translated by Jessica Spengler)
The Military-Peace Complex: Gender and Materiality in Afghanistan
Hannah Partis-Jennings
Politics of Impunity: Torture, The Armed Forces and the Failure of Transitional Justice in Brazil
Henrique Tavares Furtado
Conscientious Objection in Turkey: A Socio-legal Analysis of the Right to Refuse Military Service
Demet Çaltekin
Poetic Prosthetics: Trauma and Language in Contemporary Veteran Writing
Ron Ben-Tovim
The Gendered and Colonial Lives of Gurkhas in Private Security: From Military to Market
Amanda Chisholm
Martialling Peace: How the Peacekeeper Myth Legitimises Warfare
Nicole Wegner
Inhabiting No-Man's-Land: Army Wives, Gender and Militarisation
Alexandra Hyde
Settler Military Politics: Militarisation and the Aesthetics of War Commemoration
Federica Caso
Mobilising China's One-Child Generation: Education, Nationalism and Youth Militarisation in the PRC
Orna Naftali
The Cultural Politics of Veterans' Narratives: Beyond the Wire
Nick Caddick

Forthcoming:

War and Militarisation: The British, Canadian and Dutch Invasion of Southern Afghanistan
Paul Dixon
The Militarisation of British Democracy: The Iraq and Afghan Wars and the Rise of Authoritarianism
Paul Dixon

Mobilising China's One-Child Generation

Education, Nationalism and Youth Militarisation in the PRC

ORNA NAFTALI

EDINBURGH
University Press

Edinburgh University Press is one of the leading university presses in the UK. We publish academic books and journals in our selected subject areas across the humanities and social sciences, combining cutting-edge scholarship with high editorial and production values to produce academic works of lasting importance. For more information visit our website: edinburghuniversitypress.com

© Orna Naftali, 2024, 2026

Edinburgh University Press Ltd
13 Infirmary Street
Edinburgh EH1 1LT

First published in hardback by Edinburgh University Press 2024

Typeset in 11/13 ITC Giovanni Std by
Cheshire Typesetting Ltd, Cuddington, Cheshire, and
printed and bound by CPI Group (UK) Ltd,
Croydon, CR0 4YY

A CIP record for this book is available from the British Library

ISBN 978-1-3995-1941-0 (hardback)
ISBN 978-1-3995-1942 7 (paperback)
ISBN 978-1-3995-1943-4 (webready PDF)
ISBN 978-1-3995-1944-1 (epub)

The right of Orna Naftali to be identified as the author of this work has been asserted in accordance with the Copyright, Designs and Patents Act 1988, and the Copyright and Related Rights Regulations 2003 (SI No. 2498).

CONTENTS

Acknowledgements	vi
Introduction: Nationalism, Militarisation and Youth Education in China	1
1. The Militarisation of Education in Modern China	31
2. War and Peace in China's History Textbooks	64
3. 'Don't Get Soft': Youth Military Training in China	91
4. Military Entertainment, Gender and the Nation	117
5. Youth Notions of Armed Conflict: 'If Peace Is Our Goal, Why Use War to Attain It?'	145
6. Youth Views of the PLA: 'You Can Serve the Country in More Than One Way'	171
Conclusion: Rethinking the Militarisation of Chinese Youth in the Xi Era	197
References	206
Index	254

ACKNOWLEDGEMENTS

This book is the product of more than a decade of research, as well as numerous discussions with colleagues working on childhood, youth and militarisation in East Asia and beyond. First and foremost, I owe an immense debt of gratitude to my long-time research associate in China, JH. Our close collaboration over the years has been a true inspiration and has reshaped my thinking on many of the issues covered in the book. Moreover, without JH's sustained help throughout the years, the collection of field data presented in the book would not have been possible. I am additionally indebted to Sabine Frühstück at the University of California, Santa Barbara, who first pointed me in the direction of the book's topic, and whose groundbreaking work on the militarisation of childhood in Japan and elsewhere, along with her generous advice throughout the years, have been invaluable in helping me chart the trajectory of my argument.

I am also grateful for critical conversations about different themes which inform my writing of this book, with Louise Edwards at the University of New South Wales, with Dafna Zur at Stanford, as well as with the various participants and audience members in workshops and conferences at which I presented my work on the militarisation of Chinese childhood and youth over the past decade or so. These include the 'Education, War and Peace' conference (University of London, 2014); the 'All I Need Is Love? Nation, Affect and Aversion in a Post-Imagined-Community Asia' workshop (National Taiwan Normal University, 2015); the 'Studying Rural Chinese Society in the 21st Century: Emerging Themes and New Challenges' workshop (Hebrew University, 2015), and the 'Army, Politics, and Society in East Asia' workshop (Hebrew University,

2020). I am also thankful for the productive exchanges at panels presented at the annual meeting of the Association for Asian Studies (Honolulu, 2012); the European Social Science History Conference (Glasgow, 2012), the Social Science History Association (SSHA) (Montreal, 2017), the Conference of Asian Studies in Israel (Hebrew University, 2018), and the International Convention of Asia Scholars (ICAS) (Leiden, 2019).

As always, the support of my colleagues in the Department of Asian Studies at the Hebrew University of Jerusalem has meant a lot to me. In particular, I would like to thank Nissim Otmazgin for the many fruitful discussions on the role of popular culture in shaping popular nationalism and international relations in the East Asian region. A sabbatical from the Hebrew University and research grants from the Spencer Foundation, the Israel Science Foundation (grant 405/12), and the Harry S. Truman Research Institute for the Advancement of Peace at HU facilitated support for this project.

I am also grateful to Brendan Maartens at the University of Liverpool for first directing me to the Advances in Critical Military Studies Series at Edinburgh University Press (EUP), and for putting me in touch with the co-editors of the series, Victoria Basham at Cardiff University, and Sarah Bulmer at the University of Exeter. Victoria and Sarah have been the most wonderful series editors, and I am thankful for their encouragement and sustained support for the project. I also wish to thank Ersev Ersoy, Sam Johnson and the rest of the editorial team at EUP, as well as the anonymous reviewers of the initial book proposal, who made crucial suggestions on how to better articulate the book's arguments. Fiona Cole has been an assiduous copyeditor – thank you for your patience and your meticulous work. I dedicate this book to my father, Gideon, who has inspired my passion for academic enquiry, and to my husband and daughters who have supported my work throughout the years.

INTRODUCTION

Nationalism, Militarisation and Youth Education in China

In May 2023, a Chinese stand-up comic made a joke that landed him in trouble. Li Haoshi, a 31-year-old Shanghai comedian who performs under the stage name House, had joked that seeing his adopted stray dogs chasing squirrels reminded him of the slogan 'Forge exemplary conduct, fight to win' (*Zuofeng youliang! Nengda shenzhang!*). The phrase came from a 2013 speech by Chinese leader Xi Jinping praising the work ethic of the People's Liberation Army (PLA), and over the past decade has become a motto Chinese soldiers shout during parades. Li's joke also recalls a famous scene in a 1956 propaganda film, 'Battle on Shangganling Mountain (in Chinese, *Shangganling*)', which depicts Chinese fighters in Korea chasing a squirrel (Boyd 2023, Che and Wang 2023).

The joke appears to have gone well – at first. On an audio recording of Li's show, the crowd can be heard laughing. Later, however, an anonymous audience member took to the popular microblogging website *Weibo* to claim that Li had disparaged 'the People's soldiers'. The post became viral and ignited a heated debate on Chinese social media. Some commentators argued that there was no insult to the military while others accused Li of mocking 'martyrs' of the Korean War (Boyd 2023; Ye 2023). Li hurriedly apologised on social media for his 'incredibly inappropriate metaphor', but it was too late. Beijing authorities accused the comedian of 'severely insulting' the PLA, a criminal offence under Chinese law.[1] Li was detained by the police (at the time of writing his whereabouts are still unknown), and some of his online defenders also found themselves in trouble with the authorities. All shows by the comedy studio that employed Li were suspended. The authorities confiscated the profits from the show in which he made the offending joke and fined the studio nearly $USD2 million (Boyd 2023; Ye 2023).

The scandal which developed around a seemingly minor remark attests to the Chinese government's heightened sensitivity about the military's image and its efforts to control all forms of public speech about the PLA. The incident underscores the role of the military in shaping modern Chinese nationalism. It further demonstrates the tension between official and popular constructions of the military and armed conflict in contemporary China.

These themes are at the centre of this book which sets out to explore how the Chinese government presents the tropes of war and the military to its youngest citizens and to discover whether these official representations contribute to the militarisation of youth and their education in twenty-first century China.

Over the past several decades, the Chinese government has implemented a systematic Patriotic Education (PE) campaign and an expanded National Defence Education (NDE) programme. Both programmes encompass the entire populace, but they have an explicit focus on the country's youngest citizens. The stated aims of the PE and NDE programmes are to foster 'love' for the nation, the army and the Communist Party of China (CPC), to inculcate national defence values and knowledge, to mobilise the population to fight modern wars in the information age and to encourage well-educated youth to join the military. Additionally, China's National Defence programmes are meant to teach youth 'discipline' and temper their willpower, foster their 'organisational ability', and develop their collective spirit (Zhonghua renmin gongheguo jiaoyu bu [Ministry of Educationof the PRC] 2021).

How have Chinese schools applied these goals in practice? What role has the PLA played in the implementation of the PE and NDE programmes within and outside the school? And how do Chinese youths of diverse backgrounds react to the programmes' messages about the role of the military and war-waging in the protection of the country's national interests? By providing answers to these questions, the book aims to address the broader issue of whether Chinese education encourages youth to admire the military and regard military intervention as both justified and necessary, issues that have become particularly important amid China's worsening geopolitical environment in the Xi Jinping era.

National Security, the 'China Dream' and China's Foreign Relations in the Xi Era

Over the past decade, China has stated its aspirations for global leadership on various issues of international governance while building a growing number of international partnerships (Hass 2022). It has also pursued an increasingly assertive foreign policy. This trend, which began in the latter years of the Hu Jintao era (2002–12), intensified under Xi Jinping's administration (2012–), leading to concern among China's neighbours and especially in Western countries, where commentators and politicians have called Chinese policies 'high reaching', 'intransigent' and 'aggressive' (Coutaz 2019, 36).

Shortly after assuming his post as the CPC's top leader in 2012, Xi Jinping presented a new vision of the 'China Dream (*Zhonggguo meng*)' which stakes the Communist Party's persistence in power on the restoration of China's greatness. Promoting 'an unwieldy combination of individual dreams for the good life, and collective dreams for a wealthy and powerful nation' (Callahan 2017, 253), the 'China Dream' vision, which also features the building of a strong military, reiterates China's claim to take its rightful 'place in the top tier of the international power hierarchy' (S. Zhao 2023, 2).

As part of this vision, Xi launched an ambitious international cooperation programme under the banner of the Belt and Road Initiative (2013–). China has reportedly committed one trillion dollars of capital to the programme, which at the time of writing encompasses more than 150 countries, with more than 200 agreements signed. Some government officials and economic actors in recipient countries, particularly in the Global South, have welcomed Chinese investments. However, in many signatory countries, China's investments have also generated pushback related to issues such as the 'debt trap'; the use of Chinese contractors, labourers and raw materials instead of local resources; environmental and social impacts; and corruption (Nathan and Zhang 2022, 61).

Moreover, some analysts see China's Belt and Road Initiative as a cover for strategic self-interest. In Africa, some speculate that China collaborates with coastal countries as a step towards establishing bases that will enable it to project naval power into the Indian Ocean on the east and the Atlantic on the west. In Latin America, China has built a giant satellite and space mission control station in Argentina, a potential source of militarily useful intelligence on the continent (Nathan and Zhang 2022, 61). Closer to home, in the South China

Sea, China under the leadership of Xi Jinping has raced ahead of other territorial claimants in building large, militarily fortified artificial islands (Nathan and Zhang 2022, 61).

These actions have been accompanied by a noticeable shift in China's military policy under Xi Jinping. Wide-ranging military reforms introduced over the past decade include downsizing the PLA ground force through a reduction of 300,000 personnel and expanding the technology-intensive services, steps which some experts claim, are intended to enhance the Chinese military's capability to carry out external missions. Indeed, besides safeguarding what China perceives to be its sovereignty and security interests regarding Taiwan and the Yellow, East and South China Seas, China's 2019 Defence White Paper highlights the role of the PLA in providing security for the country's expanding development interests overseas, including energy and resources supplies, vital sea lanes, and overseas Chinese personnel, property and investment (Li 2022, 99).

Concurrently, in recent years, the Chinese leadership under Xi has begun to shift the party's discourse beyond an emphasis on the primacy of the economic development model of the 1980s onwards to an equal emphasis on 'comprehensive national security' (*zongti guojia anquan guan*) (H. Wang 2023, 529). This concept did not emerge out of thin air (Drinhausen and Legarda 2022, 6). Rather, it follows a continuous expansion that dates to the foundation of the People's Republic of China (PRC) in 1949. Since the Mao era (1949–76), the Communist Party of China has maintained its overarching goal – retaining its hold on power – which rests on the conviction that only the CPC can return China to its 'rightful place in the world' (Drinhausen and Legarda 2022, 6).

Xi's current notion of 'comprehensive national security' similarly emphasises the interaction of 'international security, domestic security, and regime security' (Pu 2022, 181–2). This holistic view embraces both traditional risks such as threats to China's territorial integrity and threats emanating from foreign military power, as well as non-traditional risks, ranging from climate change, pandemics and mass migration to 'cultural' and 'ideological security'. The last two challenges are seen as equally likely 'to emanate from within China as they are from without', and are related to the effects of social modernisation and the deepening of economic, financial and technological globalisation since the launching of economic reform and Open Door policy in the 1980s (Blanchette 2022, 3).

Over the past decade, 'military and territorial security' has focused not only on a defence of the PRC's claims in the South and East China Seas, but also on competition with the United States for primacy in the Indo-Pacific (Drinhausen and Legarda 2022, 6; Hass 2022). In 2020, the PLA engaged in its first lethal border conflict with India since 1975 followed by a sizeable military build-up along the disputed border. China also increased its hostile behaviour across the region with escalated military coercion against Bhutan and Japan; the sinking of a Vietnamese boat in the South China Sea where it made sweeping new claims; the imposition of economic sanctions on Australia and South Korea; cyberattacks on Australia and India; and the promulgation of the Hong Kong National Security Law following waves of anti-Beijing demonstrations in the city (Saunders 2020, 189; H. Wang 2023, 539).

Under Xi Jinping, CPC rhetoric has also given unprecedented urgency to 'reunification' with Taiwan – by whatever means. While previously unthinkable, the prospect of the PLA prevailing in a cross-Strait conflict has become an increasing possibility in the wake of decades of military reforms and modernisation (West and Insisa 2023, 1). Amid the rise in cross-Strait tensions after the visit of US House Speaker Nancy Pelosi to Taiwan in August 2022, many observers, particularly in the USA, have become convinced that China will attempt to take the island by force, though at the time of writing there is disagreement over the timing of such an action.

When Russia invaded Ukraine in February 2022, some predicted that the attack presaged China's own assault on Taiwan. Three weeks prior to the Ukraine invasion, Xi reaffirmed China and Russia's strategic relationship against the USA, while the PLA conducted naval war games with Russia, launched China's third-largest air-force incursion around Taiwan, and flew a fighter jet within metres of US military aircraft in the South China Sea (S. Zhao 2023, 6). Some observers believe the attack could happen by 2027, the centenary of the founding of the Chinese military, a milestone that Xi Jinping planted for the transformation of the PLA into a 'world-class' military. Others suggest 2049, the second centenary of China's 'great rejuvenation (*weida fuxing*)' (Drinhausen and Legarda 2022, 6; S. Zhao 2022, 705).

But some China and military experts have pointed out that the PLA would struggle to subjugate Taiwan at acceptable costs and risks (S. Zhao 2022, 705). In the first three decades after the establishment of the PRC, the military was mired in external conflicts involving

China's neighbours. The country fought a costly war in the Korean peninsula in the early 1950s, small border wars with India in the 1960s and contended against the former Soviet Union in the early 1970s. And yet the Chinese military has not experienced serious warfare since 1979 when it invaded Vietnam – and was routed. Taiwan, protected by a strait, armed with American weapons and supported by the US military, would pose the PLA's biggest challenge. Its success is not guaranteed (Shambaugh, 2020).

Previous studies of the PLA's likely fighting capacity often assume negligible resistance to service in the event of a cross-strait conflict, but China analysts have raised the possibility of resistance within the military should the country attack Taiwan (Hundman 2023, 573). Most of Taiwan's population is (Han) Chinese, and many trace familial descent to the Chinese mainland. Moreover, the CPC's enormous political investment in the mission of reunification might stir a domestic backlash if the operation struggles (S. Zhao 2022, 705; Liu and Li 2023, 3–5). China's military budget has ballooned over the past decade,[2] yet according to some estimates Beijing still spends more on domestic security than it does on the PLA, which suggests that public legitimacy remains vital to the CPC (Hass 2022, 13; Pu 2022, 185).

The party's growing concerns about 'ideological security' are further illustrated in a new 'Patriotic Education law' (Zhonghua renmin gongheguo aiguozhuyi jiaoyu fa, adopted October 2023, effective January 2024). While the contents of the law are not fundamentally novel, it offers a legal framework for existing practices while underscoring the continuous tightening of ideological control under Xi Jinping. The law requires that all educational institutes, cultural, and media bodies, including Internet information service providers, strengthen the creation and dissemination of patriotic content among citizens of all ages. It targets specific groups for focused patriotic education, including religious groups, overseas Chinese, and residents of Hong Kong, Macao, and Taiwan. Minors (defined in China as persons under 18) are another key group, and parents are urged to 'include love of the motherland in family education' (National People's Congress 2023). Stipulating that patriotic education should 'combine carrying forward the spirit of patriotism with expanding openness to the world', the law nonetheless highlights the importance of 'national security and defence'. It further lays out a list of punishable offenses that range from 'undermining the dignity' of the national anthem, flag, and emblems to 'distorting' or 'negating the deeds and spirit of heroes and martyrs', 'denying acts of aggression' by foreign countries, and 'destroying or defiling patriotic education facilities' (Ibid.).

And yet, even as the Chinese government has increased its reliance on 'nationalism and repression' in response to mounting challenges at home and abroad (Hass 2022), these ideological efforts have not been entirely effective. A growing number of studies demonstrate that although state-led nationalism has fed into and even encouraged expressions of popular nationalism in China, much of the nationalist activity of the past several decades has come from intellectuals with no official affiliation or from independently organised, grassroots movements (Gries 2004; Weatherley and Zhang 2017). Nationalist expressions in academic circles, in the media and popular culture spheres, on the Internet or in street demonstrations have not always aligned with the narratives – or the strategic interests – of the Party-state (Gries 2004; Nyíri 2009; S. Zhao 2013; Zhang, Liu and Wen 2018; Zhang and Ma 2023).

Before discussing the results of these studies and their implications for the book's discussion of the militarisation of Chinese youth and education, it would be useful to situate the inquiry within the broader theoretical framework of Critical Military Studies and specifically the recent work on the militarisation of childhood in different national contexts.

The Militarisation of Children in Conflict and Non-conflict Zones

Militarisation is a controversial concept. Though scholars sometimes employ it synonymously with the term 'militarism', the latter is much narrower in scope and focuses on the political realm, often referring to the ability of martial values to drive government policies and priorities (Hughes 2017, 54). In contrast, 'militarisation' draws our attention to both the material and non-material nature of military dominance. This broader definition, which has been used by scholars in critical military studies, sociology and anthropology, and international relations, understands 'militarisation' not only as the 'intensification of the labor and resources allocated to military purposes' (Lutz 2018, 321–2), but also as a discursive process through which military objectives and priorities extend into civilian life and contribute to the production of a 'militarised ethos' among non-combatants (Shepherd 2018; Enloe 2000; Pennell 2020). A 'militarised ethos' is understood as a set of values and beliefs according to which 'the world is a dangerous place'; 'having enemies is a natural condition'; a militarised response to threat is both 'normal' and 'justified'; and warfare is a particularly effective solution to international disputes (Enloe 2004, 219; Pennell 2020, 384). In this broader sense, militarisation can also imply the spread of the military's characteristic organisational techniques, routines and attitudes into civilian realms (Enloe 2007).

Drawing on these definitions, the discussion in this book assumes that militarisation is connected not only to the increasing size of armies and/or the resurgence of militant 'nationalism', that is, an ideology based on the premise of the individual's loyalty and devotion to the nation-state, but also to the formation of hierarchies of ethnicity, class, gender and sexuality in a society.

Scholarship in Critical Military Studies has demonstrated that the armed forces are a gendered institution. Their structures, practices, values, rites and rituals reflect conventionalised and widely accepted images of masculinity and femininity (Thomas 2009, 97). Military and warfare have never been exclusively male domains, but even where the military has opened to women soldiers, this process has not disrupted patriarchal gender relations (Yuval-Davis 1993, 626; Enloe 1983). Women have been 'relegated to minor, often symbolic, roles in nationalist movements and conflicts, either as icons of nationhood, to be elevated and defended, or as the booty or spoils of war, to be denigrated and disgraced' (Nagel 1998, 244; Enloe 1990).

The legitimisation of war and the military is often accompanied by the circulation of a hegemonic masculinity model (Connell 1987). Although there have been variations in these hegemonic masculinities around the world, the model commonly identifies men with the 'army', 'strength', 'domination', 'endurance and bravado', and 'heterosexual virility', while devaluing the 'feminine' and women for their association with 'weakness', 'peace' and 'peacefulness', and the 'civilian realm' (Thomas 2009, 99, 101; Higate and Hopton 2005; Kao 2017; Nagel 2017). In societies in which the maintenance of a strong army and war-making is associated with the advancement of national interests, the pursuit of 'military masculinity' is frequently equated with the attaining of a patriotic citizenship ideal (Nagel 1998, 251–2; Hemment 2015; Carlson and Tanci 2017). Women may be excluded from the achievement of this ideal, and even those who 'enact masculine roles' in military spaces do not 'feminise' or change the masculine cultures and practices associated with the army (Nagel 2017, 1453–4). At the same time, not all men are able to achieve the military masculinity ideal either. Indeed, hegemonic masculinity often stands in contrast to other class-, race- and sexuality-based masculinities (Connell and Messerschmidt 2005). Even so, hegemonic masculinity may still constitute the standard against which other masculinities compete or define themselves (Nagel 1998, 247; Nagel 2003).

Recent work on militarisation processes in capitalist democracies has additionally explored the centrality of a culture of 'military entertainment' (or 'militainment'), and the ways in which this culture may legitimise a 'martial masculinity' ideal and the 'military normal' (Lutz 2009) – the possession of a vast military force and the employment of military models and solutions to a range of issues (McSorley 2013, 2; Thomas 2009). Noting that public support for the military and/or war-waging is shaped through popular culture – films, television shows, music, video games, museum exhibitions and even fashion – scholars have examined how popular culture products (which may or may not receive support from military establishments) can convey a heightened sense of patriotism and the perception of a threat to the nation. These products can help generate the public support necessary for the extraction of resources for military purposes and the acceptance of war as a means to solve conflict (Regan 1994, 48; Thomas 2009, 97).

Children and youth constitute a key demographic in this process in both the Global South and the Global North. In its broader meaning, the militarisation of childhood subsumes 'combatant children in state and non-state forces, such as paramilitaries, militias, rebel, and warlord groups'. At the same time, militarisation also embraces 'non-combatant children's involvement in preparation for war'. This involvement includes the less tangible dimensions of militarisation such as the impact of ideologies which normalise the deployment of organised political violence as a means of solving domestic and/or international conflict (Macmillan 2011, 63).

In countries and territories with a mandatory conscription system for men, 'doing soldierhood' is often promoted as a 'rite of passage' for all boys and is presented as necessary for their 'transformation into adult men' and 'the performance of military masculinity' (Kao 2017, 203). Where recruitment is voluntary, military establishments often seek 'to attract the younger citizenry – defined as individuals of pre-recruitment age – to the armed forces or at least to have them accept the armed forces as a normal and normative component of the nation-state' (Frühstück 2020, 399).

Going beyond conflict zones where children are directly involved in fighting and/or victimised by warfare, scholars have examined the social and political process through which persons under 18 are mobilised to support the military or armed conflict, and how children's daily behaviour is shaped to conform with martial values, such as bodily discipline, obedience to authority or 'courage to fight against enemies' (Zheng 2021, 105).

As noted, this process can occur through youth consumption of war and military-themed popular culture products. It can also happen at the school. Studies worldwide (Giroux 2004; Cheney 2005; Blair, Miller and Tieken 2009; Beier 2011) have noted the importance of education in the production or curbing of a militarised ethos and documented how schools in conflict and non-conflict zones mobilise 'children's thinking and emotional readiness to accept the use of power as an answer to political problems' (Gor 2010 [2003], 209).

This mobilisation can take different forms, including specialist camps and military schools, as well as cadet forces and various versions of National Defence Education (Blair, Miller and Tieken 2009; Beier 2011). The legitimation of warfare can also take place through school rituals and memorial ceremonies to honour fallen soldiers; through organised school trips to war sites, military cemeteries and historical museums; and through the general curriculum (Davies 2005; Lomsky-Feder 2011; Abajian 2016; Sen and Starkey 2019). War histories taught at school can teach children and youth how to view their relations with outsiders and can even propagate hatred between different peoples (Hein and Selden, 2000).

Drawing on a Foucauldian approach, some scholars (McSorley 2016; Riggan 2016) have considered these activities as sites of 'disciplinary power' (Foucault 1977) where children and youth are trained to regulate and control their behaviour, gestures and movements. A regime of 'bio-politics' seeks to optimise students' mental and physical capacities while producing (or attempting to produce) 'docile bodies' (Foucault 2008) who are willing and able to fight. Others have drawn attention to the agency and subjectivity of youth in connection with militarised practices within and outside the school (Beier 2011; Basham 2016; Frühstück 2017; Beier and Tabak 2020). These studies have shown that youth do not always embrace the messages that they receive about war and the military at school or through the media. Instead, they engage with and even challenge (implicitly or explicitly) official narratives and/or the military-style disciplinary practices imposed on them (Bellino 2017, 8; Sheehan and Davison 2017; Pennell 2020).

Building on these crucial insights, in this book I examine the militarisation of education in China: a non-democratic, non-Western country in which the state posits children as the interlocutors of 'sovereign power' – the power to coerce with impunity (Foucault 1977) – while employing an array of disciplinary and biopolitical techniques to produce patriotic, docile citizens with optimal skills and the dispositions to support the Party-state and protect the nation. I explore how high school students of different backgrounds engage with these various forms of power while constructing their own notions of the nation, war and the military, notions which do not always align with those of the Party-state.

Popular Nationalism, Education and Chinese Youth Notions of Armed Conflict

Compared with the literature on the everyday militarisation of childhood and education in Western Europe and North America, the study of children and youth, and the process by which these groups have been implicated in militarisation processes in modern and contemporary China, is less developed (Zheng 2021, 104). Nonetheless, the past two decades have seen an increase in studies on two related issues: the nature of Chinese popular nationalism and its complex relationship with state nationalism; and the role of schooling and education in shaping Chinese youth notions of the national collectivity and its relationship with the world. The growth of scholarly interest in these topics is in turn related to two phenomena: the increasing emphasis on nationalism in the CPC's ideology and policies; and the rise of popular expressions of nationalism in post-1989 China.

In the aftermath of the 1989 crackdown on the student-led pro-democracy protest movement, the Chinese government systematically promoted patriotic ideology to bolster its legitimacy, to counter the threat of 'consumerist decadence and individualism' (Vickers 2009, 80) generated by its market reforms and Open Door policy and to reinforce social cohesion in the face of rapid socio-economic change and widening inequality. Studies have sought to ascertain the evolving nature of this state-led nationalism and its impact on public perceptions and practices in China. Noting the role of young participants in recurrent waves of anti-Western, anti-Japanese and anti–South Korean protests on city streets (at times turning violent) and on the Chinese Internet over the past couple of decades, some scholars have posited a direct link between official and popular practices.

Conventional wisdom, particularly in the fields of international relations and political science, maintains that the circulation of historical narratives of 'anti-imperialist patriotism' and the promotion of 'a social Darwinian view of the world as both hierarchical and competitive' (Gries 2020, 64) through a concerted Patriotic Education (PE) campaign and an expanded National Defence Education (NDE) curriculum (Hughes 2017), have socialised young Chinese of the post-1990s and post-2000s generation 'to harbor desires for revenge and restitution' against the nation-state's external enemies (Callahan 2010, 194; Gries 2020, 81; S. Zhao 2021; S. Zhao 2023), while expressing 'xenophobic' and even 'aggressive' attitudes towards the world (Gries 2004; He 2007; Z. Wang 2012; Yang and Zheng 2012; Weiss 2014; Wallace and Chen Weiss 2015).

These studies further argue that 'state-led nationalism', coupled with the government's tightening control over the media, culture and educational spheres in the Xi era, has been especially successful in spreading its message to 'millennials and Generation Z in China', who have grown up 'witnessing a remarkable rise of living standards and rapid modernization' (S. Zhao 2021, 149). China's younger generation have consequently been described as 'more fiercely patriotic and loyal to the party-state' than older cohorts (S. Zhao 2021, 150).

Other scholars have challenged this view by drawing on longitudinal survey studies (Johnston, 2017). Indeed, an overview of various large-scale studies conducted over the past two decades reveals a mixed (and at times contradictory) picture concerning the positions of young adults (aged over 18) towards China's foreign relations and specifically to armed conflict (e.g. Chubb 2014; Pan and Xu 2017; Weiss 2019; Pan and Xu 2020; Sinkkonen and Elovainio 2020; Zhong and Hwang 2020; Mazzoco and Kennedy 2022; Pang, Pan and Lin 2022; Qi, Zhang and Lin 2022).

A growing number of qualitative studies have simultaneously highlighted the existence of complex, ambiguous attitudes towards the nation and its relations with the world among Chinese of the post-1990s and post-2000s generation. These studies show that young Chinese, particularly those residing in urban, affluent areas, may express love for the nation and occasionally take part in anti-foreign street demonstrations, online grassroot campaigns, or consumer boycotts of international companies perceived to hurt the 'national dignity'. But they may also exhibit a cosmopolitan outlook and a keen desire to work and study abroad (e.g. Fong 2004; Liu 2012; Qian, Xu and Chen 2017; Naftali 2018; Yan et al. 2021; Ho 2022).

These and other studies suggest that twenty-first century Chinese youth who have grown up in an increasingly market-oriented and fragmented social environment may feel less connected to official ideologies and to values such as 'selflessness, prioritization of collective interests, [and] loyalty to the Party, the people and the motherland' (F. Liu 2008, 204; Sun and Wang 2010; Lian 2014; Fu 2018). Instead, contemporary youth have internalised the neoliberal values of 'autonomy', 'self-enterprise', 'responsibility and free choice' that both the government and Chinese schools have promoted alongside patriotic-collectivistic values (F. Liu 2008, 203; Hansen 2015).

This generational value shift is partly related to demographic processes caused by China's One Child policy (1979–2015). While the total fertility rate in China had already dropped from 5.8 children per family in 1950 to 2.3 children in 1980, the new phase in the Chinese government's population policy introduced in 1979 radically reduced the number of children per family, especially among the urban population. Official data from 2017 has shown that 19 per cent of the post-1980s generation and 32 per cent of the post-1990s generation in China are single children. For the post-2000s generation – which are the focus of this book – the figure is even higher (over 60 per cent). In general, the majority of Chinese urban children are now single children (cited in Li 2020, 3). In rural areas, where the policy has been implemented less strictly, the majority of the post-1980s and post-1990s generation have at least one sibling, yet the fertility rate has also declined significantly, with single children and 'second-born children' accounting for 61 per cent of the post-1980s generation, and 81.6 per cent of the post-1990s generation in the countryside (Ibid., 3).

The continuous decline of China's fertility rate, which in 2021 dropped to 1.2 (World Bank Group 2021), and the growing prevalence of smaller families in both urban and rural areas have in turn contributed to a transformation of the traditional generational relationships and parenting styles in Chinese families. For much of China's history, families have constituted a hierarchical system in which 'individuals were classified and ranked by generation, age and gender. Power, prestige and privilege, as well as the flow of material resources, were allocated to individuals according to their hierarchical positions' (Yan 2021a, 5). The introduction of the One-Child policy arguably inverted this long-standing feature. While some scholars (e.g. Liu 2022, 614) posit that the demographic shifts of the past four decades or so have not altered the basic 'authoritarian nature of parental guidance and teaching' in China, others maintain that contemporary families are characterised by a more equal and 'intimate' intergenerational relationship, with parents 'paying more respect to children's needs and individuality' compared to previous generations (Li 2020, 4; Naftali 2014b; Naftali 2016).

These and other studies show that while intergenerational solidarity and mutual dependence remain key features of Chinese familial relations, the singleton child, particularly in the cities, has in recent decades become known as the 'precious little emperor', pampered by parents as well as grandparents on both sides (Yan 2021a, 6–7; Liu 2020). This transformation has arguably contributed to a reshaping of the intergenerational relationship in wider society as well, with youth, particularly those of the post-1990s and post-2000s generations, exhibiting greater 'self-confidence, independence, and open-mindedness' (Li 2020, 4) and an enhanced desire for high achievement and individual self-realisation (Liu 2020). Concurrently with these developments, domestic labour migration and increased social mobility in general have had an equally profound impact on intergenerational relations, further contributing to a trend of individualisation among China's younger generations (Yan 2021a, 7, 9).

For the Communist Party leadership, this trend has been a cause for concern. As young people exhibit 'more individualistic values and lifestyles', the party has increased its efforts to strengthen ideological and political education of youth (Svensson 2023, 76). Most recently, for instance, party leaders have criticised the so-called 'lying flat' (*tang ping*) phenomenon: that is, young people's 'withdrawal from the career rat race of society by doing only the bare minimum'. Chinese state media have urged youth to renounce this trend and 'to strive hard and make efforts for national rejuvenation rather than taking it easy' (Svensson 2023, 76). Concurrently, the party has heavily invested in 'ideological work' among youth, combining 'Marxist ideology' and 'Xi Jinping Thought' with nationalism and the celebration of Chinese history, heritage and culture (Svensson 2023, 83).

These observations have been extremely useful in revealing the multidimensional nature of Chinese youth values, and specifically youth nationalism, and the factors shaping these values over the past several decades. Nonetheless, empirical studies that focus on the role of the school in shaping the political attitudes of young people in China remain scarce. Most of the studies we do have on this topic were conducted among urban elite students, and their findings may not be applicable to other populations. Indeed, as several studies document, increasing economic inequality may have eroded the loyalty of some young Chinese, particularly children of rural migrant workers who are faced with limited opportunities in the cities (Ling 2017; Chen 2020; Naftali 2021a).

Much of the existing work also neglects the military dimension in the construction of Chinese youth nationalism. A noted exception is a pioneering study by Hughes (2017) who looked at China's current National Defence Education (NDE). The study suggests that military training programmes implemented in Chinese schools and colleges as part of NDE constitute part of a new phase of the ongoing militarisation of Chinese society in the modern era. Nonetheless, the study does not include an empirical component, and the author recognises that one of the current challenges of the NDE programme is to make military knowledge appealing to the current generation of Chinese youth (Hughes 2017, 66).

A 2019 qualitative study by Juliette Genevaz offers a rare look into the views of urban Chinese college students regarding the military training course they took before college. The study finds that the elite urban youth were pleased about the physical and mental aspects of the programme, and Genevaz concludes that the college military training course successfully conveyed the authority of the Party-state and instilled 'a sense of discipline and commitment to the group' (Genevaz 2019, 466). The applicability of this finding to younger student populations or those of different locals and backgrounds remains unclear, however. Nor can we assume that embracing the value of group commitment equals – or necessarily leads to – an endorsement of a 'martial ethos', a key component of militarisation.

Finally, although scholars have offered insightful analyses of China's revised historical narratives of specific conflicts, in particular the shifting treatment of the Second Sino-Japanese War (1937–45), in school textbooks, in public sites, in children's literature and in various popular media (e.g. Denton 2007; Vickers 2007; Reilly 2011; Nie 2013; Yau 2014; Chen 2016; Mitter 2020; Chang 2021; Chew and Wang 2021), at the time of writing we still have no systematic study of how Chinese youth education constructs the general concepts of war, peace and the military. Several studies have noted the gendered dimensions of Patriotic Education in China, and in particular the circulation of a 'military masculinity' model in contemporary government, education and media works (e.g. Song and Hird 2014; Zheng 2015; Zhang 2019; Wen 2021; Song 2022). But these studies do not address the question of how young audiences engage with these gender-specific images when constructing their idea of military service or armed conflict.

This book seeks to address these gaps. Building on the valuable findings of previous work on popular nationalism and education in China, and on the theoretical insights of critical studies on the militarisation of childhood and youth worldwide, I consider the role of war and the military in Chinese state narratives of patriotic citizenship and in the formation of youth attitudes towards the nation and its relations with the world. Drawing on the analysis of empirical data and a wide range of primary sources, the discussion highlights key themes within the narratives of war and the military which young people encounter in school textbooks, organised PE and NDE activities, and government- and military-sponsored media. It explores how youth perceive, negotiate and/or challenge these narratives while forming their views of the PLA as an institution and of military service specifically. The discussion further considers youth notions regarding the use of armed force to address China's current territorial disputes.

Based on the analysis of Chinese-language government, military, media, academic and educational publications of the past several decades, the book documents a growing emphasis on military values and techniques in Chinese education of the 2000s and particularly the 2010s. The discussion further demonstrates the link between this trend and recent shifts in official and public conceptualisations of patriotism and citizenship, masculinity and femininity. Data from interviews with Han (Chinese) high school students of different social backgrounds nonetheless illustrate a variety of attitudes and contestations of official narratives about war, the military and the 'martial masculinity' ideal currently circulating in PRC youth education.

These findings complicate our understanding of youth notions of war, peace, security and the factors which shape these notions in this authoritarian global power. Highlighting the distinct manifestations of the militarisation of education in the PRC, the book underscores key similarities between the Chinese case and militarisation processes worldwide. Above all, I seek to demonstrate the importance of positioning young people's experiences and subjectivities at the centre of critical military inquiries rather than engaging youth only as objects or victims of militarisation processes. In so doing, I hope to further decenter the West/Global North in studies of everyday militarisation of youth in non-conflict areas by opening the possibility of theorising this process from an East Asian/Global South context (cf. Abebe, Dar and Lyså 2022; Twum-Danso Imoh, Rabello de Castro and Naftali 2022).

Data and Methodology

The study examines education as a cultural and political practice that occurs both within and outside the school. It further assumes that state education in China constitutes a critical institution that enforces the government's ideology on the next generation. Combining this notion with an anthropological perspective that conceptualises youth as consequential, agential subjects, and a Critical Military Studies approach that employs fieldwork to examine how people engage with military power while drawing on their own critical capacities to reflect on their experiences (Basham and Bulmer 2017, 68), the objective of the book is to explore the link between macro policies and discourses of militarisation and the meaning-making processes of individual youths of diverse backgrounds.

Specifically, the main goals of the inquiry are to evaluate whether and how China's Patriotic Education (PE), National Defence Education (NDE) and related state initiatives promote the militarisation of youth education in the 2010s; investigate the nature of youth engagements with the messages of the PE and NDE programmes and these related initiatives; and explore youth subjective perceptions of other factors which may have affected their notions of war and the miliary (e.g. peers, family members, news media and popular culture).

To address these issues the study drew on both empirical and non-empirical data, collected through two research projects conducted in 2012–19. The first project on the topic of 'Education and the Formation of National Identity in China: The Effects of Schooling and "Patriotic Education" on Youth of Different Socioeconomic Backgrounds', was sponsored by the Israel Science Foundation (ISF) (grant number 405/12), and an individual research grant of the Harry S. Truman Research Institute for the Advancement of Peace at the Hebrew University of Jerusalem (2012–16). A second project, titled 'War and the Military in Contemporary Chinese Education: The Effects of Schooling and the "Patriotic Education" Campaign on the Attitudes of Middle-School Students towards Armed Conflict' (2016–19), was supported by a Spencer Foundation research grant.

Non-empirical sources for the study included PRC government and military public documents; newspaper and magazine articles; and academic articles published in the Chinese mainland since the 1980s, with a particular focus on the past two decades. Another key resource examined in the study are high school modern history textbooks published in the Chinese mainland in the 2000s and 2010s. In addition, I explored select visual media products sponsored by the PLA in the 2010s. The discussion examined hundreds of government and military documents, all of which were obtained from official Chinese websites that are accessible to the public. Chinese media materials were retrieved online using a simple keyword search. Articles in specialised mainland magazines on education and/or the military were retrieved from CNKI (China National Knowledge Infrastructure) database, China's most comprehensive repository of magazines and academic publications. The same database also provided access to Chinese academic articles published in mainland professional journals, some of which were analysed as a primary source as part of the inquiry into the academic discourse on military-themes in Chinese education (see in particular Chapter 3). An additional key source are high school modern history textbooks published by the People's Education Press (PEP) in Beijing in 2007, 2009 and 2019 (See Chapter 2 for detailed information on the textbooks).

Empirical data for the study were collected through a semi-structured interview procedure with open-ended questions. Interviews were conducted in China in 2013 and in 2017–19 with a total of 155 Han (Chinese) students (ages 16–18, 51 per cent male; 49 per cent female) attending grades 10–12. The interviews included preliminary close-ended questions which collected basic information on the demographic background of students and their families, and whether informants knew a family member and/or a member of their close social circle who had served in the military. The interview protocol included a series of open-ended questions about the following issues:

(1) Students' experiences during various Patriotic Education (PE) and National Defence Education (NDE) activities, including school rituals and events, organised visits to PE and NDE sites,

as well as the mandatory military training course students had attended prior to their entry into junior and senior high school. Students were prompted to reflect on the messages these various activities conveyed regarding the issues of war, peace and the military.
(2) Students' views on the general messages their teachers and textbooks divulged about war, peace and the military.
(3) Students' personal views regarding the means through which China should resolve its territorial disputes, and the sources of information students reported shaping their views on this issue.
(4) Students' general impression of the military, of army life and of PLA soldiers, and the sources of information that shaped their views on this issue.
(5) Students' attitudes towards military service (i.e. their willingness to enlist) and the sources of information that shaped their views on this issue.

To consider the potential role of students' social backgrounds in shaping their attitudes towards war and the military, the study sample consisted of informants who attended different types of high schools in two geographic locations: the globalised metropolis of Shanghai on China's eastern coast; and a rural county-seat in Henan province, a relatively impoverished, peripheral area in central China. Below I provide information on each of the study sites, the type of school the informants had attended and the general demographic backgrounds of students in each site.

Located at the very centre of China, Henan province is set in the middle and lower reaches of the Yellow River. Its area is 160,000 square kilometres. A traditionally agricultural province, Henan is known as 'the granary of China', and produces over one-quarter of the country's wheat. Other chief industrial crops are cotton, tobacco, vegetable oils and silk. In 2021, Henan's population was approximately 98.83 million, making it one of the most populous provinces in the country. The majority of Henan's population lives in rural areas, and most are Han (Chinese). There are no autonomous minority groups such as those found in China's western provinces, as the small number of Hui (Chinese Muslims), Mongol and Manchu have long been integrated into the province's broader population. The high schools which the Henan respondents attended are in a county-seat in a relatively poor, agricultural region in the northeastern part of the province. In 2021, the annual per capita disposable income of rural residents in the county was approximately CN¥13,500 ($USD1,861), putting them in the lower income bracket in the country; the national figure was more than twice as much that year.

Henan informants (N = 85) were attending three academic-track schools – institutions that prepare students for China's University Entrance Examination (*gao kao*) at the end of Year 12.[3] Although the schools were in a county-seat, more than 85 per cent of their students hailed from villages and neighbouring rural townships. Owing to the considerable distance between their hometowns and the school campus, many boarded at school during weekdays, returning to their villages only on weekends and holidays. A majority of informants' parents had attained only nine years, or fewer, of education and worked as either farmers or migrant manual labourers in towns and cities within or outside the province.

Shanghai is one of the four municipalities of China directly controlled by the central government, and is also an international commercial, cultural and communication centre. Located on the coast of the East China Sea at the heart of the Yangtze Delta, Shanghai has a land area of 6,341 square kilometres. The municipality's area includes the city itself, surrounding suburbs and an agricultural hinterland. One of the first Chinese ports to be opened to Western trade in the nineteenth century, the city has long dominated the country's commerce and continues to serve as China's major trading port and the gateway to inland China. Since the launch of market reforms in the 1980s, Shanghai has attracted a large amount of foreign investment, and many multinational companies are headquartered in the metropolis.

Shanghai's current population is 24.75 million. Most of the population is Han (Chinese). Within metropolitan Shanghai there are few, if any, concentrations of ethnic minority groups but a significant proportion of people in the city are internal migrants from rural provinces who arrived in search of work in the service sector, construction, factories and/or in other types of manual labour. A majority of these internal migrants are not permanent residents. There is also a small but significant number of people from Taiwan and from other countries who mainly are involved with foreign-owned or foreign-operated enterprises located in and around Shanghai. In 2021, Shanghai's overall per capita disposable income was CN¥79,610 yuan (approximately $USD10,975), which is almost six times as much as the figure recorded in the Henan county where the study was conducted.

Shanghai study participants (N=70) attended more than a dozen schools, both academic and vocational. Like the Henan participants, students in the Shanghai academic high schools (N=43) also received preparation for the *gao kao*. However, their parents had at least twelve years of education, and were employed as white-collar workers, professionals, private entrepreneurs, or high-ranking managers in state-owned, privately owned, or foreign enterprises. The remaining Shanghai participants (N=27) attended vocational-track schools in the city. Vocational schools are generally considered inferior on the Chinese educational ladder since they are required to admit local urban students who have failed to gain admittance to academic high schools. At the time of the study, domestic migrant youth who lacked a local Shanghai registration (*hukou*)[4] were also exclusively channelled into the city's vocational high schools regardless of their academic abilities. Second-generation migrants without a local Shanghai registration constituted 35 per cent of the Shanghai vocational school sample.

Unlike their peers in the academic high schools, the vocational school respondents did not receive any preparation for the *gao kao*. Instead, they were offered training in electronics, car repair, cooking, hairdressing and beauty salon work. A majority of vocational school students came from families of relatively lower socio-economic backgrounds. Only half the informants in these schools had parents who had completed more than nine years of education and very few had completed more than twelve years of schooling. Most students' parents were employed in low-paying jobs in the service sector or as manual workers.

Informants were selected through a non-random, convenience (snowball) sample. A Shanghai research assistant who is originally a native of the area in which the Henan schools were located, approached teachers in each school and asked them to introduce the study and recruit willing participants. Students were then asked to introduce other youths who might be willing to take part in the study. The practical ease of access to some youths rather than others might mean that the voices of certain categories of students may have been undervalued or overlooked (Hill 2010). Nonetheless, the political nature of the research topic necessitated the use of this selection method (cf. Fairbrother 2003).

To minimise linguistic and cultural barriers and reduce potential informant bias when speaking to a non-native interviewer about issues that concern China's military and its territorial disputes, the

Chinese research assistant also carried out the interviews with students in each location. Informed consent was obtained from students as well as from their parents. Participants received an explanation about the purpose of the study and were instructed to freely express their thoughts and feelings. Youths were assured of the anonymity of their responses and were instructed that no information from the interviews would be divulged to their teachers, parents, or any other third party.

All interviews were conducted off-campus. Participation in the study was not compulsory, and informants were assured that they could withdraw from the study or avoid answering questions they were not comfortable with. As the discussion in Chapters 5 and 6 will demonstrate, some informants did use this option and avoided answering certain questions. In such cases, the interviewer did not pressure students to respond or explain their reluctance. Other informants employed state slogans which appeared in their textbooks or in the general media in response to some of the questions. Still others offered responses which according to students' own testimonies diverged from the messages they had heard in class, in school activities, or in the state-backed media. Finally, there were also students who explicitly criticised official messages. That the interviews were conducted by a person informants categorised as 'a cultural insider' may have helped teenagers feel more at ease, but it may have also prevented some interviewees from giving a more detailed explanation to someone they presumed shared the same background knowledge (cf. Liu 2006, 48). Nonetheless, the diversity of informants' responses can attest to the degree of rapport the Chinese interviewer was able to achieve with the study participants.

To ensure accurate rendering, all interviews were recorded and later transcribed by another native Chinese speaker. I then translated all the Chinese transcriptions and performed the data analysis. The analysis of student responses was informed by the principles of constructivist grounded theory which focuses on people's perceptions in constructing their social worlds (Charmaz 2008). Specifically, I sought to identify recurring categories, patterns and themes in the interviews while exploring the language informants used to make sense of the messages and information young people received about war and the military within or outside the school. The analysis paid particular attention to how individual students of different backgrounds and locations interact with, interpret, reproduce and/or subvert different aspects of the official narratives they were exposed to.

I further examined how students related these official narratives to information they gleaned from alternative sources, including social media, popular media, family members and other people in their close social circle. The analysis of non-empirical data was likewise grounded in a constructivist approach. The aim was to identify emergent patterns of meaning in order to illustrate how a certain social construct develops within the text or visual media product. I therefore sought to uncover not only explicit but also latent meanings in the different sources, which may in turn reflect deeper, underlying assumptions and ideologies (Boyatzis 1998).

Several caveats regarding the research design and its potential impact on the data presented in the book are in order. First, the discussion mainly relies on interview data, as the field projects which form the basis for the book did not include participant-observations in classrooms or during various PE and NDE activities. The importance of observing everyday school practices when examining the impact of education on youth attitudes on issues such as war, peace and the military has been well established (Welty 2014). However, due to practical limitations and the political sensitivity of the topic in Xi's China, the research design did not include an observation component. As noted, students were asked to describe their experiences and impressions, and such descriptions offer insights into school practices. Ultimately, the data presented in the book reflects students' subjective interpretations of these practices.

Second, the discussion focuses on students' perspectives and for the most part, does not cover the views of teachers. While the initial study design included interviews with teachers in each of the study locations, it quickly became clear that asking teachers to comment on how schools and textbooks represent war and the military to students would be unattainable. According to China's Ministry of Education guidelines, primary and secondary school teachers must not only be 'patriotic and law-abiding' but also support 'the leadership of the Communist Party of China'. Teachers' 'words or deeds' must not 'violate the policies of the party and the state' (Ministry of Education of the PRC 2008). These guidelines illuminate the Chinese state's general vision of schools as key institutions to socialise youth thinking to align with state ideas, while eliminating access to alternative notions (Yiu and Yu 2022, 529; Yan et al. 2021). As a result of this limitation and amid the diminishing space for free expression in China's educational system under Xi Jinping, especially since the mid-2010s, teachers were increasingly reluctant to take part in the study. That said, the discussion does include the views of several teachers in Shanghai and Henan, while students' testimonies regarding the messages they heard in class and during school activities provide insight into the perspectives and practices of their teachers. Youth testimonies can also shed light on the views of their family members, another population that was not included in the study.

As further noted, the study presents the views of Han (Chinese) informants and does not include ethnic minority students. Due to the political nature of the topic and the increasingly tense relationship between the Chinese government and some of the country's ethnic minorities, particularly Tibetans and Uighurs, access to ethnic minority students was curtailed by the teachers who had helped recruit the study participants. As a result of this limitation, the study sample includes Han youth only. The latter nonetheless constitute more than 90 per cent of students in the two study locations and in China more generally.

The study sample also does not include students in Hong Kong and Macau, as the structure and contents of the school curriculum, and the historical, social, economic and political conditions in Hong Kong and Macau are qualitatively different from those in the Chinese mainland. Additionally, the book does not provide information on the educational policies or attitudes of youth in Taiwan. While the PRC government claims Taiwan as part of its territory, this claim is disputed (as the discussion in the following chapters will highlight). Moreover, Taiwan's education system, as well as its historical, social, economic and political conditions are starkly different to those of the Chinese mainland. The perspectives of Taiwanese youth therefore remain beyond the scope of the present inquiry.

Finally, a note about terminology. The PRC's armed forces are made up of three formations: the People's Armed Police (PAP); the People's Militia; and the PLA (People's Liberation Army). The first two groups played a vital role in the CPC's genesis and its emergence as a victorious revolutionary movement (Scobell 2022, 349). As Chapter 1 elaborates, the People's Militia was particularly influential in the militarisation of China's civilian population, including youth, during the Mao era (1949–76). The book mainly focuses on the activities of the PLA, however. Essentially the armed wing of the CPC, the PLA constitutes the most prominent component of China's security forces and has had a particularly important role in recent decades (Scobell 2022, 349; Clay and Blasko 2020). Unless stated otherwise, the term 'military' will be used throughout the book as a synonym for all armed forces – the PLA, the PAP and the People's Militia.

Organisation of the Book

A key concern of this book is to evaluate whether China's education system is experiencing increased militarisation in the twenty-first century, and particularly in the Xi era. To properly address this issue, it is crucial to situate recent developments in China within their appropriate historical context. The book therefore begins with a general overview of militarisation processes in Chinese education from the turn of the twentieth century to the end of the Mao era in 1976. Drawing on secondary sources as well as the results of my earlier inquiries into the militarisation of Chinese education in the 1950s–1970s (Naftali 2014a; Naftali 2014b; Naftali 2021b), Chapter 1 traces the roots of the militarisation of youth education in China to the first half of the twentieth century when the country's successive military defeats to imperialist forces in previous decades had motivated China's elite to advocate not only for the strengthening and modernisation of the military but also the promotion of a military ethos in the country's newly established modern education system. As the discussion will note, this military ethos was applied non-uniformly to students of different backgrounds and genders.

Moving on to focus on the first three decades of CPC rule, the discussion in Chapter 1 will posit that the development of youth education in Maoist China was marked by a growing preoccupation with war preparation, as well as the increasing spread of the military's techniques and routines to Chinese youth education, a process which reached its zenith in the 1960s. The chapter will also highlight key contestations and limitations of this militarisation process, while demonstrating how class and gender continued to shape (and arguably undermine) the effects of this process on youth attitudes and practices in the Mao era.

Following the death of Mao Zedong in 1976, the Chinese government under the leadership of Deng Xiaoping adopted a more pragmatic approach to the country's development. This shift led to the launch of market reforms and an Open Door policy in the late 1970s–early 1980s and was accompanied by a de-emphasis on revolutionary politics in favour of academic standards and an emphasis on international cooperation and openness to the world as preconditions for the modernisation of China's science and technology and the country's economic growth. Despite this change in the political and ideological dimensions of Chinese education, militarised themes did not disappear from PRC schools of the post-1978 era. Rather, they changed form to suit the shifting needs of the CPC and the PLA. Indeed, from the 1990s onward, themes of war and the military gained increasing importance in youth education amid the rise of various threats (domestic as well as external) to the strength and stability of the regime. Chapter 2 will describe the Chinese government's reactions to these threats, including the launch of a systematic Patriotic Education (PE) campaign and a National Defence Education (NDE) programme targeting the entire population, with a particular focus on children and youth. The bulk of the chapter will discuss a key component of these government programmes: the promotion of 'patriotic sentiments' and 'national defence' values through the school curriculum.

Using history teaching as a case study, the chapter will examine how modern history textbooks used in schools of the 2000s–2010s present the themes of war, peace and the military to Chinese high school students. Drawing on original analysis, the discussion will show that although contemporary school materials highlight the 'cruelty of war' and promote the image of China as a 'pacifist' country, history textbooks used in Chinese high schools over the past two decades also justify the country's past military interventions while glorifying the role of armed conflict in the construction of the modern Chinese national collectivity. The textbooks suggest that a strong army would guarantee China's domestic stability, protect the country's national dignity, and ensure its leading international standing in the future.

An additional key component of the Chinese government's PE campaign and NDE programme is the compulsory military training course (in Chinese, *junxun*) that all youth are required to take while attending junior and senior high school as well as in college. Chapter 3 focuses on this programme. Drawing on secondary sources and on analysis of a wide array of government, military, media and academic sources published in China from the 1980s onwards, the discussion describes the goals, contents and techniques of the compulsory military training course. The chapter also notes the intersection between the expansion and consolidation of the government-mandated course as part of PE and NDE, and the concomitant rise and proliferation of various 'martial pedagogies' and 'military-style therapeutics' employed in privately owned educational and care facilities catering to different categories of 'deviant' and 'problematic' youth. Noting the distinct class and gender aspects of these various programmes and therapeutics, the discussion identifies key themes within Chinese public discourse surrounding the uses – and, significantly, also abuses – of these interventions, while demonstrating that the use of military-style methods in educating and caring for youth constitutes a controversial issue in present-day China.

Another important channel for the propagation of soldierly behavioural models and the circulation of patriotic war stories in contemporary China is popular culture, the subject of Chapter 4. The discussion observes that like military establishments in capitalist democracies, the PLA over the past two decades has begun to collaborate with commercial companies to perform its propaganda work. Drawing on the insights of previous studies and on original analysis, the chapter considers how PLA-backed commercial productions of the Xi Jinping era present the tropes of war and the military to audiences, while highlighting tensions and contradictions within these representations. Focusing on four case studies – the reality TV show, *Takes a Real Man* (*Zhenzheng nanzihan*, 2015–17), and the three war-action blockbuster films, *Wolf Warrior*, *Wolf Warrior II* (*Zhan lang*, 2015, 2017) and *Operation Red Sea* (*Honghai xingdong*, 2018) – the discussion demonstrates how these military-backed productions seek to promote not only patriotism and support for the CPC and the state (the traditional functions of PLA propaganda work). They also attempt to 'market' war and military service as exhilarating experiences through which individuals can gain 'maturity' and 'personal development'.

Adapted to the changing sensibilities and priorities of contemporary Chinese youth, these messages remain specifically gendered. The media productions examined in the chapter espouse a 'military masculinity' model which excludes alternative notions of manhood and denigrates women. Further, these productions often convey contradictory and even misleading messages about the nature of army life and the functions of the military in China's international relations.

How do contemporary Chinese youth interpret the messages they receive through school textbooks, military training courses and related activities, and various PLA-backed media? And how do youth perceptions of these messages affect their attitudes towards war and the military? Drawing on the analysis of empirical data from field interviews with high school students in Shanghai and Henan, Chapters 5 and 6 address these questions. I begin with a discussion of youth notions of the messages they receive in and outside the school regarding the use of armed force in international disputes, and specifically the employment of the military in resolving China's territorial disputes.

The analysis in Chapter 5 demonstrates that most youth participants in the two study locations exhibited a relatively circumspect attitude towards military violence. While an overwhelming majority viewed China's past involvement in international armed conflict as both just and necessary, most study participants regardless of gender and social background, rejected the use of violence in China's current territorial disputes. Those who did endorse a military intervention maintained that it should be employed only as 'a last resort' and for 'defensive' purposes. Identifying some of the key rationales students offered in support of their position, the discussion further highlights those points on which students' views either converge with – or depart from – the messages they received about armed conflict within and outside the school.

Chapter 6 moves on to explore informants' general image of the PLA and of soldierhood, as well as youth attitudes towards military service. The analysis shows that even though a majority of informants in the two study locations professed a highly positive (and even idealised) image of soldiers and the Chinese military as an institution, many were nonetheless quite ambivalent about military service. The chapter describes the key reasons students argued for or against enlistment while highlighting the differences in informants' attitudes along the lines of gender, social background, type of school and geographic location. The analysis further notes the role of school textbooks, military training courses and PLA-backed popular media, while highlighting the importance of alternative sources of information in shaping youth attitudes about the army and military service.

A central finding of the chapter is that Shanghai students, particularly those in academic high schools, were less enthusiastic about joining the military compared to their counterparts in the city's vocational schools or those attending academic high schools in Henan. The chapter offers an explanation for this finding while situating the results of the analysis within the existing scholarship on the PLA's conscription challenges in the twenty-first century.

Taken together, the book's findings suggest that Chinese students of the 2000s and 2010s are exposed to military values and soldierly practices through the school curriculum, military training courses and PLA-backed media productions. As the book's closing chapter will nonetheless argue, the underlying logic which drives the militarisation of education in Xi's China is far from new. Rather, it reflects earlier assumptions about youth education, patriotic citizenship, masculinity and femininity whose roots extend to the previous century.

While the Communist Party might have managed to systemise and expand the militarisation of youth education to an unprecedented degree in the 2000s and 2010s, this trend is undercut by concurrent shifts in the values and aspirations of different sectors of Chinese society, in particular, urban populations of higher socio-economic backgrounds. The interview data presented in the book further illustrate youth informants' non-uniform responses to – and at times, even contestations of – the messages they hear about war and the military in school textbooks, military training courses and PLA-backed media. These diverse responses, which in some cases are predicated on gender and socio-economic background, suggest that even if education in the Xi era is becoming more militarised, we cannot assume that Chinese youth are embracing this trend. Much like youth in other countries, young Chinese are able to form their own ideas about the necessity of war or the role of the military in the construction of the national collectivity.

Highlighting the ambiguities and contradictions that animate the logic and lived experiences of youth militarisation in the PRC, the book further underscores the importance of engaging with ethnographic work in the field of Critical Military Studies (cf. Basham and Bulmer 2017, 63). I argue that it is this type of work that allows us to document and fully explore the complex ways of resisting war and militarisation in China and beyond.

Notes

1. The 2021 Chinese law bans the defamation of military personnel, adding to an array of legal tools that already ban defamation of revolutionary 'martyrs', including revisions to the country's criminal code and a 2018 Law on the Protection of Heroes and Martyrs. For more details about the latter law, see Chapter 2.
2. A recent report suggests that from 2012 through 2022, China's official defence spending more than doubled from 670 billion to 1.45 trillion renminbi (roughly $USD106 billion to $USD230 billion). Approximately 40 per cent of this was

allocated to the procurement budget, where it funded programmes such as aircraft carriers, fighter modernisation and the expansion of China's nuclear arsenal (Wuthnow 2023). In March 2023, the Chinese government announced a military budget of 1.55 trillion yuan (roughly $USD224.8 billion) for 2023, a 7.2 per cent increase from the previous year. Some commentators nonetheless believe that China underreports its defence expenditures (Pomfret and Pottinger 2023), and that the figure for 2023 is closer to $USD298 billion (CSIS 2023).
3. The names of the schools and their precise location are withheld to protect informants' identities.
4. Established in 1958, the *hukou* system originally entailed a strict distinction between rural and urban households in order to control migration to Chinese cities. It has also been used to control access to urban education, health care and housing. Since the 1980s, the *hukou* system has been gradually relaxed to allow for economic growth, especially in China's booming coastal regions. However, in cities like Shanghai, the distinction between permanent and temporary household registration remains largely intact. Attaining a permanent registration for rural migrants and their family members is an extremely onerous process.

CHAPTER 1

The Militarisation of Education in Modern China

> To be civilized, citizens need a warlike spirit that serves as the essence of a nation. Without this warlike spirit, a nation cannot stand.
> Liang Qichao, 'Xin min shuo' (On new citizenship), 1902.¹

The militarisation of youth education is not a recent trend in China. Rather, the roots of this process can be traced back to the early decades of the twentieth century when leading Chinese reformers and revolutionaries such as Liang Qichao (1873–1929), whose words are cited above, came to believe that schools must foster students' fighting skills and martial spirit so that children and youths can become 'modern', 'civilised' citizens ready and able to defend the nation. The conviction remained constant throughout the twentieth century even as China underwent two revolutions and successive rounds of educational reform. What prompted the rise of a martial educational ethos in early twentieth-century China? To what extent was this ethos translated into concrete programmes of National Defence Education in schools? What were the goals and contents of these programmes, and how effective were they in shaping the views and practices of Chinese students of different backgrounds? Finally, what role have such programmes played in the militarisation of Chinese society in the modern era?

The chapter addresses these questions. Drawing on previous scholarship as well as the analysis of Chinese media and educational publications, the discussion provides a historical overview of key issues in the development of National Defence Education (hereafter, NDE) programmes in Chinese schools from the final decades of the Qing Dynasty (1644–1911), through the Republican period

(1912–49), to the Maoist era (1949–76). As we shall see, the growing frequency of military conflicts in modern Chinese history has played a large role in the development of youth NDE at school, but the militarisation of Chinese youth education throughout this period has also been characterised by notable tensions and contradictions. These tensions at times stemmed from economic limitations and an ineffectual governing capacity. Occasionally though, they were also a product of divergent notions about the social and political capacities of children and the goals of civic education in China. These contradictions were themselves a result of the refraction of the martial citizenship ideal through the dual lenses of gender and socio-economic class.

'Throw Away the Brush and Pick up the Sword'

From the mid nineteenth to the mid twentieth century, China experienced recurrent domestic and external conflicts resulting in prolonged periods of semi-colonial occupation. Following the defeat of the Qing Dynasty by the United Kingdom and France in the first and second Opium Wars (1839–42, 1856–60), China was forced to sign the 'unequal treaties'. The treaties required the Qing to relinquish or lease territories, including Hong Kong and Macau, which were ceded to the United Kingdom and Portugal respectively. The post-war agreements further enabled several foreign powers, including Britain but also Russia, Germany, France, Belgium, the United States and Japan, to form special zones of influence to facilitate the exploitation of China's resources. Foreign pressures and domestic rebellion deepened in the latter part of the nineteenth century, culminating in a momentous Chinese defeat in the First Sino-Japanese War (1894–5). Members of the Qing court and the civil officialdom who constituted the Qing Empire's political and social elite, attributed this humiliating event to the systematic incompetency and widespread lack of morale among Qing troops (Zarrow 2015, 12). Chinese literati, government officials and military leaders of the period further criticised the 'pacifist and civil orientation' of Confucian high culture, which, they argued, had dominated China's moral and political thinking for two millennia. With its emphasis on scholarly and literary achievements, they charged, Confucianism had fostered a lack of interest in physical culture, martial deeds and valour on the battlefield, resulting in 'the bodily degeneration of the Chinese people' and 'excessive effeminateness' of Chinese men (Zarrow 2015, 12; Schillinger 2016, 2).

Prominent European and American thinkers, including the social theorist Max Weber (1864–1920) adopted this view, arguing that 'traditional Chinese culture' essentially despised the military and only waged war as a last resort. Both Chinese and Euro-American intellectuals of the period invoked the Chinese phrase 'emphasise culture, de-emphasise the military' (*zhong wen qing wu*), allegedly prominent since the Song Dynasty (960–1279), as proof of China's lack of military ambition (Schillinger 2016, 8). Another oft-quoted idiom, 'Good iron is not used to make nails, and good men do not become soldiers' (*hao tie bu da ding, hao nan bu dang bing*), was further used to illustrate the long-standing prejudice against soldiers and military achievements in China's traditional culture (cited in Edwards 2016, 13).

The assumption that China's imperial culture was essentially 'pacifist' in nature is in fact a serious oversimplification (Schillinger 2016; Waley-Cohen 2006b). In large part, the notion originated in the political influence of the Confucian civil bureaucracy, which defined high culture and social values through its dominance over written records and texts. Chinese scholar officials wrote the histories and established a textual tradition in which they garnered social prestige while their military counterparts did not – despite the latter's centrality in the formation, expansion and defence of China's imperial dynasties (Schillinger 2016, 8). Historians have further observed that pacifism was never represented as official state policy or the social norm in pre-modern China. Although revered works such as the *Art of War* by Master Sun (*Sunzi bingfa*) and other pre-modern military texts in China viewed martial issues in the larger context of maintaining social order, and for the most part idealised avoiding battle, in practice, warfare was never just 'a ritual affair' in imperial China (Schillinger 2016, 8). While some imperial dynasties may have preferred to subordinate military to civil matters, throughout pre-modern Chinese history, various ruling houses used military force offensively to check enemies and conquer new territories (Schillinger 2016, 8; Waley-Cohen 2006a).

Moreover, political culture in late imperial China generally recognised the need to maintain a balance between civil/cultural accomplishment (*wen*) and military (*wu*) virtues (Louie and Edwards 1994; Louie 2002; H. Yang 2006). Accordingly, elite men would learn various forms of martial arts for fitness and to cultivate a meditative self-control alongside calligraphy and poetry. This was not in preparation for enlisting in the standing military forces but was rather a marker of cultivated status (Edwards 2016, 13). Both *wen* and *wu* (culture/miliary) were regarded as ideal masculine qualities in late imperial Chinese culture, and either or both attributes were expected to be found in men of high standing (Hird 2019, 350; Louie and Edwards 1994).

Military strength and the associated martial virtues were particularly crucial to the self-image of the Manchu-ruled Qing Dynasty (1644–1911), which at its zenith ranked among the most powerful in the world (Waley-Cohen 2006a, 97). The rulers of the Qing had from the outset expressed their desire to preserve the 'martial prowess' of the Manchu people against the 'insidious effects' of 'Chinese civilisation'. In other words, the Qing made it clear that they wished to favour *wu* over *wen* (Waley-Cohen 2006a, 99). Yet, amid the successive military defeats of the Qing Dynasty in its encounters with foreign powers in the mid–late nineteenth century, many of China's elite begun to criticise the Qing court for its weakness, while turning to Western military technology and the science that underlay it in their search for a means to strengthen the empire. After China's defeat in the First Sino-Japanese War (1894–5), the court was obliged to recognise the independence of Korea, over which it had traditionally held suzerainty; to cede Taiwan, the Pescadores Islands and the Liaodong (south Manchurian) Peninsula to Japan; to pay an indemnity to Japan; and to open several ports to Japanese trade. The defeat prompted China's elite to intensify their demand for a 'national awakening' and for military modernisation. These demands increasingly drew on the (allegedly) 'scientific' logic of Social Darwinism and the assumption that 'a united national people must be able to fight and be willing to die for their country' (Büttner 2023, 682).

Additional foreign military intrusions in 1900 following the failed Boxer Uprising, and Japan's triumph in the Russo-Japanese War in 1904–5 further prompted members of China's elite to adopt the phrase the 'sick man of East Asia' *(dongya bingfu)*, a description foreign – particularly Western – observers of the period had used to portray China as a backward country with an ailing and incompetent government. In China, however, the term began to refer to physically weak Chinese men, who lacked 'courage, military spirit, martial aspiration, and true masculinity' (Schillinger 2016, 2). In the last decade of the Qing Dynasty, Chinese revolutionaries, who now sought to supplant imperial rule with a modern republic, traced the origins of this masculine malady back to the periods of Mongol and Manchu rule, when 'alien dynasties' tried to 'declaw' their (Han) Chinese subjects by forbidding them from engaging in martial pursuits (Green 2011, 155).

As in Wilhelmine Germany (1890–1918) and Meiji Japan (1868–1912), the military became a model for a modern, cohesive and orderly Chinese society (Schillinger 2016, 5; Green 2011, 153; Zarrow 2015, 28). Flirting with militarism as a solution to the country's weakness, China's progressive elite came to see the army as a vanguard institution in the nation's struggle to modernise. Young men from the wealthy, educated and politically potent elite were now called on to 'throw away the brush and pick up the sword' (*toubi congrong*) – to pursue a military career instead of a life in the civil bureaucracy, and strive for martial glory instead of scholarly refinement. Chinese elite of the period sought not only to elevate the social status of officers and common soldiers but also to introduce a martial consciousness (*junren de jingshen*) and positive attitude towards the army and military values through all levels of society. The acquisition of this mentality was to be supplemented with physical training and military drills (Schillinger 2016, 5; Büttner 2023, 684).

These ideas were adopted by reformers and revolutionaries alike. Key thinkers like Liang Qichao regarded modern education, the fostering of a spirit of nationalism, political reform and the revival of martial attitudes 'as part of the same package', while radicals like Cai E (1882–1916) – a disciple of Liang, who took part in the 1911 Revolution and later became an influential warlord – asserted that militarist education would 'nurture the forces of revolution'. As Cai wrote in 1902: 'to train a good soldier is actually to train a good citizen' (cited in van de Ven 1997, 357).

Within this context, youth martial education became a key area of reform in the final decade of the Qing Dynasty. From the late nineteenth century onward, Chinese reformers both in and out of the government came to see the introduction of universal schooling for boys as a panacea for China's problems. A popular education system, they argued, would not only equip youth with a new set of skills but also teach them that they were part of a 'nation'. In the first decade of the twentieth century, the Qing court finally responded to these calls. Through a series of education edicts introduced in 1902–6, the imperial court sought to establish a modern state school system modelled after those introduced several decades earlier in Europe, South America, as well as in Meiji Japan. Simultaneously, in 1905, the Qing abolished the long-standing civil service examination system which had been in place in China for more than a millennium. A major shock to the country's traditionally educated elite, the move signalled the passing of an entire knowledge order based on mastery of the Confucian classics in favour of modern science and technology (Zarrow 2015, 16–19; Morris 2000). The abolition of the civil service examination also paved the way for the gradual ascendence of military values and skills in Chinese education.

Drawing mainly on Japanese pedagogical theories and models – themselves largely inspired by continental Europe – the newly established mass education system set up by the Qing emphasised discussions of Chinese and world history, politics and modern technology. It further reflected a new concern with developing students' esteem for 'public consciousness (*shanggong*)', 'the practical arts (*shangshi*)', as well as 'the military arts' (*shangwu*) (J. Chen 1989, 31; Zarrow 2015, 17, 19; Morris 2000). The new curriculum aimed at encouraging a martial spirit and included military training as part of physical education classes (mainly calisthenics and gymnastics) for students in grade 6 and above. Reform plans of the period also included putting military lessons into literature, history and geography classes – and even into art and music classes (Zarrow 2015, 20; Zheng 2021, 106).

These plans mainly targeted boys. Late Qing reformers promoted the cause of female education but mainly as a means of turning girls into 'good mothers' of (male) citizens. Reformers promoted the introduction of physical training for girls while seeking to abolish the age-old practice of women's foot-binding, now regarded as a key factor in the physical decline of 'the Chinese race' (Judge 2002, 32). New schools for women established in the first decade of the twentieth century included some form of physical education in their curricula. A few even taught weaponry skills as part of a revolutionary agenda that combined modern education for women with anti-Manchu dissent (Edwards 2016, 47).

Textbooks used in these new girls' schools further presented students with exemplars of Chinese and foreign female martial figures. These included Hua Mulan (c. 500 CE), the legendary warrior first celebrated in a sixth-century Chinese poem, who disguised herself as a man and fought in her father's place when he was ill, as well as Joan of Arc (1412–31), who masqueraded as a man in order to lead her French countrymen into battle against the British. Students were also presented with exemplary women figures who served heroically as women to defend the honour of family, community or nation.

Yet these figures generally acted alongside their husbands (Judge 2002, 40–1; Edwards and Zhou 2011). Moreover, school texts of the period did not appeal to girls to take on military roles. For instance, a lesson in a women's reader on the citizen's duty to serve as a soldier, ended by admonishing 'all mothers to encourage their sons, and all wives to rouse their husbands to sacrifice themselves for the army and exert their duties' (cited in Judge 2002, 41).

Moreover, in the years preceding the 1911 Revolution, boys remained the majority of students in China. The small number of girls who did attend school during this period learned not only academic subjects and physical education, but also household management and infant and childcare knowledge to hone their 'traditional feminine skills' (Zarrow 2015, 18–19). Ultimately then, late Qing schools reinforced, rather than undermined, the gender specificity of martial citizenship. As will be discussed below, this remained a common feature of educational texts and military training programmes in Chinese schools at least until the 1960s.

'Bravely Sacrifice for the Nation': Militarisation in the Republican Era (1912–49)

The Revolution of 1911 toppled the Qing Dynasty and brought an end to two millennia of imperial rule. In early 1912, a provisional government of the Republic of China was established, with revolutionary leader, Sun Yat-sen (1866–1925), as its president. Sun quickly abdicated the role in favour of the military general, Yuan Shikai (1859–1916). In subsequent decades, China was plagued by domestic political chaos, making the country vulnerable to foreign military encroachments. Following the end of World War I, the Versailles Treaty of 1919 turned Germany's concessions in Shandong over to Japan, in spite of China's participation in the war on the side of the Allies. The event sparked a significant upsurge in patriotic sentiment in China. Beginning with a demonstration of college students in Beijing on May 4, 1919, a national movement (which came to be known as the May Fourth Movement) emerged. Sweeping not only educated elite but also city merchants and workers, the movement drew on anti-imperialism while focusing on the ineffectual Beijing government.

In the following decade, known as the Warlord Era (1916–28), China witnessed a particularly tumultuous period, characterised not only by external threats but also by the breakdown of social, economic and political order, and destruction brought about by endemic warfare between domestic army factions. As regional forces across the country degenerated into armed gangs, and officers forsook loyalty to any cause except their own self-interest, much of the Chinese population's faith in the military as a positive institution shattered (Green 2011, 154–5; van de Ven 1997, 361). The 1910s and early 1920s witnessed the emergence of a critical stance against militarism among Chinese intellectuals. Some Western-trained or Western-influenced reformers and educators began to shift their attention from military models to liberal, pacifist pedagogies (Fong 2022, 484). This stance was influenced not only by domestic developments but also by global trends, most notably the emergence of pacifist and antimilitarist movements in the West following the end of the First World War in 1918 and the establishment of the League of Nations in 1920. Already in 1919, China's National Federation of Educational Associations had passed a resolution to abolish civic–military education as one of China's main educational goals. China's 1923 New School System curriculum also did not include military education as part of students' mandatory physical training (Culp 2007, 198).

Yet some of the country's key political leaders, including Sun Yat-sen, who had founded the Chinese Nationalist Party (*Kuomintang* [KMT], also known as *Guomindang*) in 1919, continued to uphold a 'militarized paternalistic view of China's modernization' (Meyskens 2020, 23). This view was illustrated in the comprehensive development plan Sun devised in 1920, a plan which endorsed a period of military tutelage during which the KMT would remould China's population from a 'heap of loose sand' into 'disciplined citizens devoted to building the nation and protecting it from foreign harm' (cited in Meyskens 2020, 23).

Sun's vision also affected the educational agenda of the period: a combination of civic–military education remained one of the chief objectives of leading Republican education officials such as Cai Yuanpei (1868–1940) (Fong 2022, 484). A significant avenue of youth military education was the Chinese scouting programme. First introduced to missionary schools in the 1910s as an elitist form of civic training, the programme became prevalent across coastal provinces in the 1920s. Based on the English Boy Scout programme founded by the British Army officer Robert Baden-Powell (1857–1941), China's scouting programme offered an eclectic collection of lessons that combined collective military drills and jamborees with hygiene and etiquette classes, arts and crafts, outdoor experiences, practical skills training and social services (Culp 2006).

The emergence of this new type of youth organisation was facilitated by Chinese educators' growing rejection of indigenous texts and approaches grounded in Confucian thinking, which treated children as incomplete human beings subordinate to their elders and seniors. In its earlier stages, this intellectual movement, known as the New Culture or the May Fourth Movement, was dominated by romantic notions of the innocent, defenceless child and by the liberal ideas of American Progressive Education (Naftali 2021b, 255; Anagnost 1997; Farquhar 1999; Jones 2002; Plum 2012). Over the course of the 1920s, however, Chinese progressive reformers increasingly cast children as epitomes of Darwinian 'naturalness'. In a war-torn society that many intellectuals viewed with despair and shame, youth became the perfect image for reformers who believed that China's salvation from internal political instability and foreign imperialism lay in the empowerment of its young people (Farquhar 1999, 36–7).

This view was shared across the political divide in the Republican era (1912–49). Following the establishment of the Communist Party of China (CPC) in 1921, Communist educators and activists – like their KMT counterparts – came to regard childhood as a pivotal period for cultivating future revolutionaries and instilling proper political consciousness in citizens. But CPC leaders also saw youth as intermediaries who could spread socialist and patriotic messages to the entire society (Tillman 2018). Reflecting the influence of modern conceptions of the child imported from the West, which emphasised children's capabilities and the central role of youth in nation-building processes (Plum 2012, 256), this conviction contributed to the growing militarisation of Chinese education from the late 1920s onwards (Zheng 2021, 107). After the May Thirtieth Incident of 1925 – a nationwide series of strikes and demonstrations precipitated by the killing of thirteen labour demonstrators by British police in Shanghai – Chinese educators and students of different political convictions began to demand large-scale military training for students. Their calls received further impetus as youth became involved in a new wave of nationalist movements targeting Japanese imperialist aggression against China (Fong 2022, 484).

After the establishment of a new Nationalist regime in 1927 under the leadership of KMT military general, Chiang Kai-shek (1887–1975), youth military education received an even larger push; the KMT government was dependent on the support of the military. By the late 1920s, Chiang's central army had managed to defeat most separatist warlord armies. Its success placed the whole of China under the general's centralised authority, at least in theory. With Communist forces and provincial warlords still vying for control, Chiang and his government needed to legitimise their rule by strengthening ideological and cultural control. Constructing a heroic discourse of the soldier figure and extending this discourse across society became an important step in their effort (Y. Xu 2019, 5).

Under the new regime set up in Nanjing, military training became compulsory in high schools and colleges nationwide. Students, specifically boys, had to undergo three consecutive weeks of a military education course in each summer vacation under the guidance of military officers (Chen 1989, 31). After Japan's invasion of China in 1931, the KMT began to explicitly promote 'militarisation (*junshihua*)' as part of its popular mobilisation drive. Chiang had hoped that compulsory military service would disseminate martial virtues across society but by the early 1930s, it was clear that China's tremendous size and huge population made a viable conscription system almost impossible. Faced with his government's inability to reshape civilian attitudes through conscription, Chiang initiated the New Life Movement (*Xin shenghuo yundong*, 1934–7) which aimed to promote patriotic martial values and impose military norms of behaviour on the civilian population (Green 2011, 180).

The New Life Movement (NLF) represented the KMT's attempt to inculcate individual self-discipline, collective responsibility and national loyalty among citizens by popularising a combination of Chinese neo-Confucian 'traditional' virtues – namely 'propriety, justice, integrity, and shame' – and a foreign-inspired ideology modelled in part on the Fascist regimes of Italy and Germany and in part on the military ethic Chiang Kai-shek had experienced as a cadet in Japan (Gerth 2020 [2003], 292–4). Whether, or to what extent, the Nanjing regime under Chiang Kai-shek should be characterised as 'Fascist' remains a contested issue (Fong 2022, 508; Wakeman, 1997; Culp 2007). While interwar fascism in Europe was undergirded by an ambition for military expansion and an aestheticisation and glorification of military violence, the KMT's military and political vision arguably lacked an expansionist ideology or the 'cult of war' found in European fascism (Fong 2022, 509). That said, Chiang Kai-shek's NLF used the constant threat of violence not only to convert untrained and undisciplined conscripts into ideal soldiers but also to extend the ideal of the citizen-soldier to the rest of society (Flath and Smith 2011, 7).

As Chiang himself put it, 'In the home, the factory, and the government office, everyone's activities must be the same as in the army.... And everyone together must firmly and bravely sacrifice for the group and for the nation' (cited in Gerth 2020 [2003], 294, n20). The KMT's total militarisation (*chedi junshi hua*) drive attempted to reach into the familial sphere and in theory even extended into citizens' bodies (Gerth 2020 [2003], 296). Intellectual and cultural publications associated with the NLF linked bodily discipline and hygiene to the regeneration of the country, and contrasted 'the virtues of austerity, physical strength, and moral force' to the 'degenerate habits' and '"effeminate" bodies of China's Confucian scholars' (Dikötter 1995, 125).

Within the context of the NLF, martial pedagogies became a core part of youth education. As was the case in other Fascist regimes (e.g. Ehs 2013; Ponzio 2015), militarised physical education was intended to cultivate a sense of discipline and 'tire the body into submission' – prescriptions which mainly targeted elite youth in China's big cities (Culp 2007, 197; Zheng 2021, 108; L. Xu 2015). Secondary schools were ordered to step up military education and to conduct two hours of daily training. By 1936, military training had been implemented in 522 middle schools and 97 specialised schools and universities across 18 KMT-controlled provinces. From 1929 to 1936, a total of 284,467 students were enlisted in the training programme, of which 87,674 had participated in the centralised summer military training enacted in 1934 (Fong 2022, 482). After the outbreak of a full-scale war with Japan in 1937, the KMT Education Ministry reiterated the importance of military training for youth from junior high school onward. At the college level, martial training was extended to two to three months to meet wartime needs (Chen 1989, 31–2).

The implementation of these training programmes was nonetheless riddled with problems and contradictions. While fetishising a regimented society, the KMT's military training initiatives incorporated a relatively heterogeneous set of tactics, reflecting the different ideals and interests of students, educators and various state actors (Fong 2022, 508). For instance, alongside the emphasis on instilling military discipline through collective military drills and regimented daily routines, the programme also drew on Confucian-style moral mentorship as well as on liberal ideals of voluntarism and individual competition, features which undermined the goal of imposing order, discipline and uniformity (Culp 2007, 198, Fong 2022, 483). A recent study further shows that the KMT or the central government did not have dominant control over the military training programme. Rather, it was a field in which different local stakeholders, including military drill organisers, students, parents and headmasters, negotiated with each other (Wang and Li 2022, 368).

Moreover, from the mid-1930s to the mid-1940s, the KMT regime prioritised the fight against Chinese communism over the fight against Japanese imperialism under the paradigm of 'internal pacification before external resistance'. While espousing a military ethos, the KMT's youth training programme deemphasised the urgency of actual armament. Instead, it underscored daily manners and personal moral character as a means to counter Communist influence (Fong 2022, 484). Published testimonies of students who took part in the KMT's military training during the 1930s demonstrate that this divergence undermined the mobilisational potential of the training programme and created space for student trainees to pursue their own agendas and even criticise aspects of KMT rule (Fong 2022, 484; Wang and Li 2022). The programme was further marred by discrepancies between the virtues of 'soldierly self-sacrifice' and 'endurance', and the practices of some KMT leaders. A testimony by a Hangzhou senior middle school student published in a quarterly student magazine in 1935 notes for instance that the three weeks of summer military training he and his classmates undertook felt like 'hell' compared to the 'heavenlike' conditions under which some KMT leaders had been living, 'dallying with their mistresses under electric fans' (Fong 2022, 482).

As noted, the KMT's military education scheme mainly applied to boys. Girls were exempted from military training and instead were to take a 'military nursing course' (Chen 1989, 31–2). Youth culture of the 1930s and 1940s further propagated this gendered form of militarisation, as it placed an emphasis on male military heroism, whereas girls played a relatively small part in works targeting children and youth (Farquhar 1999, 180). This distinction in turn reflected the KMT's recognition of Confucian notions of female virtues (Zheng 2021, 108). The patriarchal authority advocated by the KMT government in the 1930s and 1940s required men's fighting on the battlefield and women's cooperation in the household. Women's duties nonetheless included disciplining children 'to be good citizens for the national survival' (Zheng 2021, 108–9).

Unlike the KMT, Communist Party leaders and activists sought to challenge these traditional gender norms and were willing to allocate women a much more active part in the struggle against domestic and foreign enemies. Yet, CPC leaders shared the KMT's belief that the War of Resistance against Japan constituted an opportunity to cultivate a new society and a new type of citizen. Already in 1927, the Communist Party of China started to construct its own armed forces. On 7 August 1927, at an emergency CPC meeting following the KMT's decision to attempt to exterminate the CPC (cited in van de Ven 1997, 361) Mao Zedong (1893–1976) famously declared that 'power comes out of the barrel of the gun'. Mao's words reflected the notion that the training and organisation of militarily skilled and politically aware citizens is important both for external defence as well as for internal revolution. Army and civilian militia were needed to fight a united People's War against class enemies. They could also support the formal military forces as part of a strategy that would draw an external enemy deep into China's hinterland, mobilise the population for total war, and wage guerrilla and mobile warfare to erode the enemy's strength in a protracted war (Joffe 2008, 356). Indeed, During the War of Resistance against Japan and the Civil War, CPC-backed militia groups mounted guerilla operations in support of the regular army, provided the Red Army with rear services and served as a source of recruits (Dreyer 1982, 65).

As the Communists engaged in guerrilla warfare from base areas in northern China, the CPC's education policies (inspired by Soviet models) emphasised the importance of both labour and war preparedness among the youth (L. Xu 2015) and Party ideologues promoted 'national defence literature' (*guofang wenxue*) as the official theme for cultural products aimed at children and youth (Y. Xu 2019, 7–8; M. Chen 2016). Thus, from the 1930s onward, youth military education was carried out simultaneously in both KMT- and CPC-ruled areas (L. Xu 2015). On both sides of the political divide, media, literary and educational texts portrayed children and youth not only as victims of armed conflict but also as courageous fighters in their own right (Plum 2012, 240; M. Chen 2016, 23; W. K. Chan 2007; de Giorgi 2014; Miao and Song 2021). This was not mere rhetoric. According to official PRC historiography, children as young as 13 or 14 had joined the CPC's Red Army (Guo 2015), while the KMT had recruited thousands of children and youths with an average age of 15, the youngest no older than 9, to make up for shortages of adult fighters during the Battle of Mount Song (also known as the Battle of Ramou) against the Japanese military in 1944 (Liu and Huan 2013).

After the Japanese surrender in September 1945, the Nationalists and Communists resumed their civil war. During this period, which lasted until 1949, the KMT consolidated its earlier attempts to militarise society by calling on 'educated youths' (*zhishi qingnian*) to join the army. The efforts proved ineffective. In KMT-ruled areas, youth military training became increasingly politicised, as the KMT employed military training instructors as spies against students who supported the CPC (Chen 1989, 32). The period also saw the emergence of a Chinese students' antiwar movement, which demanded an immediate end to the civil war, an end to US backing for the KMT government in that war and a shift in public expenditure from military to civilian needs. Although student protests aroused nationwide attention and response, the KMT government refused to accept overt opposition to its civil war policy and became increasingly ruthless in its efforts to suppress the students (Y. Xu 2019, 9).

In contrast to the KMT, the CPC enjoyed increasing popular support throughout the 1930s and 1940s. Nonetheless, it too politicised youth military education in the areas under its control. For the CPC leadership the objective of NDE was not only to foster national unity, resist foreign aggression and strengthen national defence, but also to garner popular support for the socialist revolutionary case. As the armed force of the CPC, the Red Army was therefore accorded a key role not only in ensuring victory in the 'People's War' but also in popularising Party principles and policies among the population, including children and youth (H. Lu 2005, 11). As the discussion below will demonstrate, military values and techniques would play a key role in the Party's ongoing propaganda and educational efforts after the Communist victory over the KMT in 1949.

'Chinese Children Are Far from Naïve': War Education in China of the 1950s

On 1 October 1949, Mao Zedong declared that the Chinese people had 'stood up'. The establishment of the People's Republic of China (PRC) followed more than two decades of intermittent civil war between the CPC and KMT forces and prolonged struggle against Japan. Yet in the early 1950s, the new socialist regime faced enormous problems. It had to achieve political consolidation, rebuild a war-shattered economy and unify the country. In the first few years after the founding of the PRC, millions of KMT troops were still in the country's southwest and southern regions and on its coastal islands. Some displayed stubborn resistance against the new regime, while others resorted to banditry (J. Chen 1996, 1).

And yet, just a year after the establishment of the PRC, Mao and the CPC leadership sent about three million 'Chinese People's Volunteers' (CPVs) to fight against UN forces moving towards the Chinese–Korean border.[2] Although China's intervention saved the North Korean Communist regime from collapse, it was unable to fulfil the Beijing leadership's hopes of overwhelming the UN forces. When the Korean War ended in July 1953, Korea's political map remained virtually unchanged. America's military intervention in Korea and China's rush into a conflict with the US brought the Cold War in Asia into a new era characterised by confrontation between the PRC and the United States that would last nearly twenty years (J. Chen 1996, 1).

The Korean War was a period of heightened political mobilisation in China (Zheng 2021, 112). In military strength and industrial capacity, China was no match for its opponent, the well-equipped and well-supplied United Nations Command (UNC), under US leadership. What China could rely on, however, was its massive population and its political propaganda apparatus (Naftali 2021b, 259). To galvanise its citizens into fighting 'a just war' against American imperialism during a contentious land reform programme, the Chinese government launched a vigorous media and educational campaign under the slogan 'Resist America and Aid [North] Korea' (*Kang Mei yuan Chao*); 'Defend the Homeland and Protect Our Country (*Baojia weiguo*)'.

Propaganda works of the period typically demonised the American enemy while beautifying the sacrifice of Chinese volunteers on the battlefront. In a famous 1951 essay published in the *Renmin ribao* (*People's Daily*) under the title 'Who are the most beloved people?' reporter Wei Wei eulogised the heroic deeds of Chinese fighters in Korea through several moving accounts, including the rescue of a North Korean boy in the aftermath of an air strike. The essay – which would become required reading in the Chinese school curriculum in decades to come – emphasised that peace at home is impossible without the sacrifices of PLA soldiers – 'the most beloved people' (West, Levine and Hiltz 1997, 184, 195, 198; Gao 2001, 186). The term 'the most beloved people (*zui kei'ai de ren*)' became synonymous with PLA soldiers in China's public discourse, while many other poems, fiction and dramas of the Korean War period constructed a similarly romantic conception of the war. Media reports of the era further provided graphic depictions of the US bombing of China's border cities, including images of bloody bodies and burned houses, highlighting war atrocities and making the war in Korea personal to the Chinese people (Gao 2001, 198–9; Rawnsley 2009, 306; Chin 2023, 25; Zhu 2014).

These propaganda efforts targeted not only adults but also children, who were cast in the role of revolutionary successors (M. Chen 2016, 98–9; Brzycki 2019; Naftali 2021b; Chin 2023). Children's publications of the period, such as the primary school children's magazine, *Little Friends* (*Xiao pengyou*), presented young readers with ideas for military-themed games, riddles, and arts and craft projects, and encouraged children to participate in war-related activities, such as preparing military-themed propaganda posters, writing letters to soldiers, collecting military donations and partaking in the nationwide 'Patriotic Hygiene Campaign', which called for the systematic extermination of pests in order to ward off 'American germ-warfare' during the Korean War (Xia 1951, 12–13).

The magazine also included regular sections detailing the heroic tales of Chinese fighters in Korea and in previous military conflicts. Most of the accounts featured adult fighters but some stories also included children, albeit in different capacities. One common role was that of innocent victims. However, some writers presented a different image of children: that of active, heroic fighters. Noted examples include the story of a primary school student who managed to catch a spy and deliver him to PLA soldiers (Fang 1951, 4–5) or of a North Korean boy who single-handedly struck down an enemy plane with a shotgun while managing to kill all adult crew members in the process (Xiao 1951, 5). A 1951 children's poem, 'Good Older Brother, Good Younger Brother' illustrates the construction of children as political agents:

> Older brother marches forward; younger brother follows behind / 'Older Brother! Older Brother! Where are you going?' / 'I am going to military school to learn how to beat the enemy' / 'Why beat the enemy?' / 'In order to defend peace!' / 'Older Brother, you are so glorious ... / You are marching forward; I will study hard / when I finish my studies / I will join you, and together we shall defeat the enemy and kill the Americans!' (cited in Naftali 2021b, 260)

The poem emphasises that the younger child is busy with the task of studying. Nonetheless, the child – notably a boy – is depicted as being mentally prepared to fight for his country just like his brother. The gender distinctiveness of the child is typical of the period's war-themed educational and media materials. While children in general were discursively central to the 'Resist America, Aid Korea' propaganda campaign, boys and girls were differently and unequally positioned within these works, with boys more typically at the centre of war tales aimed at children.

The idea that children (specifically boys) can and should play a key role as political agents and even as fighters was by no means universal among educators and children's writers of the period. In fact, an article published in 1952 in the CPC mouthpiece, the *People's Daily*, complained that many contemporary children's authors display an 'incorrect appreciation of children's capabilities and level of awareness'. Whereas some are influenced by a 'child-centred' ideology and depict children as 'superior little heroes', while overlooking their age limitations or mental and physical immaturity, 'others "erroneously" believe that writing about war . . . is beyond children's life experiences' (He 1952). This ambiguous view of children and war was evident in other socialist countries, where alongside the trope of the child as self-reliant and always ready to defend the revolution, images of children as innocent, docile and in need of protection persisted in media and educational materials (Kelly 2007; Peacock 2015).

Maoist-era education was also ambiguous in its treatment of nationalism and internationalism when teaching youth about historical conflict. In the Maoist-era curriculum, historical materialism was considered the only way to understand past events. Workers and class struggle were the makers of both domestic and world history. The Maoist view of armed conflict, which drew on Marxist ideology, catalogued wars into 'just' and 'unjust', the former being wars against capitalist, imperialist forces who initiate 'unjust' conflicts to maximise their interests (Mao 1961 [1936]).

Accordingly, history textbooks produced in China from the 1950s onwards portrayed international military conflict as an inevitable product of the excesses of the capitalist system, which requires endless expansion to overseas markets and leads to unavoidable struggles for world hegemony. According to this narrative, in the War of Resistance against Japan, the CPC had 'led the Chinese people to victory in a war waged not against the Japanese nation as such, but rather against a ruling clique of Japanese militarists aided by Chinese feudalist traitors – that is, the KMT' (cited in Chang 2021, 1154–5). At the same time, the stated aim of school history teaching in Maoist China was to educate children and youth not only for the 'internationalist communist world view' but also for 'patriotism' (*aiguozhuyi*). Thus, in a departure from Marxist orthodoxy, school textbooks in the new socialist state portrayed the struggles of Chinese people against foreign imperialist forces as expressions not only of 'class contradictions' but also of 'righteous patriotic indignation' (Naftali 2021b, 258).

It is hard to ascertain the effects of these messages on the attitudes of Chinese children and youth of the early 1950s. Stories in PRC official media of the period suggest that war enthusiasm overwhelmed Chinese citizens. In June 1951, for instance, the Chinese government issued calls for donations of weaponry to the war front; by May 1952, civilian contributions had reportedly reached a sum large enough 'to purchase more than 3,000 fighter jets' (cited in Zhu 2014). A 76-year-old janitor from Hunan Province purportedly sent in earnings from fetching water to buy weaponry for the war, while school children gave their pocket money hoping to buy a jet in their names (Zhu 2014).

Verifying such stories is difficult, not least because their circulation constituted part of the propaganda efforts of the period. Indeed, several studies suggest that students' responses to the Korean War propaganda were in fact varied, ranging from genuine (or feigned) compliance, to indifference, or even resistance (Chin 2023, 25; Masuda 2016). For instance, a 1950 report of the Propaganda Department of Jiangning District in Shanghai indicates that 'about 80 percent of the students of Nanping Girls' Middle School' who were exposed to the educational efforts 'did not pay attention to current affairs, did not read newspapers daily, and only cared about their schoolwork'. The report further notes that some students even argued that 'American imperialism did not invade China'. Others 'had animosity toward the Soviet Union' and could not 'clearly distinguish between friends and enemies' (cited in Chin 2023, 45). Drawing on oral testimonies and memoirs, other studies claim that systematic exposure to war narratives in class and participation in patriotic propaganda activities in and outside the school may have succeeded in inculcating a martial mentality in Maoist-era students (Unger 1982; A. Chan 1985; Honig 2002; Yang and Yan 2017). Such a transformation may have also been facilitated by the military training activities youths were required to attend as part of a nationwide campaign in the late 1950s.

Youth Military Training and the 'Everyone a Soldier' Campaign

In the first decade of socialist rule, the CPC regime placed an emphasis on a systematic implementation of National Defence Education (NDE) as a means of consolidating the new regime and to ensure civilian readiness to face the regime's enemies. In articles and speeches published in the early 1950s, Mao warned against harbouring 'unrealistic illusions' concerning the diminishing threat of 'foreign imperialism' or 'domestic reactionaries' and cautioned that 'the Party and the people' must maintain their 'vigilance' against these persistent threats (H. Lu 2005, 11–12).

During the 1950s, a potential conflict with Taiwan and/or the United States constituted the primary threat. Taiwan, which had been under Japanese rule since 1895, was returned to the KMT government after Japan's defeat in the Pacific War in 1945. However, it was cut off from the mainland in 1949 when the KMT was driven by the CPC to the island during China's Civil War. While the PLA was prepared to 'liberate Taiwan' in 1950, it was forced to call off the attempt after the outbreak of the Korean War and President Harry Truman's order of the US Seventh Fleet to patrol the Taiwan Strait. Given the CPC's other priorities during this time, Mao and the other Party leaders were willing to postpone the attempt to (re)take Taiwan by force.[3] Nonetheless, Mao ordered the PLA to shell the offshore islands of Jinmen (Quemoy) and Mazu (Matsu) occupied by KMT troops twice in 1954 and 1958 to keep the civil war alive (Suisheng Zhao 2022, 707).

Mao's emphasis on National Defence Education was further related to the strategic concept of the 'People's War', which remained relevant even after the CPC transformed itself from a 'party-military revolutionary movement' into 'a governing party-army-state' after 1949 (Scobell 2022, 357). Accordingly, a January 1955 editorial published in the CPC mouthpiece, *Renmin Ribao* (*People's Daily*), under the title 'Promote Conventional National Defence Education among the People' (*Xiang renmin qunzhong Jinchang jinxing guofang jiaoyu*), stated that college students should conduct 'military training' over the summer vacation and carry out 'national defence sports' where 'conditions permit'. Such activities would ensure that youth acquire 'basic military knowledge', and develop a spirit of 'patriotism and revolutionary heroism' as well as 'a healthy and strong body' (cited in Lu, 2005, 12).

The announcement laid the foundation for the launching of the PRC's first pilot programme of student military training at the college level. In the summer of 1955, a report of the Central Military Commission of the CPC proposed that military training should be carried out in colleges and universities to train a 'reserve force', with students focusing on the study of 'relevant military professional knowledge'. The same year saw the promulgation of the first 'Military Service Law' of the People's Republic of China. Article 54 of Chapter VIII of the law lays out the foundation for the college military training programme (M. Zhang 1988, 16). The focus on the college population, which at the time constituted a small minority of educated youth residing in urban areas, was a product of the CPC leadership's plan to transform the PLA from a mass low-tech infantry force suitable for an armed revolutionary insurgency to an armed force suited for large-scale conventional war between great powers (H. Lu 2005, 12; Scobell 2022, 361).

Between 1955 and 1957, the training programme consisted of 400 credit hours for a five-year higher degree programme, 300 credit hours for a four-year degree programme, and one training camp during the summer vacation. Out of concern that the course would 'create a heavy load on students' and hinder the pressing goal of 'national industrialisation', key higher education institutes and key majors were exempt from military training which was effectively a limited pilot programme. By 1956, the pilot was implemented in fourteen colleges and universities across the country, with more than 10,000 students undergoing training (M. Zhang 1988, 17; H. Lu 2005, 12). That same year, the Ministry of Education and the Ministry of National Defence also conducted a pilot military training programme in 127 senior high schools, with the number of trained middle school students reaching tens of thousands – again a very small minority of the middle school population in China (Xie 1989, 49; H. Lu 2005, 13).

Youth military training underwent considerable expansion when the programme was integrated into the newly established People's Militia (*minbing*) in 1958 (Ge 1987, 66; Z. Zhang 1987, 26; Xie 1989, 49). As noted, before 1949, the CPC relied on civilian militia organisations to aid its struggle both against the Japanese and KMT forces. After the 1949 Revolution, the People's Militia was retained as a para-military body with detachments, battalions and companies at the appropriate civil level, while its highest command remained with the People's Liberation Army. Before 1958, the militia functioned as a reserve force for the PLA, suppressed bandits and protected crops. Local militia forces also acted as the 'spearhead' in class struggle and social reform, including the Suppression of Counterrevolutionaries and land reform movements of the early 1950s. During the early years of the PRC, the militia nonetheless served as an elite organisation. According to non-Chinese estimates, in 1954–7, its size ranged from six to twelve million (roughly 4 per cent of the population) (Gittings 1964, 102; Dreyer 1982, 79; Perry 2006).

The status and functions of the People's Militia changed during the Great Leap Forward (1958–61). Spurred on by the Taiwan Straits crisis of 1958 and the growing possibility of a war with the United States, CPC leaders launched the Great Leap Forward (GLF) to make China into a major industrial and military power by severely curbing consumption and directing all resources into a large, militarised campaign to increase heavy industry. Simultaneously, the Party headed by Mao stressed the role of the civilian militia in promoting the People's War. In the context of a re-assessment of China's defence in the nuclear age, the civilian militia was seen as vital for deterring foreign invasion (Perry 2006, 185; Meyskens 2020, 61–2). Mao as well as Lin Biao (1907–71), who had replaced Peng Dehuai as China's minister of defence in 1959, maintained that China's geographical size and its relatively dispersed industry would allow the country to survive a nuclear attack. A conventional 'follow-up' to a nuclear blast would encounter popular resistance of massive proportions. The civilian militia was to serve as a solution for the 'contradiction between a small-sized army in peace time and a large-sized army required in wartime by forming an inexhaustible reserve for the PLA' (cited in Gittings 1964, 105).[4]

Drawing on this strategic vision, in August 1958, the CPC Centre adopted a decision which called for 'arming all the people – rural and urban alike'. A month later, in an interview with a Xinhua reporter, Mao stressed that 'every factory, school, government agency, and enterprise must establish a militia' in preparation for a potential 'imperialist invasion'. This marked the beginning of the Everyone a Soldier (*quanmin jiebing*) campaign, in which all men and women between the ages of sixteen and fifty (excepting those with 'bad class labels' or physical handicaps) were expected to train with weapons as members of their local militia movement (Perry 2006, 185–6).

A smaller number of militia members aged sixteen and thirty would be further assigned to the hard-core or 'basic-level backbone' units and supplemented by demobilised servicemen and veterans. Weapons, in addition to those made available from army warehouses, were to be manufactured by all provinces, municipalities and autonomous regions. The goal was one gun for every four people (Gittings 1964, 109; Perry 2006, 186, 189). For the ordinary populace, summer camps would serve as the main mode of training. In addition to participating in irregular spare-time training sessions, all militia members were expected to spend at least ten days each year undergoing full-time instruction. Militia training sessions would stress ideological commitment (or 'redness') as much as – or more than – technical skills (or expertise) (Perry 2006, 188, 190).

Alongside the national defence aspects of the militia, the Everyone a Soldier campaign also emphasised the militia's expanded role in increasing economic production, including tasks such as fighting drought and producing iron and steel as part of the GLF (Dreyer 1982, 67, 73; Noth 2021, 158). The extensive social aims of the campaign were illustrated in a statement by General Fu Qiutao, the man in charge of militia work, who explained (in language reminiscent of the New Life Movement of Chiang Kai-shek) that the Everyone a Soldier campaign was 'to strengthen the organization, discipline, and militancy of the people and transform the disunity and backwardness inherited from the old society' (cited in Perry 2006, 186).

The plan was for a people's militia of 300 million (out of a total population then estimated at 700 million). In practice, however, only 220 million militia members were officially enrolled by the end of 1959 (approximately a third of the country's population at the time). Of these, only a small proportion – 10–15 per cent at the most in some provinces – belonged to the hard-core, and only the hard-core appears to have been systematically drilled and instructed in the use of firearms (Gittings 1964, 110; Dreyer 1982, 78; Perry 2006, 187). Because it was closely connected to the establishment of the people's communes in the countryside during the GLF, the militia of the Everyone a Soldier campaign was for the most part a rural rather than urban movement. Militia members also tended to be male even as contemporary state media circulated images of women as militia fighters and told heroic tales of figures such as Liu Hulan (the 'youngest female martyr of the socialist revolution') to highlight the total mobilisation of Chinese society (Edwards 2016, 175–8; Noth 2021, 159, 161; X. Wang 2023, 4–5).

The Everyone a Soldier campaign was undermined by several problems, including the apathy and abuse of power by local Party or military cadres. The enormous expansion of the militia was accompanied by an increase in disciplinary problems, particularly in the countryside. In some cases, militia captains used the cover of the militia to commit criminal acts that ranged from robbery to rape (Perry 2006, 189). But the campaign was particularly undermined by the disastrous outcome of the GLF movement. The GLF was supposed to create a Communist society and rapidly boost heavy industry. Instead, it produced economic depression and widespread famine, which according to some estimates killed up to 30 million people (Meyskens 2020, 6–7).

The agricultural disasters which followed the GLF hindered the militia's work and created doubts among some CPC leaders about the wisdom of 'arming the people' (Gittings 1964, 111). With the halting of the GLF in the early 1960s, the militia resumed its auxiliary role of guarding strategic points, such as railways, communications, seacoasts and frontiers; maintaining law and order; and assisting the security forces (Gittings 1964, 115; Noth 2021, 159). Militias were still called upon to partake in economic tasks, but the role may have reflected a sense among the army's leadership that 'time spent training the militia was time lost from other activities that were more beneficial to the national defense' (Dreyer 1982, 73).

The militia remained large, however, and Mao and other radical Party leaders continued to affirm its value in the 1960s. Signalling the growing penetration of the military into civilian life, the Everyone a Soldier campaign constituted an important milestone in the state-advocated militarisation of Chinese society (Perry 2006, 194–5). The campaign, which involved youths aged over sixteen, attempted not only to strengthen national defence but also – and no less importantly – to 'induce the broad masses of civilians to apply a military like workstyle enthusiastically to all of China's problems, domestic and otherwise' (Dreyer 1982, 78). As the next section will show, this approach would reach its zenith by the mid-1960s amid the deterioration of China's security environment and the eruption of a massive domestic conflict known as the Cultural Revolution.

'Learning from the Military' in the 1960s and 1970s

From the early 1960s, China experienced worsening national security conditions. During the China-Soviet split in 1960, Chiang

Kai-shek launched several commando raids into southeast China as part of Taiwan's plan to retake the Chinese mainland. In 1962, China became involved in a border war with India, and in the wake of the Sino-Soviet split, the USSR stationed hundreds of thousands of troops on China's northern border. After the Gulf of Tonkin Incident in 1964, the United States ramped up its military involvement in Vietnam, threatening China's southern border. Even though China successfully tested an atomic bomb in October 1964, its nuclear arsenal was small, and it had no delivery system that could bomb Moscow until the 1970s or the United States until the 1980s. There was also no viable way of quickly improving the technological abilities of China's military since the Soviet Union was now its enemy, and Western countries had placed an embargo on trading arms with China from the early 1950s (Meyskens 2020, 9, 45–6).

In preparation for a possible war with both the United States and the Soviet Union, the CPC leadership upheld its former strategy of a ground war whose purpose would be to draw enemy troops deep into Chinese territory where they would then become targets for PLA and civilian militia attacks. Drawing on this 'protracted people's war' tactic, in 1964 Mao initiated the Third Front (*sanxian jianshe*) project (Meyskens 2020, 61–2). The most expensive industrialisation campaign of the Mao era, the project 'reconceptualized the entire country as one giant battlefield in which society and economy were to be militarized' in preparation for the perceived threat of 'a surprise attack' (Meyskens 2020, 26).

Alongside these growing foreign security threats, in the early 1960s, Mao became increasingly anxious about the state of domestic politics and ideology. In particular, he feared that the policies issued by the CPC's centre after the debacle of the GLF exhibited signs of 'Soviet revisionism' and that his colleagues in the Party leadership were 'steering China towards a Soviet-style capitalist resurgence' (Meyskens 2020, 6–7). To foster civilian readiness to detect and defeat the internal enemies of the socialist cause, Mao initiated a 'socialist education programme' in 1963. A massive propaganda campaign aimed at reversing 'capitalist trends' in Chinese society by promoting 'collectivism, patriotism, and socialism', the campaign emphasised the ideological education role of the People's Militia, while critiquing 'bourgeois' tendencies within the PLA. In 1965, the military rank system was abolished, and emphasis was placed on the PLA's role in civilian society (Dreyer 1982, 74).

At the same time though, the 'socialist education campaign' employed militant heroes and models to reintroduce 'socialist values' into Chinese society. The entire nation was called upon to 'learn from the People's Liberation Army (*xue jun*)' and to 'learn from Lei Feng (*xue Lei Feng*)'. The most famous model-hero to emerge during this period, Lei Feng (1940–62) was an army soldier whose dedication to Mao and attitude of self-sacrifice epitomised the values the CPC sought to inculcate in the nation's citizens, in particular youth (Lanza 2012; Kauffman 2020).

While military models were already present in educational materials of the 1950s, they became even more prevalent in the 1960s, with authors deploying war stories and military models to address the concern that Chinese youth were acquiring too much 'petty bourgeois knowledge' (Yang and Li 1986, 5; Z. Zhao 2003, 579). As one study documents, numerous stories in school textbooks for first and second graders depicted how PLA army 'uncles' live 'a life of service to the people' (Martin 1975, 259). In one such story, soldiers go to great lengths to post back a kitchen knife they had borrowed from a villager on an overnight encampment. In another story, soldiers 'exhaust themselves saving the lives of fishermen caught in a storm and then provide the men with much technical assistance to repair their boats' (cited in Martin 1975, 259). Other stories were set during the wars against Japan and the KMT. Storybook heroes were either youth helping the PLA or were soldiers themselves, often martyrs who died for the revolution and/or the nation (Unger 1982, 85).

Students were encouraged to identify with the soldiers' heroism and to see the patriotic/socialist cause as worthy of their sacrifice. They were taught that China is surrounded by external and internal enemies – a theme which received increased emphasis after the Sino-Soviet split of 1960 (Unger 1982, 85; Edwards 2016, 175–97). Compared to earlier school history materials, the subject's textbooks of the early to mid-1960s contained lengthier discussions of military battles while highlighting historical incidents in which adolescents of different genders aided in the fight against domestic and external enemies, mainly in auxiliary capacities such as fetching food and water for adult combatants (Naftali 2021b, 265).

This period also witnessed the introduction of military training to younger student populations. Instead of simply being taught bodily movement during physical education, as was the case in the 1950s, boys and girls aged six to twelve were now issued sticks to use as rifles and taught games such as 'little people's militia,' 'small air force pilots' and 'learning to be the People's Liberation Army' (White 1989, 205–8, 215–16; Honig 2002, 262). When relations between China and the Soviet Union further deteriorated into armed conflict in 1969, children as young as seven or eight were encouraged to dig deep trenches in preparation for a potential war (S. H. Lu 2004, 762; Naftali 2021b, 264). All middle school and college students continued to participate in short-term military training courses as part of militia training (Z. Zhang 1987, 26; Xie 1989, 49). While only core members of the militia were capable of performing combat duties, much of the rest of the population, old and young alike, had by the mid-1960s received at least a rudimentary military education, which included some experience of handling firearms (Perry 2006, 194–5).

The launch of the 'Cultural Revolution' in 1966 brought Chinese youth to the forefront of armed political struggle. Initiated by Mao Zedong, who feared that the initial fervour of the socialist revolution was being lost to more conservative, bureaucratic elements within the CPC, the Great Proletarian Cultural Revolution received its name from Mao's call to the Chinese people, particularly youth, to attack all 'traditional values' and 'bourgeois' elements and to publicly criticise Party officials to restore the revolution to its rightful path. Chinese children, who in Confucian tradition were required to respectfully submit to their elders and seniors (including teachers), received a new role as Chairman Mao's 'foot soldiers'. They were now responsible for enlightening the older generation, especially on political matters (Naftali 2014a, 87; Finnane 2008; Lee 2011).

The Cultural Revolution (hereafter, CR) started in May 1966 with the posting of the first *dazibao* (big character poster) at Beijing University. By August 1966, the movement extended to senior and junior middle schools as well, where the first groups of Red Guards (*Hong weibing*) were formed. Millions of youths heeded Mao's call to 'go out, face the world and brave the storm' and temper and transform themselves through class struggle. Youths denounced and physically attacked teachers, school leaders and 'bourgeois academics' as counterrevolutionaries. The chaos soon spread outside the schools, as students organised as Red Guards, mobilised against authorities in factories and government offices, and 'exchanged revolutionary experiences' in other parts of the country (MacFarquhar and Schoenhals 2006).

So-called 'struggle sessions' orchestrated by Red Guard youths often turned violent and at times led to suicides or the long-term detentions of the accused. It was also not uncommon for children as young as eight to 'struggle' against their own parents in these mass denunciation meetings, during which individuals were made to wear dunce hats and paraded in their work-units in a ritual of public shaming. In some cases, young children were even induced to spy on their parents and report them to their radical peers, occasionally with fatal consequences (MacFarquhar and Schoenhals 2006; Naftali 2014a).

At the height of the CR, schooling was halted, industrial production considerably slowed down, the administration was paralysed, and anarchy and terror spread across the country. In early 1967, the CPC leadership finally decided to bring in the PLA to end the widespread violence between rival Red Guard factions and people's militias, which had triggered civil war–like conditions (MacFarquhar and Schoenhals 2006; Y. Wang 2019). In some cases, PLA soldiers themselves played a role in causing chaos and violence (Walder 2016; Y. Wang 2019). Yet, gradually, military forces took the lead in restoring order through the establishment of so-called Revolutionary Committees (RCs) across the country. RCs were formally composed of CPC officials, representatives of mass organisations and army soldiers. In effect, however, the PLA took over administration at the provincial, local and grassroots levels to fill the vacuum created by the collapse of party and state structure (Scobell 2022, 353).

The violence started to fade in 1968–9 when, on Mao's orders, millions of middle school graduates and university students who had participated in the revolutionary movement were voluntarily or forcibly moved to the countryside to be 're-educated' by peasants. Younger children were recalled to their classes and shortly afterward, middle school and college students resumed their studies (MacFarquhar and Schoenhals 2006, 179, 247). In 1971, after the death of the military leader Lin Biao who had supported the CR, the country started to recover from the political chaos and economic stagnation. Nonetheless, the CR ended only in 1976 when Mao died and the movement's radical leaders – the 'Gang of Four' – were arrested.

From the early to mid-1970s, children and youth of various ages continued to be implicated in waves of heightened political campaigns and the public persecutions of various 'class enemies' which plagued the country. These activities further promoted the militarisation of Chinese youth and their education. A *People's Daily* (*Renmin ribao*) news report from 1967 noted, for instance, that primary schools in Shanghai and Wuhan included both 'military training' (*junzheng shunlian*) and 'military physical education classes' (*junshi tiyu*) (*Renmin ribao* [*People's Daily*] 1967). Another media report from 1974 notes that Beijing primary school students were instructed to hold small group discussions on 'the military thinking of Mao' and took part in a 'military training field camp', during which they completed a rapid 'military march' (*jixingjun*) (cited in Naftali 2014a, 89). These reports notwithstanding, it should be noted that according to academic studies published in China of the post-Mao era, organised military training did not in fact feature consistently in the school curriculum in the latter part of the CR. Rather, training was carried out sporadically and without any unified guidelines (Ge 1987, 66).

At the same time, military themes continued to dominate lessons in school subjects. The 1967 People's Daily report cited earlier notes for instance that in Shanghai and Wuhan, primary school textbooks in Maths and Chinese were revised to 'better reflect the themes of class struggle' (*Renmin ribao* [*People's Daily*] 1967). History textbooks of the late 1960s to mid-1970s also highlighted the theme of military conflict while emphasising the purported leading role of 'youth (*shaonian*)' in such conflicts throughout modern Chinese history. Regardless of the veracity of such claims, the narratives conveyed the notion that rather than being passive, incomplete human beings awaiting adult indoctrination or resourceful aides to adult fighters (traditional Confucian notions of childhood), PRC youth possessed the ability to wage war and ought to enact their agency through performing politically legitimate acts of violence (X. Xu 2011, 384; David 2018; Naftali 2021b).

This view was equally prevalent in media and cultural works targeting adults as well as children of all ages (Naftali 2014a). Public discourse of the period generally condemned the liberal notion that children should be protected from the brutality of adult life as part of a 'bourgeois mode of thinking'. Instead, it emphasised the importance of allowing children to forge and develop their character by facing difficulties under tough conditions, or as one newspaper writer phrased it: 'Loving your children means posing stringent requirements on your children' (cited in Naftali 2014a). Accordingly, the few cultural works for children and youth that appeared during the CR were stern, militant and overtly political in their content (Naftali 2014a; Naftali 2021b).

While the 'small soldier' trope was rigorously promoted in school textbooks and children's media of the CR period, it would be wrong to assume that this view was wholeheartedly embraced by political leaders, educators and regular citizens even during this chaotic period. At the height of the violent stage of the CR, in 1968, Mao himself had made statements that attested to his continued ambivalence about young people's efficacy as political actors (Lanza 2012, 44). The ambiguous stance regarding children's militant role was further reflected in repeated reprimands in media publications of the CR period against the stubborn tendency of 'some educators' to 'over-protect' students of all ages from 'horrific war stories' due to the 'false notion of children's innocence' (cited in Naftali 2021b, 267). Demanding that readers discard this idea as nothing more than 'revisionist rubble', such admonitions circulated in Chinese official media until the end of the Mao era (Ibid., 267). These warnings indicate that despite the increasing militarisation of Chinese society and education during the CR era, and even as school students, including those in their early teens, had participated in extreme acts of violence against their teachers and other authority figures, some adults felt uneasy about the extreme militarisation of youth education at this time, an uneasiness that may have drawn on an idealised notion of childhood as a time of vulnerability (Naftali 2021b, 267).

The overall militarisation of youth and education during the CR period was further predicated on gender lines. Cultural and media products of the 1960s and 1970s extolled a new model or a style of female militancy which, according to contemporary and retrospective accounts, many young girls in China sought to emulate. The prominent sloganeering of the time claimed that 'women can hold up half the sky' (*funü nengding banbiantian*), and the myriad depictions of women doing 'men's jobs' in the media of the period promoted the idea of gender equality. Magazines aimed at adult women in China began to honour the achievements of female combatants who, to paraphrase a well-known Mao Zedong poem, preferred 'hardy uniforms to colorful silk' (Noth 2021). Similarly, almost all the art, literature, films, operas and ballets produced during the CR featured women as militant fighters or political activists. Energetic and muscular 'iron girls' (*tie guniang*) were feted for their ability to carry out strenuous physical labour in the fields and factories (Honig 2002; Evans 2008).

Amid this militant discourse, in the 1960s and 1970s, the PLA uniform became the sartorial ideal for both boys and girls, and Red Guard members sought out old PLA uniforms, which they wore with a red armband to proclaim their socialist spirit. Through their clothing, young people recalled an earlier revolutionary tradition and insisted upon the recognition of this tradition as the 'true spirit of modern China' (T. M. Chen 2001, 158). Young women of the period avoided wearing any 'bourgeois' clothing or accessories that marked them as female. The cultivation of beauty signified weakness of character, and female Red Guards therefore cut their hair short or shaved their heads, dressed like male soldiers and employed verbal and physical violence just like their male counterparts (Honig 2002; Evans 2008).

Such practices have led some scholars to argue that the militarisation of youth education produced the 'masculinisation' of girls and women in the CR period. Others suggest that the claim that women were excessively masculinised is an oversimplification of a complex situation in which girls and women were still ascribed distinct 'feminine traits' (Jiao 2022). Thus, a growing number of studies show that media and cultural works of the period often featured girls and women in the role of auxiliary fighters who rarely engaged in lethal action, whereas boys and men were portrayed as partaking in – or even initiating – acts of military violence, a distinction which maintained traditional Chinese gender hierarchies (Honig 2002; Roberts 2004; Evans 2008; Naftali 2014a; Edwards 2016; Hird 2019).

Conclusion

Modern Chinese education has been marked by an increasing preoccupation with preparations for war. As the discussion in this chapter has shown, the centrality of military practices to Chinese educational notions and activities is closely related to the country's loss of eight wars between the First Opium War in 1840 and World War II, as well as to the rise of new conceptions of the military and its role in the construction of a modern, strong nation-state (Meyskens 2020). From the late nineteenth century onward, many of China's elites also began casting (male) soldiers as ideal models for emulation in all areas of life (van de Ven 1997, 352; Green 2011, 154; Zheng 2021, 117; Flath and Smith 2011). The growing importance of martial pedagogy in twentieth-century China was also linked to the emergence of a new conceptualisation of childhood. During the Republican era, both the KMT and the CPC accorded children and youth a key role in political roles and employed military models to foster a new ideal of patriotic citizenship among the very young with the aim of coordinating and galvanising the masses in domestic and external struggles. This trend continued in the Maoist era.

The proliferation of war accounts and military models in PRC educational and media materials aimed at young people in the 1950s–1970s was shaped by the constraints of the Cold War era. China was not unique in this sense, as studies demonstrate that a militarisation of children and youth education was evident in both socialist and capitalist countries during this period (Stephens 1997; Peacock 2015). In Maoist China, as elsewhere, the spread of the military's organisational techniques and attitudes to civilian realms, including youth culture and education, further constituted an important mechanism for exerting state control over society, with the socialist state employing 'external threats to maintain an authoritarian hand on its own population' (Edwards 2016, 176; Zheng 2021).

Throughout the period in question, however, this increasing penetration of miltiary values and techniques into youth education was at times undermined by material shortages and a limited capacity to execute ambitious government plans in schools across the country. In both the Republican and the Mao era, the militarisation of education also ran up against competing notions of the proper roles and actual capabilities of children and youth, notions which were in turn predicated on the variables of gender and social background. In times of acute national crisis such as the War of Resistance against Japan and the Civil War of the 1930s and 1940s or the Korean War of the early 1950s, the spread of military ideals and practices may have reached diverse youth populations. But in Maoist-era China, students in elite colleges located in urban areas were exempt from systematic military training and it was mostly less-educated, rural youths who had participated in People's Militia training at least until the 1960s.

From the early twentieth century onward, the advent of martial ideals and practices in Chinese education was also closely linked to the promotion of a distinct model of masculinity. Girls were expected to play only a relatively minor and at best an auxilary role in the exercise of this idealised martial citizenship. These different expectations remained persistent until the Cultural Revolution, when youths of different genders and social backgrounds were called on to partake in armed struggle against revolutionary enemies. The widespread youth participation in this massive domestic conflict of the mid-1960s to the mid-1970s can be taken as evidence for the internalisation of martial values among Maoist-era youths. At the very least, it could attest to the ability of the sustained military-themed propaganda efforts of the 1950s and 1960s to discipline young people to employ speech and practices modelled after the military (cf. Chin 2023, 46).

Mao's death in 1976 brought the Cultural Revolution to its official end. The ascendance of a new CPC leadership bent on modernising China's stagnating economy through the introduction of market reforms and an Open Door policy signalled a renewed and strengthened emphasis on academic excellence in education. From the late 1970s onward, under the pragmatic leadership of Deng Xiaoping, the Party-state reintroduced the nationally unified college entrance examination and increased its investment in elite education, mostly in urban areas.

With the Chinese state ostensibly attempting to retreat from its former project of social mobilisation in the post-Mao era and amid the damage of the CR period, the Party-state turned away from martial models and the attempt to mobilise the entire society (Perry 2006, 275; Blasko 2007). As China established full diplomatic relations with the United States in the late 1970s, the state also began to engage in substantial military reform. In 1979, the PRC fought a one-month war with socialist Vietnam in which Chinese forces fared badly. Deng used China's poor performance in this conflict and the changing security environment to override resistance from military leaders to conduct a series of military reforms. Judging the PLA to be too large for China's shrinking security needs, the Party-state discharged a million soldiers in the early 1980s and placed more emphasis on professionalism. Adolescents aged 16–18 were no longer needed for militia activities. The reforms also included a decreased expenditure on national defence from 4.6 per cent of GNP in 1979 to 1.4 per cent in 1991 (Meyskens 2020, 228, 231).

Yet even as the post-Mao state moved to decrease the army's penetration of the economy and society and to depoliticise its education system with the aim of promoting a modernisation of science and technology and the development of the economy, the Party did not abandon its long-standing belief in the importance of war education and martial training for children of different ages. As the following chapters will discuss, this conviction would receive a new impetus following the 1989 military crackdown on the youth-led protest movement in Tiananmen, the collapse of the Soviet bloc and ensuing shifts in China's security environment, as well as the increasing global influences on young people's values and practices in the 1990s onwards – a trend that that the CPC regards as a threat to its political legitimacy and to China's national strength.

Notes

1. Cited in Xu, Guoqi. 2008. *Olympic Dreams: China and Sports, 1895–2008.* Cambridge, MA and London: Harvard University Press, 19.
2. The Chinese forces sent to Korea were in fact PLA soldiers. By using the term 'volunteers' in the army's name, as Stalin suggested, Mao hoped to convince the world that the Chinese force was organized by Chinese volunteers, not the Chinese government itself, and thereby avoid a state of open war with the United States and the other nations that had contributed to the UNC (United Nations Command).
3. In 1975, Mao told US Secretary of State Henry Kissinger that 'he could wait for 100 years to take Taiwan back' (cited in Suisheng Zhao 2022, 3).
4. Some top army officials, including Marshal Peng Dehuai, were opposed to the Great Leap Forward and to the militia, arguing that 'fighting is the business of the army, and the masses must not be mobilized and relied upon'. Such criticism indicates that the wholesale expansion of the militia threatened the supremacy and professionalisation of the armed forces and came at a time when they were being subjected to severe criticism (Gittings 1964, 106–7).

CHAPTER 2

War and Peace in China's History Textbooks

> In recorded human history, tens of thousands of wars have broken out around the globe, and the number of war casualties has reached as many as one billion ... Wars have caused grave disasters to the people of the world. Avoiding and eliminating war has become the common aspiration of peace-loving people everywhere.
>
> 'People of all countries love peace', *Standard Senior High School Experimental Textbook, History Elective 3: War and Peace in the 20th Century* (People's Education Press 2009, 128).

Warfare is a major contributor to the collective myths and memories on which the idea of the nation is constructed (Smith 1981). Tales of glorious battles and the sacrificial actions of heroic fighters unite members in an imagined national collectivity and define the nature of that collective (Billig 1995; Anderson 2006 [1983]). One central stage on which warfare is portrayed is the school history curriculum. In historical narratives taught at school, military conflicts are often presented as important turning points. They can even become the overwhelming focus of the stories told about the development of the nation (Montgomery 2006, 20, Lässig 2013).

This is certainly true of history teaching in contemporary China. Since the establishment of the PRC in 1949, the socialist Party-state has granted primacy to war accounts in educational texts and media publications targeting children and youth. After the death of Mao Zedong in 1976 and following Deng Xiaoping's rise to power in 1978, the CPC launched its 'reform and opening-up' policy, a retreat from the principle of constant class struggle in favour of pragmatic policies meant to boost economic growth and rapid modernisation.

The past four decades or so since have also witnessed a depoliticisation of the curriculum compared to the Mao era. And yet, the institutionalised production of war memory has continued to play a vital – and arguably intensified – role in shoring up the legitimacy of the Communist Party of China. The chapter explores this issue by examining the representation of war and peace in Chinese high school history textbooks of the 2000s and 2010s.

In the past three decades, China has implemented a systematic Patriotic Education (PE) campaign in the military, in government organisations, in mass media, in public sites, in the party's youth organisations, the Young Pioneers and the Communist Youth League,[1] as well as in the country's schools. Launched in the aftermath of the Chinese military crackdown on the Tiananmen democracy movement of 1989, and the collapse of communism in Russia and Europe at the end of the Cold War, the PE campaign has sought to shore up popular support for the political status quo by linking loyalty to the 'nation' with support for the socialist Party-state and the military. As part of the campaign, schools are required to carry out 'education in national defence and security' with an emphasis on 'strengthening the unity between the military and the government, and the military and the people'. The campaign further seeks to enhance youth ability to 'resist foreign invasion' and instil the importance of 'guarding the territorial integrity, national sovereignty and independence of the motherland' (Ministry of Education of the PRC 2016).

At school, these themes are enacted through activities such as flag-raising and anthem-singing rituals, visits to PE bases, participation in National Defence Education activities, as well as curriculum revisions. The Chinese government has marked history teaching as a primary vehicle for raising youth 'national self-esteem, self-confidence, pride and sense of cohesion'. Modern history lessons are to underscore the importance of 'celebrated battles' and 'the glorious deeds of national heroes and revolutionary martyrs' (Zhongguo guofang bao 2006). Students should learn about China's 'great efforts to strengthen itself, remaining indomitable' in the face of 'foreign aggression and oppression' while 'fighting bloody wars again and again for national independence and national liberation' (Ministry of Education of the PRC 2016).

Noting this development, scholars have explored the shifting narratives of the nation and of specific military conflicts in history textbooks published in the Chinese mainland in the past several decades (Jones 2005; Lo 2007; W. Li 2011; Z. Wang 2012; Rose 2013;

Lyu and Zhou 2023). To date, however, we have no systematic, qualitative study on how China's history textbooks present the concept of war to students, and the extent to which war representations in Chinese textbooks legitimise the use of power as a way of addressing domestic or international disputes.

The chapter addresses this crucial issue by focusing on the case study of history textbooks used in Chinese mainland senior high schools (grades 10–12) in the 2000s and 2010s. Specifically, I examine four volumes which cover the themes of war and peace in modern Chinese history, beginning in the First Opium War (1839–43) – the conflict marking the start of the period known in China as the 'Century of Humiliation' (*bai nian guo chi*) – through the Cold War era, to contemporary times.

The investigation of war representations in the four volumes seeks to highlight a collage of wars that are each somehow unique to their eras but also indicative of a general pattern of war historiography in the PRC (cf. Montgomery 2006, 22).

Drawing on a Foucault-informed critical discourse analysis, I focus on the 'ordering of knowledge' (Foucault 1974 [1970]; Foucault 1982) through the circulation of a specific narrative about war and peace in the modern era. With that in mind, I do not discuss all the modern conflicts represented in the four volumes, nor do I set out to compare the representations of the same war across the different versions. Rather, I seek to identify key themes in relation to the portrayal of three topics: the reasons wars are fought; the functions of war in nation-building processes, and the morality of war. Specifically, I explore the following questions: Do the textbooks present war as a perpetual condition, or as an anomaly? Is there a discussion of the benefits and/or the adverse effects of military conflict? Do the books attempt to address the human toll of war, that is, do they dwell on human suffering? If so, is there a focus on the plight of Chinese or of people of all nations?

In addressing these questions, my aim is to uncover explicit as well as latent meanings in the text, which may reflect deeper, underlying assumptions and ideologies (Boyatzis 1998). I consider not only the contents of the main body of text but also the tone and rhetoric which the text employs. I further pay attention to the sub-texts, that is, how pictures, supplementary readings and questions are brought together to construct a complex representational system. The analysis considers not only what is in the text but also what is absent from it, and the potential function of these omissions in the construction of a master narrative about war and peace in PRC contemporary textbooks.

As the discussion will show, PRC textbooks present China as a pacifist country while criticising the belligerent attitudes and policies of other nations. At the same time, the books justify the use of military force under certain conditions. They glorify the role of armed conflict in the construction of the Chinese national collectivity and promote the idea that a strong military serves as a guarantee for the country's domestic stability and the maintenance of its national interests in the global arena. As such, China's history textbooks send an ambiguous and at times contradictory message about the moral and pragmatic implications of using military force to address conflict.

War Histories in China's 'Patriotic Education' Campaign

All nations, to some degree, use history textbooks as a means to promote a view of the past, to enhance the collective memories of a nation, and, more often than not, to appease social and political agendas in the present. History textbooks never appear as neutral sources, while the curriculum is closely guarded and controlled by modern nation states worldwide (Langager 2009, 121). A state-supported history curriculum is often the choice vehicle for delivering a government's messages about war in general, or wars in particular (Foster and Nicholls 2005, 215, Hein and Selden 2000, Langager 2009). As noted earlier, in contemporary China, the representation of war history to children and youth is a vital element in the Party-state's PE campaign.

The PRC has had a long history of ideological indoctrination campaigns, but the PE campaign launched in the early 1990s (and still in force today) has been one of the longest of such campaigns (S. Zhao 2023). The campaign was initially rolled out in response to the pro-democracy Tiananmen movement. This student-led movement started in Beijing in April 1989, then spread to other cities in China, encompassing both university students and urban workers. Protesters demanded an end to official corruption which had become rampant after the implementation of market reforms in the 1980s. Demonstrators further demanded greater civil freedoms and political reform, with some even calling for the toppling of the CPC.

The demonstrations had partly coincided with the May 1989 state visit of then-Soviet leader Mikhail Gorbachev. The historic summit with Chinese leader Deng Xiaoping was a global spectacle and attracted media from around the world. After thirty years of a tense relationship between China and the Soviet Union, the two leaders intended to signify the normalisation of relations between the two countries. The event was derailed by the protesters whose numbers grew by the day (Ibrahim 2016, 582). Communist Party and government officials proved divided over the appropriate response. The protests persisted for weeks despite efforts by political leaders to first placate and then intimidate the student leaders.

On 4 June 1989, Deng Xiaoping and the party's Central Military Commission ordered PLA generals to end the seven weeks of peaceful pro-democracy protests by sending in troops with tanks, machine guns and flamethrowers (Coutaz 2019, 55). The initial lack of success and the seeming hesitancy of the PLA and People's Armed Police (PAP) units to end the demonstrations led to speculation about dissent within the armed forces. Despite rumours of a military coup, the reality was limited resistance within the PLA. According to reports, one army general refused to carry out his orders to lead troops into Beijing, and hundreds of PLA soldiers deserted. But most remained loyal to the CPC leadership and obeyed the order to forcefully crush the civilian demonstrations that Deng and other leaders saw as an existential threat to the regime and to the social and political stability of the country (Shambaugh 1991; Scobell 1992; Hundman 2023).

The quelling of the protest movement came at a considerable cost to civilian lives. The precise number of casualties in the violent crackdown remains unknown since no death toll has ever been officially released. Estimates by foreign sources range from several hundreds to more than a thousand dead (Ibrahim 2016, 582; Heilmann 2017, 251). While Deng Xiaoping believed the action was justified and the armed forces acted appropriately, he was concerned about national ideological contamination and saw the need for a serious rectification campaign both in the military and in China's education system. For China's leaders, the Tiananmen movement was an urgent reminder to address what they saw as a 'belief crisis' threatening the legitimacy of socialist rule. That legitimacy would now be based on two pillars: economic performance and nationalism (S. Zhao 2021, 142).

The launching of the nationwide PE campaign in 1993–4 marked the shift from socialism to nationalism as the country's dominant ideology. The campaign presented China as 'an ancient civilization with a superior cultural tradition', which nonetheless 'fell behind' in the modern era. China's defeat in successive wars (starting with the First Opium War of 1839–1842) against Western and then Japanese imperialism led to a loss of sovereignty at foreign hands through 'unequal treaties' and military occupations. Within this narrative of a nation under siege, the CPC presented itself as 'the nation's savior, defeating the reactionary forces, establishing the PRC and ending "one hundred years of national humiliation" (*guochi*)' (Lyu and Zhou 2023, 770; Z. Wang 2012; Weatherley and Zhang 2017). Shifting away from a class-based socialist identity towards a more ethno-cultural vision of nationhood, the regime further repositioned itself 'as the trustee of the ancient and glorious legacy of Chinese civilization'. State propaganda of the 1990s onwards increasingly celebrated the 'history, legends and heroes of the ethnic Han majority' at the expense of China's minority nationalities (Vickers and Zeng 2017, 58).

Since the launch of the PE in the 1990s, children and youth constituted a key target group. Indeed, the 2019 Outline on Patriotic Education in the New Era insists that PE should 'start from infancy by focusing on consolidating the roots and concentrating on the soul' (cited in Zhao 2021, 147). Over the past several decades, efforts to foster patriotic sentiments among youth have been waged through state-backed media and popular culture products, organised lectures and activities on campuses, trips to military museums, martyrs' graves and war memorial sites, as well as student military training courses. The campaign has also included the publication of patriotic school materials and a revision of textbooks in subjects such as morality, politics, Chinese and history (Vickers, 2007; Reilly 2011; Denton 2014; Mitter 2020). While Chapters 3 and 4 of this book will consider the promotion of war-related patriotic messages in military training courses and in media products, in this chapter, I focus on one key vehicle of the PE campaign: the school curriculum, specifically high school history textbooks.

The Politics of War Representation in Contemporary China

The Chinese state expends huge efforts on controlling how history is studied and researched at schools and universities. Censorship in educational settings and the media is common, with teachers often reprimanded and magazines put under direct government control or shut down when they stray too far from an orthodox reading of history (Wang and Chew 2021; Costigan 2022). Xi Jinping in particular has emphasised the crucial importance of learning from history in order to 'build socialism with Chinese characteristics', and his leadership

(2012–) has seen a resurrection of the term 'historical nihilism (*lishi xuwu zhuyi*)' as a way of criticising both historians and non-historians for questioning official versions of history (Liboriussen and Martin 2020, 320). Used by Chinese officials for decades, the term was given new importance when it was listed in Document No. 9 as one of the seven ideological threats the party faces. The document was leaked in 2013 and hinted at Xi's intellectual agenda as he began his tenure as party leader. According to Document No. 9, historical nihilism refers to the production and/or sharing of information that 'distorts the history of the party or the history of new China'. Such an act is 'tantamount to denying the legitimacy of the CPC's long-term political dominance' (Costigan 2022).

The Party's attempts to address the dangers of historical nihilism have included recent controversies surrounding the correct representation of 'heroes and martyrs'. Memorialised in school textbooks, museums and public sites, as well as in countless media works, the term refers to modern figures said to have given their lives in defence of the Communist Party or the nation. In 2018, the Politburo Standing Committee of the CPC passed the 'Law on the Protection of Heroes and Martyrs', which criminalises the act of 'slandering' China's war heroes (Xinhua News Agency 2016b; K. Zhao 2016). Since then, the law has been applied on several publicised occasions (including the Li Haoshi incident described in the Introduction to this book).

One widely reported incident took place in 2022 when veteran journalist, Luo Changping, formerly a senior editor at one of China's most influential magazines, *Caijing*, and a journalist who had won awards for exposing official corruption, was sentenced to a seven-month prison term for 'infringing the reputation and honor of national heroes and martyrs'. Luo's sentence came after he published several posts on China's social media site *Weibo*, in which he questioned China's role in the Korean War as depicted in *The Battle at Lake Changjin* (*Changjinhu*)– a 2021 blockbuster commissioned by the CPC's propaganda department as part of the Party's 100th anniversary celebration (Bandurski 2022).[2]

Holding that Luo was a 'repeat offender', the court found that since 2009, when Luo first registered his *Weibo* account, he had sent nine posts 'mocking heroes and martyrs'. As part of the sentence, Luo was also made to 'voluntarily' donate 80,000 yuan to the Memorial of the War to Resist US Aggression and Aid Korea, a war museum in Dandong, and to write public apologies to be published on Sina.

com and in the Party newspapers *Legal Daily* and *People's Liberation Army Daily* (Boyd 2022). A commentary published in the magazine *People's Court Daily* alongside the article describing Luo's sentencing argued that the Party must be on guard against 'historical nihilism'. It warned against the tendency of 'some people to treat history as "a little girl to dress up as they please" by debasing Party history, vulgarising it for entertainment, and in some cases, even engaging in criminal disparagement and defamation of revolutionary martyrs and model heroes' (cited in Boyd, 2022).

War representations in contemporary China are also related to the leadership's strategic interests. Previous studies have noted, for instance, that alongside the PE messages mentioned earlier, PRC school textbooks published in the 1990s and 2000s also advance the notion of China's 'peaceful rise' in the modern era. In Chinese foreign policy articulations of the past two decades or so, the slogan 'peaceful rise' (later relabelled 'peaceful development') reflects the notion that 'people of all countries should join hands and strive to build a harmonious world of lasting peace and common prosperity' (Nathan and Zhang 2022, 59). School textbooks echo this idea, while encouraging students to respect the 'multiplicity of word cultures' and contribute to world peace and sustainable development (Lo 2007; Vickers 2009; Zheng and Cherng 2020).

This educational message was closely related to the Chinese Party-state's approach to popular nationalism. Up until the 2010s, the CPC made use of nationalism for regime legitimacy, but was concerned that a rampant nationalist ideology would damage relations with Western powers and with the Asian neighbours on which China's economic success depended heavily after the Cold War. Since Xi Jinping's rise to power, however, the CPC has intensified the PE campaign, emphasising a state-led nationalism that has been characterised by growing hostility toward Western powers and values, and an assertiveness in pursuing expanded national interests (S. Zhao 2021, 141).

This shift is reflected in China's educational policy. On the one hand, the Outline for Promoting Patriotic Education published under Xi's leadership asserts that achieving 'peaceful development and cooperation' is the common aspiration 'of all peoples', including China (Xinhua News Agency 2019b), a theme that arguably demonstrates the current leadership's proclaimed commitment to the 'peaceful settlement of international disputes' and the pursuit of 'common development and win–win cooperation' between all countries (Chang 2021, 1165; Nathan and Zhang 2022). On the other hand, the Xi-era PE Outline also carries the message that China's citizens, including youth, must brace 'for danger in times of peace' (Xinhua News Agency 2019b).

A recent testimony by a former Chinese government official clarifies the link between Beijing's shifting strategic interests and curriculum contents at the basic education level. According to Wang Xuming, former deputy director of the General Office of China's Ministry of Education (MOE) and a spokesperson of the MOE, in the early 2000s, concerns among Chinese leaders about the state of China–US relations led to the omission of the famous Korean War essay, 'Who are the most lovable people?' from the Chinese curriculum (Wan wei du zhi wang 2021). The essay eulogises the heroic struggle of Chinese soldiers against American forces in Korea and as noted in Chapter 1, was mandatory reading material in Chinese lessons from the 1950s onward. According to Wang's testimony, posted on his social media account on *Weibo*, and later picked up by Chinese mainland media outlets, the omission of the text from the 2001 curriculum was in response to a directive 'which came from above' and reflected the desire of Chinese leaders to avoid use of a text associated with a military conflict with the USA. In a highly symbolic move, which reflects the deteriorating relationship between the two countries in the past several years, the essay was reintroduced in the curriculum in 2021, and now appears in seventh-grade Chinese textbooks used throughout the country (Wan wei du zhi wang 2021).

Studies have further noted a relationship between the CPC leadership's domestic and international interests and the depiction of the War of Resistance against Japan in official, media and educational texts. For instance, scholars have documented an increasing emphasis since the 1990s on the role of the War of Resistance against Japan not only in the formation of the modern Chinese nation, but also in the global victory over fascism in the Second World War (Jones 2005; W. Li 2011; Rose 2013; Mitter 2020; Chang 2021). This narrative supplanted the Maoist-era class struggle view in which the Chinese experience during the Second World War was no more than a 'side conflict' of the struggle between socialism and capitalism. Before the 1990s, the War of Resistance against Japan was similarly portrayed as a 'way-station on the path to CPC dominance in 1949', while the story of the wartime coalition between the CPC and KMT was largely suppressed, a narrative which served the Chinese leadership's interests in improving relations with Japan in the face of a common Soviet threat (Chang 2022, 979–80).

When the Soviet threat subsided in the late 1980s, and as the Chinese leadership advanced a more pragmatic economic policy at the expense of the ideology of class struggle, the legacy of the Second World War was reframed along nationalistic and patriotic lines, shifting the focus from the CPC's 'revolutionary fervor to the collective suffering of the Chinese people at the hands of Japanese aggression', regardless of citizens' political affiliation with either the KMT or the CPC (Z. Wang 2012; Mitter 2020; Lyu and Zhou 2023). Drawing on a narrative of national humiliation and victimhood, China's 'new remembering' of the War of Resistance against Japan was reflected in the contents of school curricula (Chang 2022, 979). Middle school history textbooks of the late 1990s and early 2000s promoted the trope of 'national victimisation' in relation to the War of Resistance against Japan. History textbooks of the 2010s produced under Xi Jinping emphasise Chinese military successes under the leadership of the CPC and re-interpret the victory over Japan in 1945 as 'a critical turning point towards "national rejuvenation"' (Chang 2021, 1159). The Xi-era textbooks further extended the length of China's war with Japan in the 1930s and 1940s by six years to include what it described as earlier Japanese acts of aggression beginning in 1931, a revision which amplifies Chinese people's heroic sacrifice and struggle against Japan (Lin 2020).

Drawing on the insights of these previous studies, in this chapter I seek to examine the portrayal of the general theme of war – rather than of a particular conflict – in PRC history textbooks published in the 2000s and 2010s. The first two volumes under inquiry were compiled and published during the Hu Jintao administration (2002–12). They are: Compulsory History 1 (*Lishi bixiu,* hereinafter CH [2007]), and History Elective 3: War and Peace in the 20th Century (*Lishi xuanxiu: Ershi shiji de zhanzheng yu heping,* hereinafter EH [2009]). Both CH (2007) and EH (2009) follow the 2003 History Curriculum Standard in General High Schools, which defines the core purpose of history education as the promotion of a value-based identification with national history and culture, and the cultivation of nationalist sentiments (Yan *et al.* 2021, 176).[3]

CH (2007) is a mandatory textbook used by a majority of high school students across the country (regardless of major or type of school) until autumn 2019 when a new version came out (see below). CH (2007) performs the daunting task of covering approximately

4,000 years of history in 136 pages, though its focus is mainly on politics. The text begins with 'The Political System of Ancient China' and ends with a unit on the 'Multipolar Global Order of the Early 21st century'.

EH (2009) is an elective text also compiled in the Hu Jintao era. Until 2019 it was used by students majoring in liberal arts in academic high schools in China. While not all students in the country have studied with this textbook, its focus on war and peace in the twentieth century is highly relevant for the present discussion. As such, EH (2009) provides a useful reference point for the analysis of the representation of military conflict in the Chinese history curriculum. Consisting of 163 pages, EH (2009) discusses various military conflicts throughout the previous century, beginning in the First World War and ending with the War in Iraq (2003–11).

The two other volumes examined in this chapter were published in 2019 following a revision in history teaching under the leadership of Xi Jinping (2012–). The revision included the adoption of a new curriculum standard, the History Curriculum Standard in General High Schools (2017 version) (*Putong gaozhong lishi kecheng biaozhun*), which was implemented in all schools nationwide from autumn 2019 (Lyu and Zhou 2023, 774).[4] For the purposes of this chapter, I focus on a book titled Outline of Chinese and Foreign History (*Zhong wai lishi gangyao*). The book contains two volumes which cover roughly the same period as CH (2007).

Volume One (hereinafter referred to OCFH1), which contains 217 pages, focuses on Chinese history. It starts with the 'Origin of Chinese Civilization and Early States', covers the different imperial dynasties and China's history in the modern era, and ends with a unit titled 'Reform and Opening Up and the Road of Socialism with Chinese Characteristics', which covers domestic developments from 1978 to the present.

Volume Two of Outline of Chinese and Foreign History (hereinafter referred to as OCFH2) discusses both Chinese and global history. OCFH2 consists of 156 pages. It begins with a unit on the 'Origin and Development of Ancient Civilization', covers the Middle Ages and the modern periods, and ends with a unit titled 'Characteristics and Main Trends of the Development of the Contemporary World'. The concluding unit consists of two lessons: 'World Multipolarisation and Economic Globalization', and 'The Trend of the Time for Development and Win–Win Cooperation', the latter phrase referring to Xi Jinping's key slogan regarding China's vision for the international world order.

All four volumes examined in the chapter were published by the People's Education Press (PEP) (*Renmin jiaoyu chubanshe*). Affiliated with the MOE, the PEP has been China's leading authorised publishing house for textbooks since 1950. PEP books constitute some of the most widely read historical texts in the country and represent the mainstream in history writing and teaching in China (Vickers 2009; Müller 2011). In 2003, the PEP lost its monopoly over publishing history and Chinese language textbooks and had to compete with other presses for adoption by provincial education bureaus. Several versions were published by local publishers, including in the city of Shanghai. Some senior high schools even used their own school-specific textbooks. It is important to note, however, that all textbooks nationwide had to be approved by the MOE, and no adaptations or changes could be made. All competing publishers were state-owned, and thus ultimately CPC-controlled. Moreover, as the Education Ministry's textbook publishing arm, the PEP retained a crucial voice in discussions of curriculum, while its texts remained the most widely used and a benchmark for competitors (Yan *et al.* 2021, 176; Vickers 2022, 161). Indeed, a preliminary analysis of the Shanghai versions of the PEP history textbooks examined in this chapter did not reveal any major difference in the narratives of war and peace. Therefore, for the purposes of the analysis, the discussion in this chapter refers to the PEP versions only.

As part of a coordinated ideological campaign led by Xi Jinping, Beijing's control over curriculum development in history and Chinese language has been reasserted, with textbook pluralism for history and Chinese language finally abolished in 2017. The new PEP textbooks for history published since are 'replete with portraits of Xi and paeans to "Xi Jinping thought"' (the latter was written into the PRC Constitution in 2017), as well as to Xi's signature slogans, notably the 'China Dream' (Vickers 2022, 161).

In what follows, I focus on the representation of war and peace in the PEP textbooks published in the past two decades. I consider whether the texts emphasise the constructive role of military conflict in the development of the Chinese nation, and the extent to which they sanction or negate the use of armed force in addressing international disputes involving China and/ or other countries.

Why Wars Are Fought

A key question in the discussion of armed conflict in any school textbook is the politics of war or the depiction of the reasons for its outbreak. As noted, until the reform and opening-up era, class struggle theory dominated the writing of history in the Chinese mainland. Ethnic conflicts in ancient Chinese history were interpreted as 'immoral fights among the elite class across different ethnic groups', resulting in the oppression of 'working people of various ethnicities'. Wars and revolutions in modern China were also viewed in terms of class struggle (Lyu and Zhou 2023, 769).

Both the Hu-era (2007 and 2009) and Xi-era (2019) volumes initially appear to promote a similar materialist view of war history drawing on a Marxist framework. Beginning with the Opium Wars, then the First Sino-Japanese War (1894–5), China's invasion by the Eight Armies Alliance (1900), the Second Sino-Japanese war of the 1930s–1940s, the two World Wars, the Cold War and the post-Cold War era, the books present international conflict as an 'inevitable' product of the excesses of the modern capitalist system which requires an 'endless' expansion to overseas markets and therefore inevitable struggles over world hegemony. These struggles produce 'justified resistance' by indigenous peoples in invaded or colonised territories. In this sense, China's contemporary history textbooks uphold the Maoist-era notion that at least under the conditions of modern global capitalism, war is a perpetual condition rather than an anomaly which can somehow be avoided.

A closer reading, however, suggests that within this overarching framework, China's textbooks present additional explanations for the eruption of wars, explanations which go beyond the excesses of modern capitalism and underscore the importance of nationalism and ethnicity. For instance, in relation to the two World Wars, the books highlight factors such as 'chauvinist militarism' and 'fascism' (People's Education Press 2007, 74–6; People's Education Press 2009, 2–17, 44–57; People's Education Press 2019c, 100–4). The latter is presented as an abhorrent ideology of 'extreme nationalism', which opposes 'liberalism and communism', advocates the 'implementation of terrorist dictatorship at home' and 'aggression and expansion abroad', while striving for 'world hegemony' through constant 'war-waging' (People's Education Press 2019c, 100).

Other factors said to contribute to the eruption of wars in the modern era include racism, ethnic conflict and religious conflict. Racism is mentioned mainly in relation to the actions of Nazi Germany and imperial Japan in the Second World War (People's Education Press 2007, 74–6; People's Education Press 2009, 44–79; People's Education Press 2019c, 101–2). Ethnic and religious conflicts are discussed in connection with local and regional wars in Asia, Africa and the Middle East following the Second World War (People's Education Press 2009, 106, 127; People's Education Press 2019b, 129). In describing modern conflicts, all four volumes designate some wars as 'just (*zhengyi*)' while others are labelled 'unjust (*fei zhengyi*)', a categorisation which builds on Maoist-era designations (see Chapter 1). However, in China's contemporary history textbooks, the 'just war' category includes not only the fight against 'imperialism' and 'fascism' (e.g. in the Second World War), but also 'national liberation' struggles driven by ethnic interests.

Unsurprisingly, China's struggles against foreign aggression from the mid nineteenth century onwards are presented as unconditionally justified. The Hu- and Xi-era volumes describe the Opium Wars of the nineteenth century as an occasion on which Chinese people heroically united to resist foreign invasion and actively saved the country from destruction. Lauding the heroic actions of patriotic Chinese generals under both the CPC as well as the KMT (Kuomintang), the books further promote the narrative that China's 'victory' in the Second Sino-Japanese War (known in China as the War of Resistance against Japan) enhanced 'Chinese people's sense of pride and self-esteem' and strengthened China's international status as the country's victory played an important role in the global war against fascism (People's Education Press 2007, 77; People's Education Press 2019c, 102). Volume 1 of the Xi-era textbook explains that during the War of Resistance against Japan,

> [T]he Chinese nation experienced national tribulations and sacrifices and won complete victory (*wanquan shengli*) through the heroic and tenacious struggle of the entire nation . . . [It] was the first complete victory won by China against the invasion of foreign enemies since modern times. It re-established China's status as a great power in the world and won the Chinese people the respect of peace-loving peoples all over the world. This great victory has opened bright prospects for the great rejuvenation of the Chinese nation. (People's Education Press 2019b, 161)

China's involvement in the Korean War (1950–3) is similarly presented as a justified struggle against US aggression (People's Education Press 2007, 109–11). EH (2009) quotes the words of China's former premier, Zhou Enlai, who explained the PRC's involvement in the Korean War by saying that Chinese people 'have never and will never be afraid' of 'resisting wars of aggression', nor can they 'turn a blind eye to imperialist aggression' against China's neighbours (People's Education Press 2009, 109). The book states that people should never 'be afraid to fight wars' to attain justice (People's Education Press 2009, 128). The Xi-era textbook presents a similar narrative. In OCFH1 students read that the USA 'manipulated the UN Security Council to pass a resolution to form a "United Nations Army" headed by the United States to cross the "38th Parallel" and invade North Korea'. The US Seventh Fleet 'invaded the Taiwan Strait of China, obstructing the Chinese people's liberation of Taiwan and seriously threatening China's national security' (People's Education Press 2019b, 176). 'At the request of the North Korean government', Chinese People's Volunteers led by commander-in-chief Peng Dehuai went to North Korea 'to fight against the US and aid Korea, defend their homes and the country, and fought side by side with North Korean soldiers and civilians'. Next to the main text, there is a quote by Peng Dehuai, stating that the victory over the US military in Korea proved that 'the era when Western aggressors could occupy a country by setting up a few cannons on an eastern coast for hundreds of years is gone forever' (People's Education Press 2019b, 176).

As these examples illustrate, China's textbooks do not satisfy themselves with a 'just the facts' approach to the history of war, but offer students elaborate commentary on the reasons war is fought as well as on the moral aspects of military conflict. Occasionally, the books not only insist that some wars are 'just' but also mention that wars may be conducive for national construction and the advancement of science and technology (e.g. People's Education Press 2009, 119; People's Education Press 2019b, 121). But the four volumes also elaborate on the negative impact of armed conflict. As the next section will discuss, this theme is particularly evident in CH (2007) and EH (2009), but can also be found in OCFH1 and OCFH2 (2019), the most recent volumes produced under the leadership of Xi Jinping.

The Costs of War

A key theme in the 2009 elective textbook which focuses on 'War and Peace in the 20th Century' is the human toll of war throughout modern history. The book employs relatively dramatic and emotive language to describe the suffering produced by armed conflict and provides photos and first-hand accounts of war atrocities. Describing the two World Wars, for instance, the book details the number of casualties on all sides as well as the destruction of homes, and the outbreaks of famine, disease and civil unrest. There are images of child soldiers who fought in the Second World War, the wounded, and the dead. In a module titled 'Modern Warfare under High-Tech Conditions', the discussion mentions the Iran–Iraq War (1980–8) while dwelling on the heavy toll the conflict placed on both human lives and the economy:

> In the nearly eight-year war, neither side has had a clear victory or defeat, but the lives and property of the two peoples and the national economies have suffered huge losses: more than 600,000 people were killed and injured in Iran, more than 400,000 people were killed and injured in Iraq, and the number of homeless refugees reached over 3 million. Both sides used a large number of advanced weapons, and the military expenditure was nearly 200 billion US dollars; oil revenue dropped sharply, production facilities were severely damaged, the comprehensive national strength of the two sides was greatly weakened, and the economic development plans of the two countries was delayed by 20–30 years. (People's Education Press 2009, 118)

This description clearly presents war as devastating, a theme that also appears in a more recent version of the textbooks. OCFH2 mentions the human suffering caused by the recent civil war in Syria (2011–) and the 'hundreds of thousands of displaced children' caused by the civil war in the Democratic Republic of Congo in 2009 (People's Education Press, 2019b, 139). In these examples, history textbooks no longer celebrate the active role of children and youth in historical conflict as they did in the Mao era (see Chapter 1). In PRC history textbooks of the 2000s–2010s, children under 18 are depicted as victims rather than as perpetrators of military violence. The concluding section will offer a potential explanation for this representational shift.

Although the textbooks provide accounts of war brutalities which occurred outside China, most of the historical war narratives describing the human toll of war centres on Chinese citizens. In CH (2007) students read for instance that during the First Sino-Japanese War of 1894–5, Japanese forces committed a brutal massacre (*datusha*) of innocent people at Port Arthur. The text is accompanied by a photo of Japanese soldiers standing next to the Chinese they had killed (People's Education Press 2007, 59). The victims of the War of Resistance against Japan receive special attention in both the required and elective volumes produced in the first decade of the 2000s. In CH (2007), students read that 'wherever Japanese soldiers went, they burned, killed, raped and looted' Chinese civilians. The depictions consist of both textual and visual references to the Nanjing Massacre of 1937 in which '300,000 civilians and unarmed soldiers were killed by the Japanese army'. There is also a reference to a 1941 massacre in a village in Hebei, in which '1,200 of 1,500 village residents' were killed by Japanese and 'Chinese collaborators' for refusing to provide information about the location of Communist forces. Students further read that the Japanese military engaged in 'germ warfare' and medical experiments which killed 'thousands of innocent people' (People's Education Press 2007, 75).

The attention to human suffering brought on by war is further demonstrated in a reflective exercise which appears in EH (2009). The text reads: 'Japanese soldiers also had families, also had wives and children, and derived happiness from being together with their families. However, after they invaded China, they committed cruel and inhumane acts of violence against unarmed Chinese civilians.' There follows a gruesome description of atrocities committed by Japanese soldiers in China, including pouring acid on civilians, using civilians for 'target practice' and gang raping a pregnant woman while killing her unborn foetus. The text is accompanied by two images of Japanese soldiers: one with his family, and the other posing with a smile next to the bodies of Chinese. The assignment asks students to deliberate 'what made' Japanese soldiers 'commit these animalistic acts' (People's Education Press 2007, 76).

The more recent volumes, OCFH1 and OCFH2 (2019), omit this reflexive assignment but include a lengthy discussion of the 1937 Nanjing Massacre and other atrocities committed by the Japanese army in China in the 1930s and 1940s (People's Education Press 2019b, 153; People's Education Press 2019c, 136–7). The new textbook also mentions the Japanese military's 'sex slavery' ('comfort women') system.[5] Describing this wartime sex slavery system as 'a government crime committed by the Japanese aggressors in violation of humanitarianism and international law', the Xi-era textbook states that the system victimised '200,000 Chinese women'.[6] There is no mention, however, of non-Chinese victims of the system elsewhere in East and Southeast Asia (People's Education Press 2019b, 154).

Alongside the elaborate discussion of the negative impact of war on human lives, especially in China, the textbooks examined here also promote the notion that 'in contemporary times', countries should employ peaceful means to address international disputes – a point demonstrated in the epigraph to this chapter which appears in EH (2009). The next section elaborates on this topic.

'People of All Countries Love Peace'

All four volumes examined in this chapter highlight the benefits of peace over war and describe China's continuous efforts to promote global peace. The EH (2009) volume explains: 'Practice has proven that peaceful settlement of international disputes through political means can truly achieve reasonable and proper conflict resolution, and help establish and maintain friendly relations' between countries (People's Education Press 2009, 129). The book further observes that 'peace and economic development are mutually reinforcing', as 'peace' is the prerequisite for the common development of all countries, while 'development' is an important foundation for maintaining world peace (People's Education Press 2009, 131–2).

The Hu-era compulsory volume, CH (2007), underscores China's contribution to the advancement of world peace. It claims that since the socialist revolution of 1949, China has pursued a non-belligerent foreign policy (People's Education Press 2007, 108) based on the 'Five Principles of Peaceful Coexistence' laid out by Chinese Premier Zhou Enlai in the early 1950s. Students read that these principles, which include 'mutual respect for territorial sovereignty; non-aggression; non-interference in another country's internal affairs; equality and mutual benefit, and peaceful coexistence', have become 'basic tenets for resolving conflicts between countries', with 'far-reaching international influence' to this day (People's Education Press 2007, 109–12, People's Education Press 2009, 123, 133). The CH (2007) volume further notes that since 1978, China has supported 'a peaceful international environment' which the country sees as crucial for economic development, a stance demonstrated by China's participation in 'UN peacekeeping forces' since the 1990s (People's Education Press 2007, 114–15).[7]

The 2019 volumes, OCFH1 and OCFH2, similarly underscore China's commitment for peace. Emphasising again that peace is 'the basic condition for development' and 'development guarantees peace', the Xi-era textbooks underscore China's role 'as a builder of world peace, a contributor to global development, and a defender of the international order' (People's Education Press 2019b, 177;

People's Education Press 2019c, 138–9, 141). A unit titled 'The Trend of the Times is Peaceful Development and Win–Win Cooperation' in OCFH2 notes, for instance, that 'China continues to hold high the banner of peace' and 'insists on developing friendly relations with other countries on the basis of the Five Principles of Peaceful Coexistence'. Presenting Xi Jinping's Belt and Road Initiative (2013–) as a project designed to promote world peace and development, the text states that following the end of the Cold War, China has sought to build 'a new type of global governance system', based on 'mutual respect, fairness and justice' (People's Education Press 2019c, 139, 141).

An emphasis on the use of non-violent means is notable in the books' discussion of Taiwan, a theme that reflects Beijing's official position on the issue at least until the 2010s. Under the leadership of Deng Xiaoping, the CPC engaged Taiwan strategically with a two-pronged policy (*liangshou celüe*) of 'peaceful unification' to build goodwill and military coercion to deter Taiwan's independence. During the Jiang Zemin era (1989–2002), the Chinese government began to articulate that it 'would not wait forever' but lacked the capacity to back up the implicit threat (S. Zhao 2022, 707). In 1992, both sides agreed 'there was one China, but each might maintain a separate interpretation of its meaning'. While Beijing focused on 'one China', Taipei emphasised a claim for 'independent sovereignty'. Concerns about the collusion between the anti-China forces in the US and Taiwan's independence forces led Beijing to launch missiles in Taiwan Strait in a series of military exercises in 1995–6: a move meant to send threatening messages and influence Taiwan's first direct presidential election in 1996 (S. Zhao 2022, 708).

Amid these developments, the Party-state PE campaign launched in 1993–4 presented 'reunification' with Taiwan as a critical element in the rejuvenation of the Chinese nation. Until the early 2010s, however, reunification was seen as a long-term goal, with the expectation that people on both sides of the Taiwan Strait, sharing a common ethno-cultural background, could come up with a resolution in the future (Lyu and Zhou 2023, 769). PRC history textbooks published in the 2000s reflect this official stance. Presented to students as a 'domestic' rather than international matter, the Hu-era books reviewed here maintain that Taiwan has been in 'a hostile state of isolation from the mainland of the motherland' during the Cold War era. However, since 1979, the PRC government has adopted a policy of 'reunifying' Taiwan with the mainland 'by peaceful means' and seeks to promote economic and cultural ties between people in Taiwan and the mainland. The CH (2007) and EH (2009) volumes assert that Taiwan's reunification with the 'motherland' is the 'common long-cherished goal of the Chinese nation'.

Recent political events produced a shift in Beijing's official stance over Taiwan, however. In particular, the CPC was alerted by the results of the 2016 Taiwanese election, which favoured the Democratic Progressive Party (DPP) which advocates for strengthening Taiwanese identity. This development has caused Beijing to strengthen the push for reunification. Placing increasing pressure on Taiwan to 'accept unification without bloodshed', China has intensified military and economic preparations for a potential military takeover. Expressions of national unity have become increasingly prevalent in official PRC discourse on Taiwanese affairs (Lyu and Zhou 2023, 769; S. Zhao 2022, 707). Reunification with Taiwan – by whatever means – has been given unprecedented urgency by linking it to the second centenary goal of achieving China's 'national rejuvenation' by 2049 (Drinhausen and Legarda 2022, 6). A 2019 defence White Paper further describes 'resolving the Taiwan issue and realizing national unification' as a 'basic interest of the Chinese people', and states that 'the PLA would resolutely defeat' Taiwan independence and 'defend the unity of the country at all costs' (Wuthnow and Fravel 2023, 1158).

China's education curriculum has also adopted a stronger tone towards the issue of 'territorial integrity'. Discussing the recent curriculum revision in PRC textbooks, a MOE official stated in 2019 that new history textbooks produced in the Xi era 'describe the historical origins of Tibet, Xinjiang, Taiwan and its affiliated islands, and the South China Sea islands, as integral parts of China's territory to enhance students' awareness of safeguarding national unity and sovereignty' (cited in Lyu and Zhou 2023, 769). The 2019 volumes examined here accordingly frame the unification of Taiwan and the mainland as a 'sacred mission' and a crucial part of 'the great rejuvenation of the Chinese nation' (People's Education Press 2019b, 70–3).

The Xi-era textbooks ignore the growing distance between Taiwanese and Chinese national identity over recent decades. And yet all four volumes reviewed here assert that reunification should be attained through mutual agreement and negotiation. In CH (2007), students read that Beijing is working resolutely to prevent Taiwan 'separatism'. However, there is no explicit mention of the potential use of force should such 'separatism' take place (People's Education

Press 2007, 102–4). While the Xi era has seen the rise of a more strident rhetoric regarding Taiwan, the 2019 history textbook examined here carries a similar message to the earlier versions (e.g. People's Education Press 2019b, 191).

In contrast to China's key role in 'advancing world peace', all four volumes examined here describe the United States' policies (including its involvement in the Taiwan issue) as an enduring obstacle for the peaceful resolution of conflict in the post–Second World War era. This message forms part of an overarching narrative which lauds China's consistent opposition to those who seek 'world hegemony'. The books explain that China's 'peaceful policies' were impeded by the power struggle between the Soviet Union and the USA during the Cold War era, and in particular by the United States's containment policy and its 'hegemonic ambitions' (People's Education Press 2007, 109–11; People's Education Press 2019c, 108). Asserting that the USA has threatened China since the 1950s by waging 'a war of aggression' in Korea, launching the Vietnam War to challenge China from the south, and using 'the Taiwan issue to assert its position in the Taiwan Strait' and threaten China from the east, both the Hu- and Xi-era volumes note that the USA has consistently attempted to employ military means to consolidate its 'superpower standing' (People's Education Press 2009, 127; People's Education Press 2019c, 133).

The volumes examined here describe a process of 'political multipolarisation' since the end of the Cold War. This process has produced 'favorable conditions for various forces in the world to strengthen coordination and dialogue on the basis of equality and mutual benefit, eliminate confrontation, and jointly maintain world peace and development'. However, the military actions of the United States have consistently undermined these efforts (People's Education Press 2007, 127; People's Education Press 2009, 124). CH (2007) condemns the United States' military involvement in Kosovo, Iraq and Afghanistan. It describes American military action in the Kosovo War in 1999 as 'unjustified' since it 'did not receive the support of the UN Security Council' and was carried out under 'the excuse of the primacy of human rights over sovereignty'. The book tells students that the underlying motive for American action was not human rights but strengthening the power of the USA (People's Education Press 2007, 127). Next to the text conveying this message, students are shown an image of anti-war demonstrations which the textbook says took place in the USA in March 1999. The photo depicts a woman holding a demonstration sign with the slogan: 'stop the bombing, stop the war' and an image of a crying infant showered by a torrent of bombs (People's Education Press 2007, 127). While the text makes a distinction between the 'belligerent' actions of the US government and the anti-war stance of (some) American citizens, the underlying message here and in the other volumes is that the United States constitutes a major obstacle for the achievement of world peace while China is a force for good.

In the Xi-era textbooks, the message regarding China's peaceful stance is reiterated but there is a new emphasis on the country's increasing military might. In the last lesson in OCFH1, titled 'Great achievements since the reform and opening up', students read that thanks to the re-structuring of the Chinese army in recent decades, the overall strength of the People's Liberation Army has 'leapt forward' and the PLA is well on the road to becoming a 'world-class army'. The development of weaponry and equipment 'has been accelerated', and 'preparations for military struggle have made significant progress'. The book further asserts that the Chinese military resolutely 'safeguards national sovereignty, security, and development interests'. It 'effectively carries out major tasks such as maritime rights protection', including the protection of 'China's rights over the Diaoyu Islands' and 'regular combat patrols in the South China Sea'. In addition, the Chinese military is involved in 'counterterrorism and stability maintenance, emergency rescue and disaster relief, international peacekeeping, transit escorts in the Gulf of Aden, and humanitarian rescue' (People's Education Press 2019b, 197).

Beneath this text, students also read, however, that 'China advocates the Five Principles of Peaceful Coexistence, supports the UN to play a central role in international affairs, and promotes peaceful solutions to international and regional hotspot issues such as the Korean Peninsula nuclear issue, the Iranian nuclear issue, the Syrian issue and the Middle East peace process' (People's Education Press, 2019b, 197). The juxtaposition of the two messages together on the same page, alongside a symbolic image of Xi Jinping in military uniform arguably sends a mixed message about the Chinese government's position on the use of military force in international disputes, specifically those involving the protection of China's interests.

This mixed message is reiterated in other educational materials of the Xi Jinping era, including those which address teachers and students in the lower grades. For instance, a teachers' handbook on morality and civic education – subjects tasked with disseminating CPC 'ideology in its purest form' (Vickers 2022, 161)[8] – instructs sixth-grade educators:

> Since its establishment, the Chinese People's Liberation Army has always been the guardian of the Chinese people, the defender of national security, and a staunch defender of world peace. A strong national defense force is an important guarantee for maintaining peace and winning wars . . . The Chinese People's Liberation Army is the 'Great Wall of Steel' that defends the motherland and guarantees our peace and happiness. (People's Education Press 2019a, 80–1)

A grade 9 textbook on the same subject similarly alerts students that China 'must build a national security system that integrates political security, homeland security, military security, economic security, cultural security, social security, technological security, network security, ecological security, resource security, and nuclear security'. It then asks learners to discuss the following question:

> Some people believe that peace and development are the global trend. They maintain that after more than 30 years of reforms, China has accumulated great strength and no longer must worry about national security. Do you agree with this point of view? Present your reasons. (People's Education Press 2017, 99)

Promoting 'national security as the prism through which everything should be refracted' and pushing 'a siege mentality' (Hope 2023, 3; Blanchette 2022), texts such as these are part of a systematic propaganda drive under Xi Jinping, which in recent years has included the launch of a public counterespionage campaign targeting college students, a 'National Security Education' book for primary and secondary schools, and the publication of commentary on 'how teachers run geography lessons on homeland security and maritime security, history lessons on cultural security, and biology lessons on ecological security and resource security' (Hope 2023, 4). These media and education efforts reflect the desire of China's current leadership to increase a sense of vulnerability to foreign and domestic threats among citizens of all ages, while propping up the Communist Party and the military as the main bulwark against these myriad threats.

Conclusion

This chapter set out to explore the representation of war and peace in PRC history textbooks produced over the past two decades. The history textbooks examined here present war in an ambiguous fashion. On the one hand, the books address the immorality of war, dwell on the damage war inflicts on individuals and nations, and promote the message that wars for material gain or to maintain domination over other nations or territories are categorically 'unjust'. Force should be used only for the sake of a 'just cause', which as the books suggest, includes the defence of one's country against a breach of national sovereignty and foreign invasion, a national liberation struggle against colonial occupation or the struggle against all forms of militarist fascism. Even in these cases, however, China's history textbooks convey the message that armed force should be used only after all peaceful and viable alternatives have been seriously tried and exhausted. Working for world peace, the texts tell Chinese students, is a continuing ethical obligation of all nations, China included. Indeed, China is presented in all four volumes as a leader in promoting global peace. In this sense, then, the underlying message in the history textbooks examined here cannot be described as blatantly 'militaristic'. The books do not categorically sanction the use of military force to address conflict.

The anti-war messages in the textbooks also highlight the cruelty of war, and its impact on innocent civilians, including children. Depicting children as victims rather than aggressors in military conflict constitutes part of a broader shift observed in official and public conceptualisations of childhood in China of the post-Mao era. As discussed in my previous work (Naftali 2014a; Naftali 2014b), Chinese educational and media materials of the post-1978 era increasingly embody a 'child-centred' approach which underscores the distinct needs and capacities of minors (defined in China as persons under 18).

As noted in Chapter 1, this approach which is grounded in a modern liberal understanding of childhood, was first introduced to China from the West in the 1910s. It was gradually eclipsed in the 1930s–1940s and the Mao era by the idea of children as agents who can and should partake in politically justified acts of miliary violence. In contrast, the reform and opening-up era has witnessed the reemergence of the romantic notion of childhood as a time of innocence and play rather than struggle. PRC educational discourse, cultural works and government legislation introduced from the 1990s onwards increasingly promote the idea that children have a right to protection from all forms of violence, and should therefore be sheltered from – rather than enticed to – partake in military conflict (Naftali 2014b; Naftali 2019).

Recent studies by Louise Edwards (2016) and Xian Wang (2023) demonstrate how this crucial change affects the representation of children and youth participation in conflict. Since the 2000s, for instance, there have been public debates in China about the depiction of heroic figures such as Liu Hulan, long extolled in official PRC historiography as 'a child martyr'.[9] According to a 2005 media report, some primary school teachers in China felt that it 'was no longer appropriate to encourage children to undertake sacrifices that should be the responsibilities of adult men' and have expressed concern at teaching children about Liu's story given the 'gruesome nature of her execution and her young age at death' (cited in Edwards 2016, 179).

The war accounts in the high school textbooks reviewed here similarly reflect the rise of new sensibilities regarding the children's role in military violence. The textbooks employ the figure of the child as war victim to advance an anti-war message. Nonetheless, China's contemporary textbooks send an ambiguous message about adults' involvement in warfare. In the depiction of conflicts involving China, war is presented not only as an event which causes loss and suffering but as a tempering experience which facilitated the emergence of a modern Chinese national consciousness. Highlighting the role of war in nation-building processes, the textbooks examined in this chapter depict modern Chinese history as a progressive story of national 'coming of age' or 'national rejuvenation', hastened and even assisted by the experience of war.

This complex, and at times contradictory, notion of war and peace echoes the ambiguous messages of official guidelines published in the past decade or so. For instance, a Chinese government White Paper issued in 2011, 'China's Peaceful Development', states that China's 'love for peace' is based on 'lessons drawn from history'. The document asserts that from 'their bitter sufferings from war and poverty in modern times', the Chinese people have 'learned the value of peace and the pressing need for development'. That is why China 'never engages in aggression or expansion, never seeks hegemony, and remains a staunch force for upholding regional and world peace and stability' (Information Office of the State Council of the People's Republic of China 2011). The most recent (2017)

History Curriculum Standard in General High Schools states that 'by learning about famous wars in history, students can objectively understand that wars are the result of the collision between different cultures, and that war causes the breakdown and destruction of human cultures' (Ministry of Education of the PRC 2020 [2017], 31). And yet, the same document asserts that through the study of China's different wars, students should develop 'homeland emotions' (*jiaguo qinghuan*) (Ministry of Education of the PRC 2020 [2017], 47).

In conclusion, accounts of past suffering and struggle in history textbooks of the Hu Jintao and Xi Jinping era may seek to promote a peaceful stance, but also and no less importantly to foster a sense of strong national belonging among youth, while perpetuating and preserving the CPC's and the military's political legitimacy. In the following chapters I discuss how military training courses at school and state-backed media produced in the 2000s–2010s attempt to achieve the same aim. I will then move on to consider how Chinese high school students of different backgrounds make sense of official narratives of war, peace and the military, and how students construct their own meaning of these issues in the process.

Notes

1. Established in China in 1951 and modelled on a similar institution in the Soviet Union, the Young Pioneers (Shaoxiandui, sometimes translated as the Red Pioneers) serve as the first Communist Party affiliation for Chinese children aged seven to thirteen. Qualified teenagers can then apply for membership in the Communist Youth League (Qingnian tuan), which recruits youth between fourteen and twenty-eight.
2. For a detailed discussion of the production of military-backed war films such as *The Battle at Lake Changjin*, see Chapter 4.
3. The textbook series produced under the 2003 Standard consists of three required textbooks and six elective ones. The compulsory courses are composed of History I (with an emphasis on politics), History II (with an emphasis on socio-economic and social life) and History III (with an emphasis on thought, culture, science and technology). The elective textbooks were also organised by themes, such as Major Reforms in History, Democratic Thoughts and Practices in Modern Society, War and Peace in the Twentieth Century, Comments on Chinese and Foreign Historical Figures, Exploring the Mystery of History and A View on World Culture Heritage. For further details on the series, (see Yan et al. 2021).
4. The Xi-era revision was also accompanied by a discontinuation of all previous local editions.
5. 'Comfort women' is a euphemism used to describe those forced to provide sexual services to the Japanese military from 1932 to 1945. The issue remained dormant until the public statements of Korean victims in 1991. In the past several decades,

historians have recorded the existence of this sex slavery system across occupied countries and territories in East and Southeast Asia, including China, Korea, Taiwan, the Philippines and Vietnam. For an in-depth discussion of the system, see, e.g. Tanaka (2002), Soh (2008), Qiu, with Su and Chen (2013) and Caroline (2016).
6. Accounts of sexual violence are found in the confessions written by suspected Japanese war criminals placed on trial in PRC courts of the 1950s. Notably, however, Chinese courts did not pursue the so-called 'comfort women' issue. Nor did the topic appear in previous versions of China's high school history textbooks. For a discussion of the CPC's position on the so-called 'Comfort Women' issue, see Hao (2020).
7. China has indeed engaged in peacekeeping, environmental protection and counterterrorism under the United Nations since the 1990s.
8. Morality and civic education is not a separate subject in the Chinese mainland's school curriculum, but rather has been included in lessons with different titles over the years, such as *Sixiang zhengzhi jiayou* (Ideological and Political Education), *Pinde yu shenghuo* (Morality and Life), *Pinde yu shehui* (Morality and Society) and/or *Sixiang Pinde* (Morality and Ideology). Under Xi Jinping, the lesson is titled *Daode yu fazhi* (Morality and Legal Rule) and is now taught as a unified curriculum in grades 1–9 in lessons carrying the same title.
9. Most CPC materials describe Liu Hulan as being 14 when she joined the party and 15 when she was executed for her participation in CPC activities.

CHAPTER 3

'Don't Get Soft': Youth Military Training in China

In August 2015, police in the city of Nanjing in China's Jiangsu province, received an urgent call from a student at Jiangsu Luhe Senior High School. The student, who was undergoing a week-long mandatory military training course before beginning senior high school, complained to the emergency service that the instructor had made the training programme too difficult. 'I'm exhausted and he's still asking me to train', the student was quoted saying by a local newspaper. The call triggered a debate. Concerned parents questioned the effectiveness of the training, saying 'one week was not going to build endurance or change habits', reported the paper. A teacher insisted that 'the training was an opportunity to show teenagers they needed to toughen up'. And the military training instructor complained that the trainees, who were in their mid-teens, 'were worse than children: even though young children have a short attention span, at least they have a serious attitude and obey orders'. The students, the instructor added, lacked discipline and 'were found snacking on junk food and sugary drinks instead of drinking water during their break time' (cited in Ng 2015).

While the student's complaint to the police was unusual, as state-mandated martial training programmes targeting youth have expanded over the past couple of decades, reports in Chinese media about incidents on these courses have increased. And it is not just the state-mandated courses that are raising concerns. The past two decades have also witnessed the growing use of military techniques in the treatment and education of youths thought to suffer from psychological, physical and/or moral ailments.

What accounts for the proliferation of martial techniques in these different settings? What are the goals, rationales and contents of the military training course which forms part of Patriotic Education (PE) and National Defence Education (NDE), and how do these intersect with the goals and contents of the military-style therapeutic techniques employed in state- and privately run youth treatment centres? Finally, to what extent do these different programmes indicate the growing militarisation of Chinese youth education? The chapter addresses these issues by drawing on the analysis of PRC government, media and academic discourse on the use of martial techniques to train young people to become loyal, disciplined and healthy citizens in contemporary China.

Scholars have examined the wide-ranging influence of military ideologies and technologies not only on the contents of school curricula but also on pedagogical practices in both conflict and non-conflict zones (Giroux 2004; Cheney 2005; Beier 2011; Lomsky-Feder 2011; Sen and Starkey 2019). Studies have considered, for instance, the myriad ways in which the army insinuates itself in the daily lives of American youth through initiatives such as the Junior Reserve Officer Training Programme (JROTC) (Pérez 2006; Berlowitz and Long 2011 [2003]; Galaviz 2011). Focusing on the programme's role in conscription, Berlowitz and Long (2011 [2003], 181) argue that the incorporation and proliferation of JROTC in US schools in the 2000s constitutes a form of 'structural violence': the programme employs economic coercion and deception to recruit disproportionate numbers of African Americans and other racially oppressed groups into the US military. Studies of cadet activities aimed at children and youth in countries such as the UK and Japan have likewise shown how such programmes often cast military roles as 'glamorous and exciting', and military service as contributing to 'personal growth', while glossing over the physical and mental risks, ethical challenges and relationship problems which may be associated with army service (Frühstück 2020). In some countries, such as the UK, youth military training further aims to increase students' 'discipline' while promising to deliver 'at-risk' youth populations (particularly working-class boys) 'from a life of violent crime' (Basham 2011, 175; cf. Trejo and Madrazo 2023).

As these and other studies further remind us, militarisation as a social and cultural force should not be conceptualised merely in terms of 'symbolic manipulations in the head', but also as an 'embodied process' (McSorley 2016, 105). Crucially, this process is also gendered (Enloe 1983; Enloe 1990; Nagel 2003; Nagel 2017). While some militaries do enlist women, an enduring legacy of women being traditionally deemed 'unsuited to combat' has meant that worldwide, girls' and women's 'bodies are suspect in military settings' – a fact reinforced through the 'denigration of the "feminine"' (Basham 2015, 130; Basham 2013) and the habitual incitement of boys and men to demonstrate 'tough masculinity' during physical military training (Thomas 2009, 99).

Building on these insights, the chapter examines China's military training programmes for youth as a form of 'bio-politics' (McSorley 2016, 103) meant to instil a correct attitude towards the army and the nation-state, improve the values and optimise the bodies of contemporary Chinese youth, specifically urban boys. Drawing on thematic analysis of Chinese-language government, academic and media publications of the past several decades, the discussion will demonstrate the links between the expansion of military training as part of PE and NDE, and the spread of martial therapeutic methods to care facilities for 'problematic' youth in China of the 2000s and 2010s. Both developments should be understood as a product of a growing concern among government and military officials, academics and media writers in China about the deficiencies of the current generation of youth, specifically urban singleton boys. The main argument of the chapter is that the proliferation of soldierly models and techniques in state schools and privately run treatment centres constitutes a new stage in the militarisation of youth care and education in the PRC. In the past decade or so, this process has come under criticism from some media writers and academics in China, making it a contested issue in Chinese public discourse.

Youth Military Training in the Post-1978 Era

Military training for youths aged sixteen and above was introduced to the PRC in the 1950s. Throughout the Mao era, the programme was implemented in a fragmented fashion, and as Chapter 1 notes, was largely disrupted during the Cultural Revolution (1966–76) when youth took to the streets to fight against 'revolutionary enemies'. After the launch of the reform and opening-up policy in 1978, the Chinese government moved to depoliticise the country's education system while emphasising the primacy of academic excellence as a way to achieve the modernisation of science and technology and the country's rapid economic growth. At the same time, however, the first decade of economic reforms also saw the re-introduction of youth military training (hereafter, MT) to educational institutes.

The move began with the adoption of a revised Military Service Law in 1984 stipulating that colleges and universities must incorporate MT into their teaching plans (Lu 2005, 10).

Between 1985 and 1989, however, only a select number of higher education institutes implemented such a programme, and by the late 1980s approximately 15 per cent of all college and university students were undergoing MT (Xie 1989, 48; Wang and Zhang 1994, 24; Lu 2005, 14; Yang 2006, 78). College level MT during this period consisted of 4–5 weeks of intensive training on campus or an army base, followed by three weeks of on-campus 'military classes', as well as basic MT and NDE classes throughout the academic year (Zhang 1987, 26).

Although the programme was implemented in fairly limited fashion, a 1988 report in the PLA-sponsored newspaper, *National Defense* (*Guo fang*) claimed that the share of students who were receiving martial training during these years was 'considerably higher' than 'it had ever been' prior to 1978, and added that in contrast to previous decades, the programme received 'more resources' and was now 'run according to clearer criteria' (Zhang 1988, 17). Another contemporary report noted that a select number of elite senior high schools in major cities, including the Tsinghua University Affiliated High School in Beijing, also introduced MT for youths under 18. These courses were shorter than the college level programmes, typically lasting only ten to twelve days (Wan and Zhou 1987, 12).

The MT programme received a significant boost following the Tiananmen pro-democracy movement of 1989, during which urban elite youth protested en masse in Beijing and other major cities. As discussed in Chapter 2, the movement was suppressed by force, and after the PLA's violent crackdown, the CPC initiated a new Patriotic Education (PE) campaign to shore up support for the regime. Military training formed a key part of the PE campaign. For the next three years, defence education radically intensified in China's two most prestigious universities, which were also most central to the protests: Peking University in Beijing and Fudan University in Shanghai (Vickers and Zeng 2017, 50). In 1989–92, all incoming students at these universities were sent to a military academy for one year before starting their studies, where they received an intensive form of defence education. In Chinese official publications, this programme was referred to as 'military and political training' (*junzheng xunlian*) (Genevaz 2019, 460).

In the years following the Tiananmen events, shorter military drill courses were expanded to additional, non-elite universities

(Zheng 1993, 89; Genevaz 2019, 460-1). By the late 1990s, more high schools and even some primary schools had reportedly begun to organise MT courses for younger students. However, even at the higher education level, MT was still conducted in only a minority of colleges and universities in the country though the numbers reached more than a thousand during this decade (Zhao 1997, 25).

It was only in the early 2000s that military drills became compulsory for all college and university students as well as for students at the junior and senior high school level (ages 12-18). Marking a shift from a pilot stage to the mass compulsory stage of the MT programme (Li *et al.* 2009, 17; Yang 2006), the development was accompanied by the promulgation and revision of legislation mandating youth MT, including China's National Defence Law (NDL) (*Zhonghua renmin gongheguo guofang fa*; adopted 1997, amended 2009, 2020), and the National Defence Education Law (NDEL) (*Guofang jiaoyu fa*, adopted 2001, amended 2018). An additional law mandating youth MT, the National Defence Mobilisation Law, was adopted in 2010 (*Guofang dongyuan fa*).

These laws require all Chinese citizens to receive 'national defence education (*guofang jiaoyu*)' (NDE) and state that NDE in school constitutes 'the basis of national defence education for all'. Schools at all levels and of all types must set appropriate NDE courses or include NDE in relevant curricula. Since one of the functions of NDE is to train 'high-quality' reserve soldiers, all institutes of higher learning and secondary schools must also organise practical 'military training (*junshi xunlian*)' for students (National People's Congress of the People's Republic of China 2020a). China's laws further stipulate that NDE should be incorporated into extra-curricular and/or summer activities at kindergarten, primary and junior high school (Wang 1998, 77; Hughes 2017, 59).

As part of this new emphasis on NDE, the Party-state has established two national days devoted to the theme of national defence. On these days, schools and workplaces must hold special National Defence and National Security Education activities for their students and employees. Those activities might include attending lectures, participating in various types of emergency drills or watching 'patriotic films' (Hughes 2017, 59; Van Oudenaren 2023). Under the leadership of Xi Jinping (2012-), the government has also mandated the establishment of NDE demonstration bases open to the public, with a special emphasis on children and youth as a target group. Visits to these bases, organized by schools as well as by the Young

Pioneers and Communist Youth League, include student speeches and knowledge competitions, film screenings and NDE sports events (Zhang 2018; Xinhua News Agency 2022; Chen and Zhang 2023).

On school campuses, official guidelines stipulate that as part of their NDE programmes, schools should promote students' reverence for the national flag, symbol and anthem, as well as for military flags, symbols and songs. Educators should give 'full play' to the theme of national defence through student activities such as touring military barracks, attending briefings with military experts, and participating in military drills. Government guidelines require schools to conduct drills during the summer break prior to students' entry into junior high school, senior high school and college. The length of the MT course ranges from one week at the basic education level to two weeks at the college level. Military drills can take place either on school campuses or in designated training bases. Participation is mandatory, and a poor performance can mark students' records (Fish 2015, 4). The MT programme includes a physical component, marching in formation, learning the correct way to stand, march, kneel and salute; map reading and orienteering, and outdoor training. Senior high school and college students must practice the use of light arms and basic combat skills. MT courses must also include lectures and classes, emergency preparation classes; listening to 'military music' (*junshi yinyue*); and 'military sports' activities (*junshi jingji*) (Hughes 2017, 57; Luo 2014).

The PLA has played a key role in the execution of MT since the 1980s. During the pilot stage of the programme, Departments for Defence Education were established in local governments across the country. These departments oversaw the implementation of NDE in coordination with the corresponding Military Region, while PLA soldiers and officers from military academies located near the university delivered the course (Genevaz 2019, 458). With the expansion of MT to additional schools and colleges and younger student populations across the country, the number of military instructors has risen from 200,000 in 2002 to more than half a million in 2014. Most trainers are now PLA reservists (Luo 2014; Jiang 2022; J. Zhang 2022). Over the past decade, provincial military commands have been instructed to create 'military–civil' linkages to support NDE 'model schools' within their respective jurisdictions. The aim is for schools to develop active relationships with local military garrisons to facilitate talks from PLA troops, military demonstrations, and training for students (Van Oudenaren 2023).[1]

Below, I elaborate on the functions and the rationales of the state-mandated MT courses as reflected in PRC government, military, academic and media publications of the 1980s–2020s. I note key changes and continuities in the discourse surrounding the programme over this period, and consider the link between the state-mandated MT course as part of PE and NDE, and the martial therapeutic techniques employed in privately run youth care facilities since the 2000s.

'Arming' Young Minds with a Patriotic Fighting Spirit

A review of Chinese official, academic and state-media publications regarding the MT programme since the 1980s reveals a recurrent emphasis on the programme's political and ideological functions. Two years after the launch of MT as a limited, pilot programme mainly in select universities in China, a 1987 report asserts the programme's importance, warning that since the launching of market reforms and the Open-Door policy in 1978, Chinese students have become 'too focused on their personal success' as a result of 'bourgeois liberal ideology influences' and have developed a sense of 'indifference to revolutionary ideals'. Military training could help address this worrying trend, the report declares (Wan and Zhou 1987, 12–13).

Other publications in the mid to late 1980s warn against the development of a complacent mentality among contemporary Chinese youth, who have lived in peace 'far too long' and need reminding that war is always imminent. Youth MT is an ideal site to deliver this message, the publications argue (see, for example, He 1985; Liu 1987; Wang 1988). In a 1987 article published in *Chinese Militia* (*Zhongguo bingmin*), a magazine run by the Central Military Commission of the CPC, the author opines:

> Youth who will attend college in the 1990s will have lived in a peaceful environment since childhood. They will be able to focus on their studies in the quiet campus without being disturbed by the sound of guns. That is great of course ... but it may also promote naive thinking, leading young people to mistakenly believe there is no chance of war in their generation, and that gunfire is only a remote news topic in some distant part of the world. Youth may love their peaceful life, but do not realize that peace can be disturbed by war. They might think that contemporary world peace could be achieved through peaceful means, but do not understand that international conditions may force us to seek peace through war.

They might hate war, but do not understand much about fighting back in self-defence. (Liu 1987, 18)

An article published in another state-run magazine, *National Defence* (*Guo fang*) in 1988 makes a similar point. Noting that 'some comrades believe that we live in an age of peace and prosperity' and that national defence education 'is no longer as important' in such an age, the author says:

Since ancient times, Chinese people have loved peace and opposed war, which is our national quintessence; on the other hand, our nation has never been afraid of war, which is also our national quintessence. From the 1920s until the 1980s, our socialist construction has been carried out in an unstable international environment . . . and even if a world war is not imminent at present, we cannot assume that wars will disappear from now on. (Wang 1998, 22–3)

Arguing that military training should start at an early age, the author suggests that at the basic education level, the focus of NDE and MT should be on 'the cultivation of a martial spirit (*changwu jingshen*)' and 'military awareness' among children and youth (Wang 1998, 22–3). Emphasising the political and ideological functions of the programme became even more important after the military crackdown on youth protesters in Tiananmen and the dissolution of the Soviet Union in the early 1990s. In an article published shortly after the crackdown, the author – a member of Tsinghua University Armed Forces Department – notes that CPC leader, Deng Xiaoping has maintained that 'the biggest mistake' the Party had committed in the past decade was in the field of ideological and political education. The article argues that the MT programme, by improving students' 'national defence awareness' and their spirit of 'revolutionary heroism', will 'arm the minds of the young' to consciously resist 'all sorts of external interferences'. It also elaborates on the type of interferences students must resist:

Currently [we do not expect another] world war. However . . . small wars and local armed conflicts may [still] occur . . . [Moreover] imperialists and foreign reactionary forces who oppose the Communist Party have not given up their ambition to overthrow a socialist China. The actions of certain Western powers and various foreign reactionary forces during the recent turmoil and counter-revolutionary riots in Beijing have sufficiently proven this point.

Therefore, we cannot sit back and relax; peace should not paralyze our thinking. (Yang 1989, 41)

A similar message appears in an article published a decade later by a Communist Party official in the Ethnic Autonomous Region of Inner Mongolia. According to the text, as China becomes 'more open to foreign capital and technology', its citizens increasingly engage in economic and cultural exchanges with people from foreign countries. This development, notes the author, may assist in China's modernisation efforts, but may also lead to a 'relatively weak national defence awareness' among youth. MT can address this problem by helping youth to realise that the current international situation is still 'turbulent'. Various 'ethnic conflicts, territorial disputes and religious disputes' in many countries and regions have become 'prominent', and in some cases have led to 'bloody conflicts and local wars', which is why China needs 'strong national defence' (Zhao 1997, 24).

Through military drills, youth can understand 'the country's foreign policy', and also acquire 'a strong sense of patriotism', which would in turn motivate them 'to fight heroically and make selfless contributions to the survival and development of the motherland'. Patriotic feelings cultivated through military training can further encourage youth to 'subordinate their individual interests to the overall interests of the country', stimulate their 'national self-esteem', 'self-confidence' and 'national unity' and prevent the influence of 'corrupt ideas' (Zhao 1997, 25). As illustrated in the article, the Party-state regards the MT programme as an important site for addressing the threat of ethnic conflict. Since the 1980s the country has seen growing ethnic unrest in China's border regions, particularly Xinjiang, Tibet, and to a lesser extent, Inner Mongolia.

Publications in state-backed media and academic journals of the 2000s onwards reiterate the notion that youth MT can function as an effective carrier of the narrative of patriotic education, and includes not only an anti-foreign aspect but also the idea of inter-ethnic solidarity (B. Liu 2005, 46; Zhang 2004; Zhang and Ma 2009). This notion has received greater stress over the past two decades amid growing concerns about dangerous global influences on Chinese youth culture and values, and the emphasis on China's national rejuvenation in the Xi Jinping era. These concerns are illustrated in a 2020 government document which specifies that NDE and MT should strengthen youth awareness of various national security threats facing the country. For instance, students at the junior high school stage (ages 12–15) should be taught about the 'problems and challenges facing national borders and maritime security', including 'China's fight for sovereignty over islands and reefs and maritime rights in the South China Sea and the East China Sea'. Senior high school students (ages 16–18) should be made aware of the various dangers to China's 'financial security' and 'political security', including not only 'ethnic separatism' but also 'international anti-China hostile forces which distort, slander, contain and suppress [the] country's development path and social system' (Ministry of Education of the PRC 2020).

'Making the Hearts of Students and Soldiers Beat as One'

Another goal of the state-mandated MT course has been the strengthening of ties between civilians and soldiers and the deepening of sympathy among youth towards the Chinese military. Acknowledging (often implicitly) that the brevity of the MT course may hinder the ability of youth to acquire extensive military knowledge and/or actual fighting skills, PRC state-media and academic publications express hope that the programme might strengthen appreciation for the military, especially among elite urban youth. This notion already appears in publications from the late 1980s, when the programme was implemented in only a select number of higher education institutes in the cities (Zhengzhi yanjiu 1988; Wan and Zhou 1987, 12–13; Chongqing University 1987) but became more pronounced following the PLA's crackdown on the student-led protest movement in Tiananmen (Fish 2015, 9).

An article published shortly after the 4 June crackdown describes how a PLA veteran arrived at Tiananmen Square on the eve of 21 May, after Beijing authorities had pronounced martial law. The veteran had served as a training instructor at Beijing's Tsinghua University. According to the report, published in the magazine *National Defence*, while 'some people, including students, had opposed the troops who had entered the city and tried to prevent them from carrying out the martial law tasks . . . dozens of students whom he had trained in the past' rushed over to greet their former trainer 'with joy', and their 'spirit of resistance to the troops dissipated' (Yang 1989, 41).

The idea that youth MT can increase support for the PLA is a recurrent theme in other state-media and academic publications of the early to mid-1990s (Yang 1989, 40; Sichuan waiyu xueyuan wuzhuang bu [Armed Forces Department of Sichuan University of Foreign Languages] 1991, 87; Li 1994, 18). One article suggests that through MT, students would adopt the idea of 'defending national sovereignty, territorial integrity and security, defending against foreign aggression and subversion', but also develop 'love for the army' and a greater willingness to 'fulfil national defence obligations' (Tang 1990, 25). This latter point alludes to another perceived function of the MT course: the enticement of youth to join the military.

Theoretically, service in the PLA is obligatory for all male citizens in China.[2] In practice, because of the size of China's population and the large numbers of individuals who volunteer to join the regular armed forces, the authorities have never enforced a draft.[3] The PLA's main challenge in the era of market reforms has therefore been to attract the best talent. Since the establishment of the PRC, the vast majority of army personnel have been undereducated and drawn from rural villages, with little understanding of modern military technology. This shortcoming was less important during the 1960s and 1970s when the PLA was preoccupied with domestic political conflicts and Mao had promoted 'redness' over technical expertise, but after Deng Xiaoping's rise to power in 1978, the Party-state prioritised the modernisation of agriculture, industry, science and technology as well as national defence. The low education level of most army recruits has posed a considerable challenge for the achievement of the latter goal (Cheung 2011; Blasko 2012; Chase *et al.* 2015). The 'personal testimony' of a student who took part in the MT programme at Fudan University in a 1987 report illustrates the problem:

> The PLA instructor is the same age as me. Although he has not been to university, he insists on self-study. He can write poetry and essays. He has also made suggestions for development and construction in his home village. He is like a candle, silently dedicating himself to others. This selfless dedication is exactly what I want to learn from PLA soldiers. (Wang and Yang 1987, 36)

Presented as evidence for the effectiveness of the MT course in creating sympathy and even admiration for the character of the soldier-trainer, the testimony also alludes to the socioeconomic gap between the speaker – a student in one of China's top universities located in Shanghai – and the military trainer who is rural and less educated. As Chapter 6 will discuss in greater detail, this gap still exists, and has widened with the growth of the economic sector and the liberalisation of government controls over job assignments since the late 1990s. Recognising this problem, state-media and academic publications about the merits of the MT programme have over the past three decades suggested that the programme could motivate youth, particularly those of urban, well-educated backgrounds, to enlist (Q. Liu 2005; Zhang and Ma 2009; Lian 2014; Zou 2015).

Building Character and Fostering Discipline

While the primary goals of the MT programme have been to promote youth patriotism, love for the Party-state and love for the army, another stated aim of the programme since its inception has been to build the character of students, specifically by teaching them 'discipline', tempering their willpower and fostering their 'organisational ability' and 'collective spirit' (Xinhua News Agency 2006). These functions are consistently emphasised in PRC academic and media writings from the 1980s onwards.

In the first few years of the launch of the MT programme in 1985, some writers noted that the programme could help to reduce disciplinary violations at school (Yang 1985, 40–1), 'hardening the character' of urban college students who are too 'soft' and 'delicate' and encouraging youth to work with their classmates as 'one big family' (Wan and Zhou 1987, 13). Publications of the 1980s–1990s describe the benefits of performing physically arduous drills as well as cleaning and kitchen duties in curbing 'adolescent restlessness' and cultivating students' ability for 'hard work' and 'self-management' (Xie 1989, 48; Yang 1989, 41; Li 1994, 18; Zhao 1997, 24).

The emphasis on the psychological and social benefits of military drills is even more salient in media and academic writings published in the 2000s as the first generation of children born under the One-Child policy came of age. Writings on military training describe urban singletons, particularly those of the post-90s generation, as 'overly pampered' by their families and lacking in opportunities to challenge themselves. Labelling youth as either 'weak-willed' and 'fearful' (Q. Liu 2005; Zhou and Li 2008; Chen and Song 2016), or conversely as too strong-minded and self-absorbed, some academics in China complain that contemporary youth care 'only for their rights' and not their responsibilities, are overly demanding and lack respect for others. Military training is presented as a catch-all remedy for these ailments (Q. Liu 2005; Shen 2008; Lu and Tan 2011; Song 2012). Soldierly practices can enhance students' 'collective consciousness' and collaborative 'team spirit', their ability to 'withstand hardship' and 'endurance under pressure', 'flexibility' and 'practical mindedness'. During military training, students can emulate the PLA instructors' spirit of 'solidarity and mutual assistance, perseverance and dedication' – qualities that the present generation of youth, particularly in urban areas, are said to lack (Zhang 2004; Zou 2015).

Another recurring theme in Chinese publications of the 2000s–2010s is that military training can help youth to cope successfully with present and future academic and career pressures (Zou, 2015), increase a child's 'self-confidence', 'problem-solving' skills and ability for 'self-care', 'self-regulation' and 'self-discipline', all of which are necessary qualities for success in workplaces from factories to large companies (B. Liu 2005; Han 2013; Zou 2015). According to recent media reports, these perceived benefits have even motivated some kindergartens and primary school educators to implement forms of martial training for young students not usually subjected to mandatory military training. For instance, in September 2020, one kindergarten in the eastern Chinese city of Hangzhou interspersed its lessons with four days of what it called 'military training' for its five- and six-year-olds (Lin 2020). According to the school's public account on the social media network, *WeChat*, the children, 'dressed in military fatigues, held Chinese flags and performed salutes', while the kindergarten principal 'said in a speech that the goal was to encourage children to be strong and to persevere like young Chinese soldiers' (cited in Lin 2020).

An article published in 2021 in a Chinese educational journal, relates how primary school students from the city of Guiyang in China's Guizhou Province, underwent six days of military-themed camp in a special training base, where 'they stepped out of their comfort zone, challenged themselves and became stronger, more confident and self-disciplined'. According to the report, the military camp experience taught children 'to respect others, work in solidarity and understand how to cherish their good life and be grateful for the protection of soldiers' (Deng 2021). A 2022 report published in the PLA-run website, *China Military Network*, describes how an eight-day military training course for primary school children in Huaibei City, Anhui Province in central China, included formation training, physical fitness exercises, safety protection skills and team-building games. Training of first and second graders focused on 'cultivating patriotic education' as well as 'life skills' and 'self-care ability' (*zili nengli*), while those in grades 3 to 6 received training focused on cultivating 'good study habits', tempering willpower and improving 'self-discipline (*zilü nengli*)' in addition to lectures on 'military knowledge' (J. Zhang 2022).

Military-style summer camps have also become a popular trend among middle class Chinese families. Run by commercial companies, these camps offer to help children develop personal and social skills, such as 'resilience', 'independence' and an ability for 'self-governance'. Pragmatic calculations rather than patriotic sentiments are what motivates some parents to send children to these 'character-building' camps. In fact, a recent media report suggests that affluent Chinese parents believe such an experience would help their children gain admittance into 'prestigious overseas schools and universities' that 'value' this type of skills (Ni 2023).

This view reflects an ethos of intense individualistic competition which has become pervasive in contemporary Chinese society (Hansen 2013). Informed and legitimated by neoliberal economic arguments, this ethos attributes ultimate responsibility for success or failure to the individual and its family (Vickers and Zeng 2017, 67; Murphy 2004; Kipnis 2007). It promotes military pedagogies and technologies not just in association with the strength of the nation, but also as 'a template for social and individual management' (Yan 2013, 90). As society comes to be seen as an unending and intensified process of market competition, martial training becomes a 'model of self-discipline and self-management' (Ibid., 90) while the optimisation of children's bodies and their mental capabilities through these soldierly techniques is touted as a way for students to engage the world successfully.

The emphasis on the social and psychological benefits of military training is also evident in media and academic articles that discuss the use of martial techniques in privately run care facilities for youths with various mental and behavioural problems. These 'problems' include medicalised disorders such as mood disorders and conduct disorders but also issues not formally diagnosed, such as school refusal, defiance against family members, as well as 'Internet addiction' (*wangyin*) (Bao 2009; Liu and Zhuang 2010; Song 2012). The next section discusses key themes in the discourse surrounding the use of military drills as a cure for these afflictions, in particular Internet addiction.

Conquering Internet Addiction with Military Drills

The Internet entered China in 1994 and its adoption is now almost universal, particularly among the younger generation. According to a report jointly carried out by the state-backed China Internet Network Information Center and the Chinese Communist Youth League, as many as 191 million Chinese aged between 6 and 18 were digitally connected in 2021. The figure represents 96.8 per cent of the country's population for that age group, up from 94.9 per cent in 2020 (Xin 2022). The Chinese state's perspective is that the Internet should be a tool for learning, entertainment and socialising, but that the mental capacities of children and youth raise a risk of excessive indulgence (Pissin 2021, 90). Chinese government, media and academic publications have blamed online addiction for deteriorating eyesight and poor academic performance, as well as for various psychological problems (Xin 2022).

Consequently, the past two decades or so have witnessed a 'medicalization of deviance' in China over the relationship between youth and their 'excessive', and/or 'addictive' use of the Internet in general and online games in particular (Bax 2014, 687). In 2008, the Chinese government designated 'Internet addiction' a clinical disorder. Recent research on Chinese adolescents concluded that 13 per cent displayed 'Internet addiction' (also known as Internet gaming disorder), a finding consistent with other research indicating higher prevalence in China than in other countries (cited in Pissin 2021, 87).[4] Since the 2000s, Internet addiction has been framed in Chinese government, academic and mainstream media discourse not only as an individual, psychological ailment but also as a moral, social and even national threat (Bax 2014; Bax 2016; Rao 2019).

Linked to phenomena such as juvenile delinquency and described as carrying the same harmful social effects as gambling addiction, alcoholism and drug addiction, Chinese media publications have presented Internet addiction as a contemporary 'opium for the spirit'. In the context of the PE campaign, this metaphor holds rhetorical power by referring to the source of China's 'national humiliation' in the Opium Wars, and as a reminder of the legacy of colonialism (Szablewicz 2010, 460). Describing the Internet as 'opium' frames the Internet as a 'foreign' element that threatens the morality of Chinese youth and the prosperity of the nation (Szablewicz 2010, 460; Rao 2019, 336, 338).

The Chinese government has since the 2000s adopted various measures to curb Internet consumption among children and youth, including regulating game design and the playing time of minors (Szablewicz 2010, 464). The most recent attempt to tackle the problem was in 2021 when China's National Press and Publication Administration, the body in charge of licensing video games, required online game providers to offer only one-hour services to minors from 8pm to 9pm on Fridays, Saturdays and Sundays, as well as on official holidays (Global Times 2022). A recent report in the state-run newspaper, *Global Times*, argues that this measure has 'largely' resolved the problem of minors' addiction to online games, but notes a new concern that the time 'originally spent on games is now being used to browse short videos' (Ibid.).

Chinese youth who have been diagnosed as suffering from Internet addiction have also been sent to special state- and privately run treatment centres. The first Internet addiction treatment centre for youth was established in Beijing's Military General Hospital in 2004 by Tao Ran, a Chinese psychiatrist, PLA Colonel and Communist Party member. Tao Ran has been a pioneer in advocating a psychiatric-based medicalised discourse for framing, explaining and solving Internet addiction but his treatment centre employs military-style disciplinary methods (Pissin 2021, 93). Tao Ran's treatment model has been adopted by other institutions in China which combine military training and psychotherapy to treat youth, most of them boys aged 14–19 (Rao 2019, 337).

According to the 'Report on Youth Internet Addiction and Its Eradication' issued by the China Youth Research Center, China had more than 300 Internet addiction treatment centres in 2017 (cited in Rao 2019, 337). The founders of some of these centres are education experts with access to youth and their parents; others are military members 'with a consistent labor supply of drillmasters' and a close relationship (*guanxi*) with the local government (Rao 2019, 337). Many of these Internet addiction centres hire military veterans as instructors and implement 'militarised management' of students, including severe restrictions on personal freedom, long hours of military drills and intensive physical training (Bax 2014; Bax, 2016; Rao 2019). The proliferation of these privately owned treatment centres suggests that many Chinese parents turn to these centres and regard military-style methods as a potential solution. As noted, such perceptions have emerged in the context of government, academic and media discourse which associates military training with the fostering of 'group conformity, national pride and moral dignity', and promotes martial drills as a means to cultivate the 'discipline, respect, strength and integrity' of 'deviant' youth, 'helping them stay healthy' and fulfil social expectations (Rao 2019, 336). As the next section demonstrates, military drills are also associated with the fostering of desirable physical qualities, particularly for boys.

Honing (Masculine) Bodies

Concerns over a perceived lack of fitness in China's population and a potential deterioration of military strength and the body politic first emerged in China amid the country's repeated military defeats in the mid nineteenth century. As discussed in Chapter 1, these concerns motivated the Qing Dynasty to introduce military training in schools in the first decade of the twentieth century. More than a hundred years later, similar concerns about the feeble bodies of youth, particularly boys, are once again a prominent feature in government, media and academic publications about youth military training.

Noting that contemporary youth lack exercise and have lived in a relatively comfortable environment since childhood, Chinese publications of the early 1990s onwards argued that performing physical drills 'under the scorching sun or pouring rain', as well as running laps, doing push-ups and other physical fitness exercises as part of MT could be beneficial for improving students' fitness (Sichuan waiyu xueyuan wuzhuang bu [Armed Forces Department of Sichuan University of Foreign Languages] 1991, 87; Zheng 1993, 90; Zhao 1997, 25).

As the first generation of singletons born under the One-Child policy came of age in the late 1990s, writers extolling the benefits of military training described what they saw as the physical deficiencies of urban only boys. Raised as 'little emperors' without the 'capacity for movement/action' (*huodong nengli*) (cited in Chicharro-Saito 2008, 39), they 'no longer play outside' and 'take little exercise', the writers argued. Academic and media writers have also warned against the problem of excessive weight gain as children of the post-1990s generation have become keen on 'Western foods' such as biscuits, buttered brioches, sugary drinks and hamburgers (Chicharro-Saito 2008, 39), as the student military trainer in Nanjing had discovered.

Military drills and the fostering of children's 'fit, healthy' bodies is further promoted in alarmist articles in Chinese media and academic journals decrying 'the decline of male authority' and the 'emasculation of Chinese men'. Some Chinese media writers and education experts have suggested that contemporary boys, particularly urban singletons, are becoming too 'gentle and refined' (*wenzhi binbin*) due to excessive doting by family members (Jiang et al. 2010, 28). Concerns about the so-called 'rise of the feminine and the decline of the masculine' (*yin sheng yang shuai*) are further compounded by the sense of Chinese men losing ground to women who are now achieving higher levels of education and greater economic independence (Hird 2019, 357). This discourse around a 'crisis of masculinity' gained increased prominence in Chinese official, media and academic publications of the 2000s and especially since the 2010s (Zheng 2015; F. Liu 2018; Zhang 2019), a trend which has coincided with the promotion of a more assertive strand of nationalism in the Xi Jinping era (a similar trend has been observed in Russia under Putin. See: Hemment 2015). Lamenting the 'dangerous dilution' of China's 'traditional martial spirit (*wu*)' in favour of 'cultural attainment ideals (*wen*)', some academics and media writers warn that like 'earlier eras in Chinese history', the trend could lead to the 'decline' of the nation and its eventual conquest by outside powers (Q. Liu 2005; Ma and Li 2015).

A related discourse links this worrying trend to the proliferation of foreign popular culture products, particularly from Japan and South Korea, which promote male actors and singers characterised by 'soft' masculinity (*naiyou xiaosheng*, literally, 'saccharine youths') (Hird 2019, 357). Associated with a gender-ambiguous appearance, delicate features and a gentle, sensitive demeanour, this masculinity model is viewed as a threat to the security of the Chinese nation since it symbolises 'powerlessness, inferiority, feminised passivity and social deterioration' (Wen 2021, 257–8). The following quote from an article originally published on a CPC-run media website and reprinted on other Chinese media websites, illustrates this alarmist discourse:

> Today, some [Chinese] men exhibit effeminate characteristics . . . If most teenagers adopt this trend, how much time and energy will they devote to learning about heroic deeds or cultivating courageousness? How could such unmanly, 'too feeble to truss a chicken' (*shou wu fu ji zhi li*) 'sissies' (*niang pao*) . . . kill an enemy on the battlefield? Once their bodies become boneless and weak and their masculinity is depleted, we will no longer have upright and courageous men, and this would be a real tragedy for the nation. (Hong, 2019)

The text, which appears in an opinion piece titled 'Advocate Heroes, Remember Struggle' (*Chongshang yingxiong, laoji fendou*), further laments the growing popularity of 'sissy men (*niang pao*)' and 'pseudo girls' (*jia nü*) in China's contemporary youth culture as harmful to 'national security' (Hong, 2019). An article in the CPC's mouthpiece, *People's Daily*, makes a similar point, and questions whether Chinese youth of this generation could exhibit the sort of 'upright and courageous (*xianxing*) masculinity (*yanggang*)' required of military soldiers (Wang, 2015). As noted in a number of studies on the construction of masculinity in twenty-first century China, these arguments are typical of a hyper-nationalistic discourse currently found on Chinese mainstream media (Song and Hird 2014; Zheng 2015; Lin and Mac an Ghaill 2019; Zhang 2019; Song 2022).

Media commentary have called on schools to foster male physical strength and capability, while re-inscribing a binary division between boys and girls as a central condition for China's national development and stability (Dauncey 2017, 360; Lin and Mac an Ghaill, 2019, 289–90). Some schools have responded to these calls by launching gender-distinctive educational programmes and the establishment of single-gender schools (Zheng 2015, 358, 360). Over the past decade, the government has also addressed such concerns about the state of masculinity in China by calling, among other things, for the hiring of more male teachers at the basic education level (Du and Chen 2021). In recent years, China's Ministry of Education (MOE) further announced its intention to strengthen sports lessons to cultivate the 'masculinity' (*yanggan zhiqi*) of boys (Zhonghua renmin gongheguo jiaoyu bu [Ministry of Education of the PRC] 2020).

The announcement came in response to a proposal in 2020 by a member of the standing committee of the Chinese People's Political Consultative Conference (CPPCC) – a top political body in Beijing. Describing the 'feminisation' of boys as a threat to the survival of the nation, the delegate warned that China's male students have in recent decades become 'weak, self-effacing and timid', a development he relates to the effects of the One-Child policy, the feminisation of childcare and the teaching profession, and the media's excessive hyping of young, good-looking popular culture icons lacking in 'macho' male features (*xiao xian rou*, literally 'little fresh meat') (Siwei Zhao 2021). A year later, in 2021, China's State Administration of Radio and Television banned 'sissy boys' (*niang pao*) from Chinese television shows or video-sharing sites to protect youth from 'harmful', 'chaotic' influences (Guojia guangbo dianshi zongjiu [the State Administration of Radio and Television] 2021).

Amid this growing preoccupation with the deficient bodily practices and behaviours of Chinese youth (particularly urban boys), official, media and academic publications have framed military drills as an important means of fighting these 'dangerous' tendencies. Contemporary publications constitute youth sexuality as a politicised site in which 'discipline' and 'regulation', the health of the individual body and the health of society, fuse into one (Foucault 1978, 139; Foucault 2008). At the same time, however, the discourse which links MT to the promotion of a 'proper' masculinity model as well as to other desirable personal qualities have come under criticism in Chinese public discourse. For instance, the MOE's 2020 announcement on the strengthening of physical education for boys stirred a heated debate on Chinese social media, with some netizens calling the policy 'sexist' (Du and Chen 2021). As the next section will discuss, criticism of youth military training also appears in some media and academic writings about the programme.

Youth Military Training in China: Problems and Contradictions

While most of the texts surveyed here underscore the myriad benefits of the state-mandated MT course for both individual youth and the national collective, some writers do highlight inherent problems within the programme. A key tension stems from a potential contradiction between the harsh environment of the MT course and the programme's goal of attracting youth to military service. While learning about barrack culture and the courageous sacrifice of individual soldiers may increase admiration for the military and motivate some young people to enlist, others might find the challenging conditions of the course a powerful deterrence. The problem was acknowledged early on.

A report published a couple of years after the Tiananmen incident lists a potential tension between students' values and the harsh discipline of the MT course. 'Foreign hostile forces' advocating individual liberty and 'absolute democracy', coupled with 'lax school management and poor ideological and political education', the report suggests, have made 'many students' used to an atmosphere of 'freedom' and 'enjoyment'. They feel that MT is 'a pointless waste of time' since the country is 'now focused on economic construction' and they themselves have come to college 'to study', not to 'learn how to use a gun'. As a result, continues the report, young people may experience 'disgust, boredom' and acts of 'disobedience' and 'rebellion' during the MT course, as well as 'excessive anxiety, insomnia, neurasthenia, lack of self-confidence, depression and other phenomena'. 'Weaker' (male) students may feel 'heavy physical and psychological pressure', while girls may be 'frightened by the loud noises during the live ammunition shooting', 'cry', or 'refuse to participate' (Sichuan waiyu xueyuan wuzhuang bu [Armed Forces Department of Sichuan University of Foreign Languages] 1991, 85). Another article from the same period notes that the MT experience may lead some college students to believe that army life is 'monotonous and tedious'. The course is unlikely to change students' common notion that 'a good man should not be a soldier (*hao nan bu dangbing*)' since 'soldiers are poor and miserable' (Tang 1990, 25).

Discussion of the problematic disconnect between the goals and contents of the MT programme, the government's push for rapid economic growth, and the values and aspirations of Chinese youth deepened in publications of the 1990s onwards. An article published in 1993 in the journal of Huazhong University of Science and Technology in the city of Wuhan observed that military training for college students has become a 'hot topic' on which 'people have mixed opinions', due to the view that the goals of the course do not match the needs of the market economy to train a large number of talents required for economic construction (Zheng 1993, 89).

An article published in 1997 noted that economic development and increasing 'exchanges with foreigners' have caused some youths to develop 'illusions about world harmony' and 'extravagant consumer desires', 'hedonism' and 'money worship'. The challenges of army life and low military pay conflict with the ambition of many young people to become 'business entrepreneurs'. Concurrently, youth also see little value in the MT course (Zhao 1997, 24). Another article observed that some young people believe that 'learning from the military, workers and peasants' was a 'Cultural Revolution' ideology negated in the reform era, so there is 'no reason to engage in military training' (Cheng 1998, 100).

Since the 2000s, writers have emphasised that the MT programme is 'unsuitable' for contemporary youth because the values it promotes contradict the new emphasis in Chinese education on innovation, critical thinking and problem-solving introduced as part of a major reform plan under the title 'education for quality' *(suzhi jiaoyu)*. Inspired in part by reforms in neighbouring countries, such as Japan, where concerns over 'skills' formation, examination stress and excessive homework' had sparked similar initiatives, calls for 'quality' in Chinese education reflected the regime's desire to nurture critical and creative thinkers for the knowledge economy. Yet these aspirations conflict with the attempt to reinforce political control through patriotic education and military training (Vickers and Zeng 2017, 59; Vickers 2022).

Noting this contradiction, a journalist in the *Guangzhou ribao* (*Guangzhou Daily*), the official newspaper of the city's Communist Party Committee, responded to the 2015 incident described at the beginning of the chapter by noting that:

> The times are advancing. Students' minds and bodies are different from those of their predecessors a few decades ago ... Today, students' awareness of rights and the legal system has also been greatly improved, and instructors cannot treat them according to old ways of thinking. Moreover, the current educational trend is to foster students' creative thinking. Therefore, military training should not place too much emphasis on obedience. Instructors must not oblige students to obey the rules by force. (Z. Zhang 2015)

This view has also found expression in academic publications and opinion columns which observe that 'in modern society', no one can accept a spirit of 'crude (*cubao*) obedience' or 'insulting behaviour harmful both to the body and mind' (Chu 2014; Ning 2014; Chen 2016). Criticism of youth military training has become increasingly prevalent following reports on various incidents during MT courses for youth under 18. According to stories circulating in Chinese social media and the general press, over the past two decades, there have been recurrent cases of high school students suffering injuries and even death from over-exertion, heat stroke, or an underlying medical problem (Fish 2015, 13; Lu 2006). Other reported incidents have involved verbal abuse of young trainees by military instructors, including male trainers making offensive remarks to girls about their bodies or scolding boys who could not perform the required drills. There have also been cases of physical abuse, including beating and other forms of corporal punishment (Chen and Hu 2017, 67; Fu and Yang 2018).

In one such case, a drill master's abuse was said to have caused the suicide of a young female trainee (*Pengpai* 2014; Jiang 2022). In another reported incident in 2014, military training at one high school in Longshan County, Hunan Province, turned violent when students resisted their drill masters (Fish 2015, 15). The facts were disputed, but a quarrel between an instructor and a female cadet appears to have ended with him threatening to beat her palm with a stick. The boys in the class intervened and were punished with push-ups, to which they protested. A group of drunk military instructors are alleged to have later sought revenge for the students' disobedience by attacking the students, leaving several hospitalised (cited in Fish, 2015, 15). Such incidents have occasionally resulted in official inquiries and the disciplining of instructors. Meanwhile, there has also been widespread public criticism in both general and social media about the abuse of 'human rights' of young patients in Internet addiction treatment centres which employ military training methods. In some cases, such criticism has even led to the closure of these centres (Fu and Yang 2018; Rao 2019).

These episodes have fuelled a continuous public debate in China concerning the logic, necessity and effects of military training and the use of martial therapeutic methods, especially for those under 18 (e.g. CRI 2016; F. Zhang 2017). For instance, in response to the 2014 Hunan incident cited earlier, Chinese artist Chen Danqing posted a comment on his social media account in which he described student military training as 'an education in how to be a slave that should only exist in totalitarian countries like North Korea' (cited in Davis 2014). The post, which was soon deleted by state censors, asked: 'Are we trying to cultivate a healthy, independent and freethinking populace or a bunch of obedient machines?' (Davis 2014). Other online commentators retorted that MT-related incidents often reflect 'the spoiled attitude and disobedience' of youth of the post-90s generation which is why 'China needs student military training in the first place' (Davis 2014).

One possible cause of the abusive incidents reported during MT may be a shortage of qualified training personnel as a result of the expansion of the programme in the last two decades. According to some reports in Chinese media, the problem has led to the employment of 'sub-standard commercial trainers' posing as 'fake ex-soldiers', or of regular sports teachers who lack professional training (Li *et al.* 2009, 18; Chen and Hu 2017). Whatever the reason, the expansion of MT to ever younger populations since the 2000s has brought anxious parents in increasing conflict with military trainers as well as school authorities. After the 2014 Hunan incident, for instance, some parents reported 'feeling powerless as they sent their children to training with no means of checking in' (cited in Davis 2014).

In the 1990s, budget shortages even forced students' families to pay participation fees for these courses (Wang 1998, 77). The practice persisted into the 2010s, but many schools have struggled to charge students of poor backgrounds (Chen and Hu 2017, 68). The insufficient funding has also led to complaints by students and their families about substandard food, daily life provisions and hygiene during the MT course, particularly for those taking place in special facilities (Li et al. 2009, 18). Some high schools have responded to parental concerns by having teachers accompany students throughout their training, and some military instructors have allowed high school students who are too tired 'to sit on the side' (cited in Fish 2015, 13).

In short, while media and academic writers in China have for the most part endorsed the use of martial techniques to promote 'correct' political attitudes, bodily deficiencies, as well as various mental ailments, the proliferation of these techniques in the past two decades or so has also stirred resistance among students and their families. The publications reviewed here note that this resistance has led some youth to skip the mandatory MT course altogether by 'feigning sickness' with the aid of their parents (Cheng 1998, 101; Li et al. 2009, 17).

Concluding Remarks

This chapter examined China's official, media and academic discourse regarding the use of military training in educational and care facilities. As noted, official formulations of the mandatory MT course list the promotion of 'love' for the nation, the Party-state and the army, as well as 'character building' among the aims of the programme. Government renderings make clear that the latter includes the fostering of self-discipline, endurance under pressure and the ability to work in a team. Since the programme's inception in the mid 1980s, most academic and media writers have followed the government's lead by highlighting the role of the MT programme in fostering a spirit of patriotism, collectivism and discipline. The past two decades or so have nonetheless witnessed a growing emphasis in media and academic writing on the individual, pragmatic benefits of military drills, including the improvement of youth ability for self-reliance, flexibility and independence (cf. Naftali 2021c).

The fact that contemporary academics and journalists feel a need to recommend military training by stressing its utilitarian ethos may attest to the ineffectiveness of one of the central goals of the programme: the promotion of 'love for the country' and 'love for the military' among the current young generation. Yet, the emphasis on the benefits of military training for the personal success and healthy development of youths could be seen as complementary to an authoritarian-militaristic strain of thinking in that it creates a crucial link between military mobilisation as a form of sovereign power and a neoliberal bio-political discourse of 'self-improvement' (McSorley 2013, 15). As we saw, media and academic publications rationalise the use of martial techniques by framing it as a panacea for the physical, psychological and gender deficiencies of Chinese youth of the post-1990s and 2000s generation, particularly urban boys. By employing various practices of 'corporeal transformation' through which specific 'martial dispositions and competencies become inculcated', China's MT programmes function as a site for the optimisation and standardisation of bodies and mentalities as well as the 'domestication' of deviant youth (cf. Chicharro-Saito 2008, 29).

Nonetheless, as indicated in the 2015 incident described at the beginning of the chapter and in the discussion of inherent tensions within the military training programme, it appears that the programme may not be entirely effective in achieving its various goals. Indeed, as Chapter 6 will demonstrate, some youth express apathy, ambivalence and even resentment towards the programme. Nor do they readily embrace the kind of 'tough masculinity' model the programme seeks to promote. Recognising this challenge, in the past decade or so, the Party-state and the PLA have been turning to popular culture products as an alternative channel for the promotion of patriotism, 'love for the military' and a martial masculinity ideal. These efforts will be discussed in the next chapter.

Notes

1. The network of National Defence Education Model schools has steadily expanded in recent years. In early 2023, for instance, the Chinese government issued a notice on the selection of '2,687 primary and secondary schools as national defence education model school' (cited in Van Oudenaren 2023).
2. For the past several decades, women have constituted approximately 5 per cent or less of the PLA (Kania 2016).
3. For an elaborate discussion of the PLA's conscription policy, see Chapter 6.

4. The most recent update of the American Psychiatric Association's *Diagnostic and Statistical Manual of Mental Disorders* (American Psychiatric Association 2013) includes Internet gaming disorder as a condition warranting further study, and, although contested, the revision of the *International Statistical Classification of Diseases* (ICD-11) by the World Health Organization (2018) includes gaming disorder under the category 'Disorders due to substance use or addictive behaviours'. Most studies about Internet gaming in relation to psychological disorders such as addiction, depression, anxiety, impulsiveness and attention-deficit hyperactivity disorder shows an incoherency of interpretation with regard to the definition of Internet gaming disorder, an incoherency that calls for caution in assessing scientific literature about the disorder (cited in Pissin 2021, 87).

CHAPTER 4

Military Entertainment, Gender and the Nation

In Spring 2023, *Born to Fly* (*Changkong zhi wang*) took Chinese movie theatres by storm. Made in close collaboration with the PLA Airforce, *Born to Fly* portrays Chinese test pilots risking their lives to perfect a new stealth fighter for combat against a foreign power that, though unnamed, speaks American-accented English (The Economist 2023a). Describing the film as 'China's answer' to the US blockbuster, *Top Gun: Maverick* (2022), an article in the Chinese state-run newspaper *Global Times* praised the film for showcasing 'the charisma of PLA test pilots' and 'the rapid development of China's aviation industry'. The article also hailed *Born to Fly* for its strong patriotic message while noting that the movie was created by 'China's modern film industry against the backdrop of continuously catching up with the production standards of top international film industries' (Lin 2023).

Born to Fly exemplifies a new type of propaganda work deployed by the Chinese military over the past decade. While media and culture have played a key role in the Party-state's efforts to shape public perceptions of war, military and the nation since the establishment of the PRC (R. Cai 2018, 781; Bao 2019), an increasingly competitive media market in recent decades have undermined this effort. In response, the PLA has turned to a new tactic: the sponsoring of 'military entertainment' – or 'militainment' (Thomas 2009) – products made by commercial companies. How do these media productions package war and the military to Chinese audiences? What sort of messages do they convey about the role of the military and the use of armed force in China's international relations? And how do such messages contribute to the promotion of a 'military masculinity' model in contemporary China?

The chapter addresses these questions while drawing on select examples of war and military tropes in four case studies: the variety TV show, *Takes a Real Man* (*Zhenzheng nanzihan*, 2015–17); and three prominent war/action films – *Wolf Warrior* (*Zhan lang*, 2015), *Wolf Warrior II* (*Zhan lang II*, 2017) and *Operation Red Sea* (*Hong Hai xingdong*, 2018). Drawing on original analysis as well as on insights from previous studies of the three films, in particular the *Wolf Warrior* series, the chapter advances the following arguments.

First, the PLA has come to recognise over the past couple of decades the centrality of popular culture in the lives of young people of the post-1990s and post-2000s generation. This realisation has forced China's military to adopt the strategies and techniques of commercial popular culture in its 'public relations, image-making and self-presentation efforts' (Frühstück 2007, 117). Like military establishments in capitalist, democratic countries such as Japan, the US or the UK (Bailey 2007; Frühstück 2007; Der Derian 2009 [2001]; Robb 2019), China's military has turned to popular culture to convince audiences, in particular youths of conscription age, not only of the army's necessity but also of its 'likability' and 'coolness' (Frühstück 2007, 117, 119; Thomas 2009, 106; Basham 2011, 187–8).

Second, in seeking to create attractive 'simulations' of war and the military for youth consumption, the PLA (again, like militaries elsewhere) engages in 'dissimulation' (Der Derian 2009 [2001]). The commercial products it sponsors convey contradictory and occasionally even misleading messages about the nature of army life and the role of the military in China's international relations.

Finally, the discussion in this chapter demonstrates that PLA-backed media typically advertise a 'military masculinity' model while linking this model to the defence of China's national interests. In doing so, these media productions build on and feed into the growing public anxiety in China about the prevalence of so-called 'effeminate boys' in youth popular culture, and the threat the trend poses for Chinese society and the nation. As such, these military-sponsored media play an integral part in the creation and circulation of popular culture that is bound to an immanent gender hierarchy (Enloe 2000, 3; Thomas 2009, 106). The case studies examined in the chapter further demonstrate that gender and sexuality are not 'exterior to the story' these media productions attempt to tell about 'China's rise'; they are 'constitutive' of it (cf. P. Liu 2018).

The Rise of Military Entertainment in Twenty-First Century China

Military-themed media played a key role in the construction of the Chinese state's ideology of patriotism and collectivism during the Mao era (Wang 2018; Chu 2022). As discussed in Chapter 1, magazines, books, films, opera and ballets of the 1950s–70s, including those targeting children and youth, sought to inspire audiences to fight for the revolution and the country against domestic and foreign enemies. The government's use of media and culture for educational and propaganda purposes persisted after 1978. The CPC and the military have nonetheless adapted their propaganda tactics to the social, cultural and economic conditions of the reform era, and specifically to the rise of a commercialised media market in China.

Since the 1990s, the use of media to promote patriotism and national security consciousness has been framed by the need to bolster the Party-state's and the PLA's legitimacy following the military crackdown on youth protestors in 1989, and by international developments perceived as threats to China's national strength, in particular, growing tensions with the United States. As these challenges grew, Jiang Zemin, who served as China's leader and as General Secretary of the CPC in 1989–2002/3, stressed the importance of ideological work, requiring media practitioners to 'guide public opinion' towards acceptance of the leadership of the CPC (Brady 2008, 51). An essential part of this ideological work has been the strengthening of Patriotic Education and National Defence Education in propaganda and culture (Wang and Klein 2022, 112).

And yet, over the past several decades, the Party and the PLA's ideological work has been crucially informed by both the commercialisation of China's media market and by the increasing flow of global popular culture into the country, particularly across the Internet and social media. These trends pose a serious challenge for the efforts of the Party-state and the PLA. Maoist-era propaganda work could rely on overt appeals to mass audiences using a one-size-fits-all approach; publicity work in the era of market reforms is much more difficult and the Chinese military now has to compete with international broadcasts, films, websites, online games, mobile applications and commercial ads for the attention of young consumers (Naftali 2020).

In response, since the 1990s, China has implemented a 'Main Melody' (*zhuxuanlü*) initiative whose goal is to produce government-sponsored films and TV shows to propagate what the

Party-state defines as the country's 'mainstream values' of 'Marxism-Leninism-Maoism, socialism, patriotism and collectivism' (cited in Guan and Hu 2021, 842). Specifically, Main Melody media productions should extoll 'the virtues of the state, military and the Communist Party of China', while propagating national spirit, pride and cohesion among audiences. While Main Melody media is aimed at audiences of all ages, youth constitute a special target group. In the mid-1990s, the PRC State Education Commission issued a list of '100 patriotic films' that primary and secondary school students in China must watch. Most of the films glorify CPC history or depict China's invasion by foreign imperial powers from the mid nineteenth to the mid twentieth century (Chu 2022, 6). Other themes include the Communist revolution, post-1949 Chinese history, including the Korean War, and contemporary Chinese politics (Guan and Hu 2021, 843; Wang and Chew 2021, 882).

Under the leadership of Hu Jintao (2002–12) and especially in the Xi Jinping era (2012–), the Party-state intensified its efforts to shape young people's ideological values through additional media initiatives. In 2009, for instance, the government launched the 'National Defence Education Ten Thousand Screenings Programme' (*Guofang jiaoyu wanying jihua*) (*Renmin ribao* [*People's Daily*] 2021), which 'provides policy, project approval and support for the creation of national defence military films' (cited in Van Oudenaren, 2023; *Renmin ribao* [*People's Daily*] 2021). Run by the China Film Foundation (CFF) under the special guidance of the NDE Office of the Central Military Commission's Political Work Department in the CPC, the program supports the production of media which focuses on 'national defence stories' (*Renmin ribao* [*People's Daily*] 2021; Van Oudenaren 2023).

In addition to facilitating engagement between the military and the film industry, the 'National Defence Ten Thousand Screenings Program' has also held online and in-person public screenings of military- and patriotic-themed films to popularise NDE among army officers and soldiers, militia reservists and students of all ages. In recent years, the program has reportedly held nearly 1,000 screenings per month in 'communities, military camps, factories, enterprises, as well as primary, junior and senior schools' and NDE demonstration bases for children (Kang and Wang 2021; *Renmin ribao* [*People's Daily*] 2021; Tu and Cui 2021). The focus on NDE among China's youngest citizens is clear. In a speech in August 2018, Xi Jinping emphasised the need to 'seize the critical period that determines and forms teenagers' values', while a 2019 document published by the State Council (China's cabinet) states that 'patriotism is the most natural and simple emotion of the Chinese. We must insist on starting from when they are babies, focusing on consolidating the roots, concentrating on the soul' (cited in Lin 2020). The document includes instructions for government and Party officials to promote movies, news and classroom lessons with Xi's plans for 'China's rejuvenation', and calls on authorities to capitalise on teenagers' interests in online games, animation and short videos 'so that patriotism can fill the Internet space' (Lin 2020).

As the 'socialist market economy' introduced media commercialisation and cultural diversification (Ma 2014, 527), these initiatives have formed part of the CPC's strategy to transform direct propaganda and maintain its appeal to young people. Since the 1980s, commercial factors have increasingly impacted media operations, financing and content production, bringing changes with important implications for the form and content of TV shows and films in China (Chu 2022, 7, 12). The production of TV content has been mainly financed by private capital since the 1990s, and television channels now depend on audience demographics and advertising revenues to fund their operations. Increased competition for revenue has encouraged channels to seek production formats which appeal to large audiences or which have already proven successful elsewhere (Wang and Chew 2021, 878; Peng 2022, 744).

As part of this trend, Chinese television has been airing an increasing amount of reality shows. Arriving from Europe and the United Kingdom in the early 2000s, the format peaked on Chinese television between 2010 and 2013. In the past decade, more reality formats have entered China from South Korea, capitalising on the popularity of the Korean Wave (in Chinese, *hanliu*) among audiences, especially young Chinese born in the 1990s onward (Keane and Zhang 2017). One of the case studies discussed in this chapter – the reality TV show, *Takes a Real Man* – is based on a format imported directly from South Korea.

At the same time, the Party-state has continued to strongly regulate state-owned media corporations, private media businesses and media content. A large part of the Chinese media system remains under the Party-state framework. Television channels are owned by the state which often exercises authoritarian power to regulate media products, including popular entertainment (Zeng and Sparks 2019). Chinese TV production is influenced by both market demands and the CPC's administration. Propaganda remains a major task for state-owned media, and private capital and market forces are compelled to compromise with state goals (Peng 2022, 745). Since the 2010s, all TV channels in China have aired numerous war dramas, most of which depict the War of Resistance against Japan. For Chinese producers, 'to be patriotic simply meant good business, since any show about fighting the Japanese would be bulletproof in the license application process' (Sun 2021, 124–5).

Until the mid-2010s, these war dramas dominated the audience ratings of many provincial satellite television channels. They also made money, and were sometimes extremely profitable (Wang and Chew 2021, 883). Scholars have explained the success of this genre by noting its appeal to the patriotism of Chinese viewers, as well as the inclusion of graphic battle scenes and big explosions. The casting of youth idols from the Chinese mainland, Hong Kong and Taiwan in starring roles might also have helped. Some studies note a bigger emphasis on the 'human factor' in these TV war dramas, a move which increases the stories' emotional appeal (Chu 2022, 7; Wang and Klein 2022, 117–18).

These new features draw their inspiration from imported cultural models, especially Hollywood (Wang and Klein 2022, 117–18). In the mid-1990s, in order to open the market and boost box-office income while protecting domestic cultural industries, the Chinese government adopted a regulatory system to govern the number of foreign blockbuster films that could enter the market each year (Chu 2022, 6). Initially capped at ten foreign films a year, the quota has gradually increased and now stands at 34. Many of the foreign blockbusters allowed in have been Hollywood movies. Popular among young Chinese audiences who now consume these films online, legally or illegally, the movies have directly inspired local productions of war- and military-themed media (Wang and Klein 2022, 117–18).

The adoption of entertainment-oriented elements in some of China's TV war dramas over the past decade has antagonised some audiences as well as the state. In 2013, official media began to criticise some of these shows for their 'consumerist cultural tendency', accusing them of 'distorting history for profit' (Wang and Chew 2021, 887). Indeed, some of the dramas about the War of Resistance against Japan portray protagonists using superior fighting skills, tactics and strategies to defeat a Japanese army that is depicted as militarily incompetent. Others have shown Communist soldiers using Chinese martial arts to defeat a much larger number of Japanese army soldiers (Sun 2021, 127; Wang and Chew 2021, 885). One recent show to draw close scrutiny is *Drawing Sword 3: Lightning Fighters* (*Lei ting zhan jiang*, 2020). Official media in China criticised the show for its 'distorted presentation of war scenes', such as the depiction of a Red Army officer 'smoking a cigar', and the Communist military headquarters as located in a 'splendid villa'. The portrayal, state media argued, was 'more typical of a Hollywood hero than a Chinese soldier in a war meant to safeguard the homeland and resist aggression' (cited in Liang 2020). An article in the CPC's mouthpiece, the *People's Daily*, derided the show's producers for attempting to attract young audiences by creating an 'idol-centred' drama 'under the guise of a patriotic war drama'. The show was cancelled after nine episodes of the planned forty had aired (Liang 2020).

The keen criticism reveals an inherent tension between the political and entertainment functions of Chinese TV shows in the Main Melody genre, but the attacks have had an effect. Amid growing censure and new government regulations meant to curb their 'excessive' entertainment, the number of commercial TV shows about the War of Resistance against Japan has fallen (Wang and Chew 2021, 887). But war- and military-themed productions have not disappeared from mainland Chinese screens. Instead, they have developed into the military-action film.

An early example is *The Taking of Tiger Mountain 3D* (*Zhiqu Weihushan*, dir., Tsui Hark, 2014). The film, based on one of the most well-known model operas of the Cultural Revolution (1966–76), depicts a battle between a PLA squad and a bandit gang in northeast China during the socialist revolution (Chu 2022, 16). But the most popular films in the genre have been contemporary. In 2015, the mainland Chinese filmmaker and actor Wu Jing brought the military-action genre to public attention with the surprise box-office success of *Wolf Warrior* (*Zhan lang*). Since then, the genre has seen a surge in both commercial profit and public acceptance. In the three years following the release of *Wolf Warrior*, several other war-action films set in contemporary times have been released, including *Operation Mekong* (*Meigonghe Xingdong*, 2016) and *Operation Red Sea* (*Hong Hai Xingdong*, 2018) directed by Hong Kong filmmaker, Dante Lam, and the second instalment in the *Wolf Warrior* series (*Zhan lang* II, dir. Wu Jing, 2017).

Some of these films have been hugely successful. *Wolf Warrior II* and *Operation Red Sea* broke numerous box-office records and were ranked second and fifth respectively in the All-Time-Mainland China Box Office (Guan and Hu 2021, 841). *Wolf Warrior II* even inspires the name of China's combative new style of 'wolf-warrior diplomacy' (Martin 2021; Yang 2023). Two other noteworthy war-action films that achieved commercial success in recent years include *The Battle at Lake Changjin* (*Changjin hu*, 2021) and *Born to Fly* mentioned at the beginning of this chapter. Co-directed by Chen Kaige, Tsui Hark and Dante Lam, *The Battle at Lake Changjin* is said to be the most expensive film ever made in China. The film depicts the story of the forced retreat of US forces by the Chinese People's Volunteer Army in one of the bloodiest battles of the Korean War, the Battle of the Chosin Reservoir (Myers and Chien 2021). The movie was commissioned by the Central Propaganda Department of the CPC as part of the Party's 100th anniversary celebrations.

All these films received the strong support of the Chinese government and the PLA during production and distribution. For films set in contemporary times, such as the *Wolf Warrior* series and *Operation Red Sea*, the support included the provision of new military weapons and equipment that have rarely appeared on screen (Jin 2018). These war-action films cannot be seen only as an entertainment product. They are also a political instrument which conveys the discourses and viewpoints that the Chinese state wants its citizens to embrace (Guan and Hu 2021, 849). The films and the TV show discussed also function as public relations tools for the PLA by reflecting the new image of the military – across sea, land and air – to domestic audiences, including potential recruits.

Military Entertainment, Masculinities and Femininities in China

We saw in Chapter 1 that during the Mao era, the Communist Party-state promoted its idea of gender equality through rhetoric and policy. Media and cultural works of the 1950s and particularly the 1960s propagated a new ideal of assertive, capable women alongside a physically robust, militant masculinity. During the Cultural Revolution (1966–76), militant masculinity became the ideal for Chinese women as well, resulting in what some scholars have described as an 'erasure of femininity' (Dai 1995; Yang 1999; Yang and Yan 2017). Other studies have documented a persistent notion of gender difference even within the militant masculinity framework of the Cultural Revolution (Honig

2002; Roberts 2004; Evans 2008; Naftali 2014a; Edwards 2016; Hird 2019; Jiao 2022).

The complexity of Maoist-era gender ideologies notwithstanding, the 'Reform and Opening Up' era ushered in a reappraisal of Maoist gender ideals (Liu 2014; Evans 2021). Beginning in the 1980s, China's cultural elite criticised the Cultural Revolution–era's repression of 'natural' differences between men and women which they argued led to the excessive 'masculinisation of women' and the 'emasculation of men' (Jiao 2022, 5). Amid this critique, Chinese public discourse, as well as media and culture products, have increasingly propagated essentialist notions of femininity and masculinity couched in articulations of a nativist patriarchal ideology. These notions, actively promoted by the state, underwrite biological differences and cast women's 'natural role' as 'vulnerable, dependent and inferior', and men as 'active and even aggressive' (Zurndorfer 2018, 491).

Over the past three decades, this discourse has contrasted with changing social attitudes, as young Chinese, especially wealthier, educated youths born since the start of the 1990s, have experienced enhanced opportunities to explore a plurality of gender practices (Li and Jankowiak 2016, 188; Liu 2019, 298; Liu 2014). Growing individualism grounded in neo-liberal formulations of free choice and the effects of the One-Child policy, together with global cultural influences and the rise of social media, have created a space for the discussion of diverse sexualities and the circulation of alternative female and male images in China (Naftali 2024, 96). Domestic cultural industries have responded – and further contributed to this trend – by creating a wider range of gender representations, including images of 'girlie boys' and 'boyish girls'. A number of studies suggest that these diverse gender representations have become increasingly popular among Chinese youth of the post-1990s and 2000s generation, especially those in urban areas (Lin and Mac an Ghaill 2019, 291; Song 2022).

The proliferation of these alternative gender representations has stirred political and public concern about the erosion of so-called 'indigenous gender values' (Peng 2022, 746). As noted in Chapter 3, these concerns have fed into a 'crisis of masculinity' discourse which partially blames media representations of 'effeminate men' and 'masculine women' for the 'dilution' of 'real masculinity' among contemporary youth. The Chinese government has responded by promoting the production of 'nationalist masculinities', a combination of Confucian and Maoist tropes of manhood adapted to the new expectations of the market reform era which require men to display an 'entrepreneurial spirit' and 'competitive toughness' (Song and Hird 2014, 11–12). At the same time, under Xi Jinping's revival of Confucianism, dominant discourse and policy have celebrated women's 'traditional' virtues and domestic roles as key for the country's national prosperity (Evans 2021, 99; Yan 2021b).

Mainstream media has followed suit. A survey of the main characters of top-grossing Chinese films between 2002 and 2011 reveals that the principal female characters tended to be 'young, sexualized and docile' (Zurndorfer 2018, 495). Television shows over the past two decades underline the importance of Chinese women's domesticity and femininity and pay little to no attention towards female achievement outside the home (Peng 2022, 746). The predominance of gender-essentialist representations in contemporary media products may reflect commercial considerations on the part of privately owned Chinese media companies. In 2018, the issue of young men's appearance and behaviour triggered a heated debate in China following a television performance of New F4, a boy band whose members were described in Chinese media as 'little fresh meat' (*xiao xian rou*), a derogatory term referring to their 'effeminate appearance'.[1] After the band performed at an annual back-to-school gala aired on CCTV, China's national state-run television network, a number of parents complained online that the band's image was 'too effeminate'. Others deplored 'the pop culture influence from Korea and Japan' which they argued led to the spread of improper gender behaviour among Chinese boys (Wen 2021, 253–4).

In addition to the public debate over gender representations in popular culture and their effects on Chinese youth behaviours, media content in China is also crucially shaped by the CPC's political interference, which occurs at both censorship and propaganda levels (Peng 2022, 746). This interference plays an important part in what appears on Chinese screens. An editorial published in the state-run magazine, *Beijing Youth Daily* (*Beijing qingnian bao*) following the New F4 incident demonstrated the state's position:

> 'Sissy boys' [in Chinese, *niang pao*; literally, 'girlie guns', a derogatory term for 'effeminate men'] have dominated our screens in recent years. Whether in talent shows, youth dramas or even some mainstream positive energy programs, the 'sissy boys' are everywhere now . . . Popular culture can have a profound impact on the healthy growth of young people, the future of the country, and the

fate of the nation. [Therefore], it is everyone's responsibility to construct a masculine society (*yanggang shehui*) and a masculine culture (*yanggang wenhua*) – a culture that is characterized by vigor, ambition, responsibility, and boldness (Beijing qingnian bao 2018).

Acknowledging that both boys and girls can be 'ambitious', the editorial calls on young people to reject the 'sissy boy trend': girls should strive to be 'gentle and beautiful (*roumei*)', while boys should avoid 'effeminate' beauty standards (Beijing qingnian bao 2018). A related editorial published by the state News Agency, *Xinhua*, similarly denounced young men for being too effeminate and issued a call 'to save boys and the nation' (cited in Wen 2021, 254).

This type of rhetoric has translated into official regulations of the media market. As noted, in 2021, China's State Administration of Radio and Television ordered that 'sissy boys' (*niang pao*) not appear on Chinese television shows or video sharing websites to protect youth from 'chaotic' gender influences. Official publications link these influences to foreign threats. For instance, a commentary published in October 2023 by the Communist Party Propaganda Department in Zhejiang Province relates the popularity of 'abnormal' gender aesthetics in China's entertainment industry to Xi Jinping's 'comprehensive national security' concerns. The article goes as far as to suggest the existence of 'a broader CIA-driven plot of "cultural castration" (*wenhua yange*)', which allegedly uses 'Japanese and South Korean talent agencies' to promote 'non-binary (*bu nan bu nü*) media stars in China in order to weaken Chinese masculinity' (cited in Thornton 2023). To address this type of threat, the Chinese government has called on domestic media producers to create content which portrays 'healthier' models of manhood (see Naftali 2024). War- and military-themed media has been accorded a key role in instructing Chinese boys how to become 'real men (*zhenzheng nanzihan*)', who display 'boldness', 'heroism' and 'willingness to fight for the country' (Chen 2019). The discussion below seeks to examine how PLA-backed media of the Xi Jinping era delineate the tropes of armed combat and soldierhood, and how these renderings construct a distinctively gendered notion of 'patriotic citizenship'.

The Case Studies under Consideration

The analysis in this chapter draws on examples from four case studies. The first is the TV variety program, *Takes a Real Man*, which aired on China's Hunan Satellite Television for two seasons (2015–17, twelve to fourteen episodes, each approximately ninety minutes). The first military-themed reality show to be screened in China, the program is based on a South Korean format titled *Real Man* (*Jinjja Sanai* in Korean), which aired on the Korean Munhwa Broadcasting Corporation (MBC) in 2013–16 (for a discussion of the original format see Han, Lee and Park 2017).

Like the Korean show, the Chinese version portrays the experiences of a group of celebrities who join the military as new conscripts. Cast members are assigned to a camp where they receive military training and complete several tasks over a limited period (in the Chinese version five days). In a 2016 press interview, the show's producers described *Takes a Real Man* as a 'National Defence Education show packaged as entertainment', in which participants of 'different personalities' are brought to army barracks where they 'eat, live and train with soldiers' to 'help them transform into "real men" (*zheng nan ren*)' (Xin Jing bao 2016). The show's narrative revolves around the physical and mental challenges that the participants undergo, highlighting the contrast between the stars' 'loose and comfortable' lifestyle and the 'disciplined' and 'high-intensity environment' of the military. In order to make the show 'more realistic', the production team reportedly implemented 'zero intervention'. Participants had to follow the directions of military commanders and undergo a program 'similar to that of the army, including the use of live ammunition' (Xinhua News Agency 2016a). Filming was conducted under the supervision of both the military and Hunan Satellite TV, with military personnel reviewing each episode before it was broadcast (Ibid.).

The show's first season was produced jointly by the Jinan Military Region, the PLA's Bayi Film Studio and Hunan Satellite TV. Participants consisted of seven well-known male Chinese actors at the average age of 30 (the youngest was 18 and the eldest 59): Zhang Fengyi, Guo Xiaodong, Wang Baoqiang, Yuan Hong, Du Haitao, Liu Haoran and Ou Hao. The second season of the show was jointly produced by the TV Art Centre of the Political Department of the PLA Air Force and Hunan Satellite TV. In this season, participants included both men and women whose average age was again 30 (though the oldest participant was in his forties). The cast included four men (Li Rui, Jiang Jinfu, Sun Yang and Huang Zitao), and four women (Tong Liya, Zhang Lanxin, Yang Mi and Shen Mengchen). With the exception of Sun Yang, who is an Olympic medallist, the rest of the cast in the second season were actors, TV presenters, musicians and/or models.

Both seasons attracted relatively large audiences at the time of their airing, with the second season achieving higher ratings than the first (Xu 2016). On *Douban*, China's main TV and film social media site, the first season of the show received a relatively high mark of 4.5 out of 5 stars (8.5 out of 10), with more than 18,000 mostly positive reviews (84 per cent gave it 4 or 5 stars). The second season received more mixed reviews and a somewhat lower score: more than 20,000 reviews rated it 3.5 out of 5 stars (7.2 out of 10).

The second case study examined here is *Operation Red Sea* (2018, 142 min.). The film was created by Hong Kong director Dante Lam (known in the Chinese mainland by his Chinese name, Lin Chaoxian), whose earlier work consists of romantic comedies and crime and gangster thrillers. Lam is also credited with a number of Main Melody films such as the 2007 animated remake of the Cultural Revolution–era children's film, *Sparkling Red Star* (*Shanshan de hongxing*) (Robinson 2011; Naftali 2014b), and more recently the film *Battle at Lake Changjin* (co-directed with renowned filmmakers Chen Kaige and Tsui Hark).

Operation Red Sea was initiated by the Chinese navy to demonstrate China's efforts at overseas counter-terrorism. The navy outsourced the production rights to private companies, and Bona Films won the bid (Yang 2023, 3). Described as 'China's *Black Hawk Down*' (Chu 2022, 152), *Operation Red Sea* is based on a real-life evacuation conducted by the Chinese navy during the civil war in Yemen in 2015. The film depicts the efforts of Jiaolong (Sea Dragon), an eight-person elite Navy squad, to counter local terrorist forces while protecting the lives of Chinese nationals.

The film begins with the Jiaolong force defending a Chinese cargo ship from pirates near Somali waters. The squad is then ordered to change course to help evacuate Chinese citizens from 'Yewaire', a fictional country based loosely on Yemen, where civil war has broken out following a military coup. The evacuation goes smoothly at first until Deng Mei, a Chinese embassy staffer, is captured by rebel forces. Members of the Jiaolong task force are sent to rescue her and the other hostages. On the way, Jiaolong's leader picks up Xia Nan, a French-Chinese (female) journalist on the trail of Yellowcake, a formula for chemical weapons. The eight-man Chinese task force penetrates the terrorists' stronghold, and battle 150 heavily armed terrorists. They save the Chinese civilians, the journalist and a local man forced to participate as a car bomber. Two Jiaolong members are killed in action and another two are seriously injured but the squad recovers the chemical weapons recipe and captures the cargo plane carrying the Yellowcake. Back aboard the Chinese fleet, the fallen soldiers are honoured for their courage under fire.

The film cost approximately CN¥500 million ($USD75 million) to make, and grossed $USD579 million, mainly in China (Sun 2021, 128). It was the second-highest grossing Chinese-language film in China at the time of its release, and the seventh-highest grossing film of 2018 globally. Described as a 'breakthrough' in the Main Melody genre and proof that patriotic films can also be 'entertaining' (Chu 2022, 152), the film got a relatively high score of 4 out of 5 stars (8.2 out of 10) from more than a million reviewers on *Douban*. It also won numerous awards in the Chinese mainland and Hong Kong, including the Hundred Flowers Award for Best Director and the award for Best Action Choreography at the 38th Hong Kong Film Awards.

The other case studies under discussion are the first and second instalments in the *Wolf Warrior* series. Both films were directed by Wu Jing, who also stars as the film's lone hero, Leng Feng (literally 'cold blade'). The first film, *Wolf Warrior* (2015, 96 min.) was produced by Beijing Dengfeng International Media (Wu Jing's film company). The two other production and distribution companies involved in its making – Chunqiu Shidai (Tianjin) Pictures and Hengye Pictures – were also private enterprises (Yang 2023). The Chinese army provided both personnel and equipment from the Nanjing Military Region of the PLA.

Wolf Warrior follows the adventures of former PLA soldier Leng Feng. In 2008, a combined task group of the PLA and the police raid a drug smuggling operation in southern China. Leng Feng, a highly skilled military sniper, ignores orders to stand down and kills Wu Ji, the leader of the operation. Leng Feng is sent to solitary confinement as punishment for his breach of orders but is approached with an offer from Long Xiaoyun, the (female) commander of the 'Wolf Warriors', an elite unit tasked with simulating foreign tactics to help the PLA train. Meanwhile, in the Philippines, crime lord Min Deng, Wu Ji's brother, has hired ex-US Navy SEAL 'Tom Cat' (played by Scott Adkins) and his group to assassinate Leng Feng.

During a training exercise in a remote region on China's southern border, the Wolf Warriors are ambushed by Tom Cat and his mercenaries, who kill one of Leng Feng's comrades. The PLA and the Wolf Warriors are tasked with hunting down Tom Cat's squad to restore their honour. They are delayed by traps set by Tom Cat and pinned down by sniper fire until Leng Feng kills the shooter. The rest of the PLA force then engages the mercenaries, who are eventually overwhelmed. Meanwhile, Long Xiaoyun and the other PLA commanders deduce that Ming Deng himself is in the training area to take possession of a smuggled cache of biotechnology which would allow the creation of a genetic weapon to target Chinese people. Leng Feng catches Tom Cat near China's southern border and kills the former SEAL with his own knife after Tom Cat mocks Leng Feng's patriotism. Eventually, Leng Feng also captures Min Deng and holds him at bayonet point at the Chinese border. Min Deng's paramilitary force approaches from the other side of the border but faced by the arrival of the Wolf Warriors and other PLA soldiers, they retreat, leaving Min Deng behind.

The film made a large profit. The budget was approximately CN¥79 million ($USD12 million), while box-office revenue reached approximately CN¥525 ($USD81 million). It won thirteen awards in the Chinese mainland and was relatively well received by domestic audiences, winning a rating of 3.5 out of 5 stars (7 out of 10) on *Douban*, where it was reviewed by more than 300,000 users. The success of *Wolf Warrior* led director Wu Jing to produce *Wolf Warrior II* (2017, 123 min.), reprising his role as Leng Feng. Like the first film, the second instalment was produced by Dengfeng in collaboration with Bona Films and a number of other privately owned companies.

Wolf Warrior II centres on the story of Leng Feng's entanglement in the civil war of an unnamed African country. At the beginning of the film, Leng Feng is sent to jail for seriously injuring the leader of a demolition team in China. After his release, he travels to Africa and gets caught in the crossfire between militarised rebel forces and government troops. Initially, Leng Feng retreats to a Chinese battleship with his godson, an African boy named Tundu, but at the request of Tundu and the Chinese ambassador, Leng returns to the city to rescue Tundu's mother and Dr. Chen, a Chinese national conducting research on a deadly disease called 'Lamanla'. Tundu's mother is rescued but Dr. Chen has already been murdered when Leng arrives, so Leng instead takes Dr. Chen's adopted African daughter, Pasha, not knowing that the little girl is the only survivor of the illness and carries antibodies that cure the disease. A group of white mercenaries under the command of 'Big Daddy' chases Leng and Pasha, but with the assistance of Chinese factory owner Zhuo Yifan and a PLA veteran by the name of He, Leng wards off the attack. Leng discovers that he has been infected by Lamanla and leaves the group, but a Chinese-American doctor, Rachel Smith, cures Leng using antibodies extracted from Pasha. Once Leng recovers his strength, he returns to the factory, rescues the rest of the workers from Big Daddy and leads them to safety on the Chinese battleship stationed in the harbour.

Hitting Chinese screens on July 27, 2017, several days ahead of the 90th founding anniversary of the PLA (August 1), *Wolf Warrior II* was an even bigger success than its predecessor. Its budget was CN¥200 million ($USD30.1 million), and its box-office revenue reached CN¥5.68 billion ($USD874 million). Most of the earnings were in the Chinese mainland, with only 0.3 per cent of the film's revenue coming from the US film market (Guan and Hu 2021, 842). The film received a similar score to its predecessor on *Douban*: 3.5 out of 5 stars (7.1 out of 10) from more than 890,000 reviewers.

Each of the media products reviewed in this chapter had to pass through military channels to ensure that the messages it promotes are congruent with Party ideology and policies and the goals of the PLA. According to a Chinese media report, the productions must establish 'correct attitudes and values', enhance the patriotic feelings of domestic audiences, and 'cultivate their self-confidence' (Zhao 2018). In what follows, I draw both on original analysis and on the insights of previous scholars to address how the different case studies perform this function. Specifically, I focus on the following issues: How do the media works envision the Chinese national collectivity and the role of the military in this collectivity? To the extent that the case study engages with the themes of war and peace, how are these themes portrayed to audiences? Is military action legitimised, and if so, on what grounds? What sort of image do the productions seek to convey regarding the nature of military life and/or soldierly qualities? Finally, how are these depictions related to the construction of a particular model of masculinity and femininity?

Projecting the Image of a Powerful, Rising China

In an interview at the PLA Navy (PLAN) TV Art Centre, the creative team involved in the making of *Operation Red Sea* described the military's goals in the production of the film, and the messages they hoped to convey:

> We wanted to create a group portrait of a commando unit stationed in a foreign country ... The soldiers are tasked with the protection

of Chinese citizens' lives, a mission which they perform heroically. We felt that this theme can reflect our ability to fight and win wars, allow audiences to understand what our navy has done, and increase people's national pride and self-confidence (Ren 2018).

The creators emphasised in the interview that the film has an 'anti-war message at its core'. The depiction of bloody battles and 'gory footage' were to let domestic audiences know that 'today's peaceful life is not easy to come by'. It is only thanks to the 'dedication and sacrifice of China's naval officers and soldiers that our people are protected'. Chinese civilians should know that the navy 'will always bring them home', and that 'terrorists' are not allowed to 'hurt even one Chinese citizen' (Ren 2018).

These messages are conveyed in the film in various ways. First, the film attempts to justify the need for China's involvement in a military operation on foreign soil. The PLAN vessel enters the harbour of the fictional Republic of Ihwea only with the consent of the local government (Guan and Hu 2021, 848). *Operation Red Sea* dwells on the brutal actions of an extremist terrorist group against innocent civilians, including children, as well as against Chinese navy soldiers and a warship anchored off-shore to rescue the Chinese nationals. The terrorists' threat to China is intensified to highlight the righteousness of China's overseas military action (Guan and Hu 2021, 846). The film ends with a warning addressed to US Navy ships that they 'are about to enter China's territorial waters', and must 'please leave immediately'. China is depicted as striving to maintain peace, but the PLA can and will fight anyone who attacks its military and impinges on its national interests.

Like *Operation Red Sea*, the two films in the *Wolf Warrior* series attempt to justify the actions of the Chinese military abroad while conveying the theme of patriotism and an assertive, even aggressive stand against those who harm Chinese interests (Y. Cai 2018; P. Liu 2018). In one of the most memorable scenes in the first film, the protagonist, Leng Feng, is engaged in hand-to-hand combat with a white mercenary solider. The mercenary says in English, 'You might not be the smartest soldier I've ever seen but you are the bravest', to which Leng Feng replies with a disdainful curse and asks whether the mercenary 'can speak Chinese'. Moments before stabbing the hero, the white mercenary mocks him by saying, 'you are nothing but a bunch of Boy Scouts' to which Leng Feng replies scornfully, 'don't even think of going back if you dare break into China'. The fight scene ends with the temporary defeat of Leng Feng, but the Chinese hero will have the upper hand.

This defiant message is repeated throughout the film and reflected in the movie's tagline: 'Those who offend China will be punished even if they are far away' (*fan wo Zhonghua zhe, sui yuan bi zhu*). The phrase alludes to a well-known quote associated with General Chen Tang who fought against the foreign Xiongnu (Hsiung-nu) during the Western Han Dynasty (206 BC–9 AD). Chen Tang is said to have assured Emperor Yuan that 'those who commit crimes against the mighty Han will be punished even if they are far away'. Chinese state-publications reviewing the film (e.g. Wang 2015) noted that the rephrasing of the quote as a tagline highlights the invincible 'martial spirit (*shangwu jingshen*) of the Chinese throughout history'.

Wolf Warrior II continues this theme, this time on the African continent. Here too, China's military actions are portrayed as a 'legitimate' intervention in contrast to US-style aggressive interventionism. One crucial reason for Leng Feng conducting the rescue mission alone is that the Chinese military cannot enter the war zone without UN authorisation (Guan and Hu 2021, 848). The surveillance and targeting of African and Chinese civilians by mercenary drones define these fighters as a 'sinister and illegitimate fighting force with no qualms about inflicting collateral damage' (Amar 2018). The rebels' intentional targeting of Chinese people not only dramatises the story and maximises commercial attraction for domestic audiences, but also provides 'rational reasons for China being "forced" to intervene in other nation's affairs' (Guan and Hu 2021, 846). *Wolf Warrior* II casts China's use of its military power as a means to maintain global security rather than as a threat to the world (Yang 2023, 10).

At the same time though, by depicting Chinese national heroism through a militarised lens, the film (like the other two movies discussed here) naturalises the use of military solutions in international conflicts (Rofel 2018). And by highlighting the role of the Party-state in safeguarding Chinese people abroad, *Wolf Warrior II* conveys the idea that the state and the military are never far away. Despite China's apparent international restraint, when its citizens' lives are at stake, the Chinese military will intervene, with or without the approval of the international community (Y. Cai 2018; P. Liu 2018; Wang 2018). As noted, the film's combative message has led to the emergence of the term 'wolf warrior' diplomacy to describe Chinese diplomats who, like the hero Leng Feng, demonstrate their fighting spirit, aggressively defending China and attacking its critics. This style of diplomacy made headlines around the world during COVID-19 (Suisheng Zhao 2021, 157). Even though Chinese 'wolf warrior' diplomats often damage rather than improve China's international image, they have been popular at home (Pu 2022, 183).

Leng Feng's saving of the Chinese factory owner and the Chinese-American doctor in Africa also suggests that the state will stand behind anyone who holds a Chinese passport even if they have left the country. The PRC flag and passport feature prominently in the film. In one highly symbolic scene, Leng Feng crosses the war zone with China's flag held high. The film ends with an image of a Chinese passport and the words 'Citizens of the People's Republic of China: Do not give up when you are in danger overseas! Remember that there is a strong motherland behind you!' (Wang 2018).

As a number of studies have noted, *Wolf Warrior II* reimagines China's position in the Global South in a manner meant to convey 'security, comfort and even superiority' among Chinese audiences (Cai 2018; Liu and Rofel 2018; P. Liu 2018). The film critiques the UN peacekeeping campaign and humanitarian aid in Africa, and also the US forces. It portrays the UN as ineffective, and shows the US retreating, ignoring the plight of innocent civilians. In contrast, Chinese fight honourably. Leng Feng befriends 'good' Africans, battles against American mercenaries, and saves Chinese and other citizens. Unlike the early evacuation of the US Embassy and the failed rescue attempt of the UN portrayed in the film, Leng Feng's 'lone-wolf operation' is more effective and valiant, his actions justified by his anti-imperialist and anti-racist sentiments (Wang 2018).

Despite this rationalisation, *Wolf Warrior II* does not resolve the basic contradiction between the ideology of 'Third World solidarity' – a principle still invoked by the Chinese government – and the exploitation of Africa's land, resources and people by Chinese companies (Rofel 2018). Set in a 'disease-ridden, war-ravaged and helpless unnamed African country', the film is ultimately 'a story about power' that seeks to foster patriotic sentiment among the domestic audience while legitimising China's rise as 'positive, humane and beneficial for the world' (Udochi 2018; Guan and Hu 2021). Like *Operation Red Sea*, Africa is shown as 'undeveloped, chaotic and vulnerable' in contrast to 'modern China' – 'a safe, developed and powerful country' (Yang 2023, 10).

The fourth case study, *Takes a Real Man*, adopts a different format, and yet the message of the reality TV show is similar to that of the three war-action blockbusters. According to a report in the PLA-run website, the *China Military Network*, the show sought to convey to audiences the 'positive energy of patriotism' while emphasising the importance of 'strengthening the army' and ensuring 'battle preparedness' (Chen 2019). A review in the CPC-mouthpiece, *People's Daily*, observed that the show demonstrates 'the army's role in serving the country and maintaining civilians' peaceful, stable life' (Yang 2016). These messages are conveyed on-screen in the statements of the celebrity participants who declare that the military training they undertook 'made them realise' the importance of the soldiers' role in 'guarding our home for us' and providing Chinese people with 'a sense of security'. At the same time, the show also highlights the Chinese military's contribution to the maintenance of world peace through its peacekeeping missions. Another key theme, discussed in detail below, is the portrayal of the military barracks as a transformative site and of PLA soldiers as models for emulation even for China's famous, wealthy celebrities.

Stars Become Warriors; Warriors Become Stars

Takes a Real Man seeks to generate a narrative in which individual competition, economic power and spectacle intersect with the values of patriotism, collectivism and self-sacrifice. The celebrity guests function as 'a cultural commodity' (Schubart 2009, 5) that induce audiences to consume the show and identify with – and compare themselves to – the stars undergoing a positive transformative experience through military training. In interviews with Chinese state media, the show's producers stated that youth were a specific target group of the production. The show seeks to show young people that soldiers 'selflessly dedicate themselves to the motherland' but are also 'flesh-and-blood'. Another stated goal was to make the PLA more attractive to young, well-educated audiences, and increase their motivation to enlist. The show's promotional activities included special screening events at China's top universities. These events were attended by some of the show's celebrity guests who related their experiences to the students while singing the praise of PLA soldiers (Sohu 2016; Xinhua News Agency 2016a).

The show conveys these themes in several ways. In Season Two, for example, male actor and model, Jiang Jinfu, makes an emotional speech on behalf of the other participants at the swearing-in ceremony: 'I knew before that the life of a soldier was very hard, but I didn't expect it to be so hard, and I was only here for a short while. Many soldiers spend three years or even longer in the army'. In the same episode, Captain Liu, who was depicted throughout the season as 'tough' and 'cool-headed', is shown responding emotionally to the transformation of his celebrity 'recruits'. He tells Huang Zitao – a rapper and former member of the South Korean-Chinese boy band Exo – that the training he underwent has transformed Huang's character from 'unruly and rebellious' to 'unyielding'. As long as Huang and the other trainees 'proceed in the right direction' they can 'bravely brace forward' no matter the challenge.

Alongside these solemn messages, the show presents the experiences of the famous trainees in a relatively humorous way. Cartoon captions, text messages and on-screen emoticons convey emotions and affect, a common feature of Chinese variety shows which closely echoes the production style of Korean and Japanese formats (Keane and Zhang 2017, 635). The inclusion of these comic elements increases audiences' identification with the trainees and highlights the show's entertainment. But the contrast between the light-hearted tone of the captions and the serious messages underscores the show's contrived nature.

The films *Operation Red Sea*, *Wolf Warrior* and *Wolf Warrior II* also employ entertainment elements to promote an appealing image of the PLA and its actions. All three films draw on the techniques of Hollywood war movies to depict real modern conflict while showcasing some of the PLA's latest weapons and up-to-date combat systems (Chu 2022, 151). Through these depictions, the Chinese military seeks to re-brand itself as a modern, high-tech military to increase the confidence and national pride of Chinese audiences but also to attract well-educated urban youths to enlist.

The importance of this recruitment goal is also demonstrated in the 2023 war-action film, *Born to Fly*, mentioned at the beginning of the chapter. The film's hero, played by Wang Yibo – a popular Chinese actor and singer known for his stint in the Chinese-Korean boyband Uniq – is first portrayed as unruly and childish. However, after visiting a martyrs' cemetery for test pilots and watching his commander sacrifice his life to avoid ejecting over a city, the hero devotes his life to the country. When he is injured, his parents ask him to quit the military and complain about his refusal of an offer to study overseas. They also express doubts that China 'can ever match Western planes' (The Economist 2023a). The young hero scolds his parents for their lack of faith, informing them that 'youth of his generation will give China back its confidence'. In another scene, the hero is shown 'designing a plane-saving technology on his laptop in his spare time', a plot device which aligns with the PLA's campaign to recruit college graduates with engineering and computing skills (Naftali 2020; The Economist 2023a).

Like *Born to Fly*, the blockbuster films and TV show reviewed here construct Chinese soldiers as possessing the qualities of courageousness and uprightness, 'a calm and tenacious fighting spirit', and the willingness to employ lethal violence to protect their country and its people (Wang 2015). As discussed below, the productions also associate these qualities with a desirable form of masculinity.

Recovering Chinese Masculinity

The case studies examined here can be understood not only as an attempt to incite patriotism and admiration for the military but also to renegotiate gender and sexual norms and reshape China's 'culture of masculinity' (P. Liu 2018). As noted by a number of scholars, the *Wolf Warrior* series constructs China's rise as 'a masculine rivalry between men' (Xiang 2018). In the first film, the rivalry is between the unscrupulous white mercenary who misjudges the strength and determination of Leng Feng (the Chinese man), and by extension the strength of the Chinese army. In *Wolf Warrior II*, the conflict is between 'the old saviour (the white man)' and 'the new saviour (the Chinese man)' (Xiang 2018). A Chinese man wins the conflict each time: a depiction that rejects the traditional Hollywood trope of Asian men as 'emasculated' and 'racially castrated' (P. Liu 2018).

The *Wolf Warrior* films further make use of female figures and alternative types of masculinity as a foil for the idealised model of a man who is neither articulate nor romantic, but a strong, passionate fighter loyal to his comrades, and ready to protect the weak. The films construct this figure in opposition to – and as a critique of – the 'soft masculinity' model circulating in China's media market. *Wolf Warrior II*, in particular, mocks 'soft masculinity' by presenting a 'delicate' male character, Zhuo Yifan, as a rich young man who owns an African factory and weapons in large quantities, but needs to be repeatedly rescued by the muscular hero, Leng Feng (Wang 2018). Unlike Leng Feng, who feels responsible towards Africans, Zhuo is also portrayed as selfish and spoiled, and focused solely on saving Chinese citizens, a stand the film presents as amoral (Amar 2018).

In an interview, Wu Jing – the film's director, lead actor and scriptwriter – stated that the portrayal was intentional. Pointing out that China has not yet produced a 'real man', such as 'Tom Cruise or Sylvester Stallone', that audiences 'can identify with', Wu complained that the domestic film industry has been taken over by effeminate 'pretty boys' (*lian zhang de huayang shaonan*) from 'Korea and Japan'. Wu added that in making a military-themed film such as *Wolf Warrior*, he sought to 'inspire men to become real men (*zhen nanren*) and encourage women to go for real men' (cited in P. Liu 2018).

Zhou Zhengtian, the head of the creative team involved in the production of *Operation Red Sea*, stated a similar goal in a 2018 interview. The film, he hoped, would not only foster patriotism and admiration for navy soldiers but also counter harmful gender practices. In response to a question about the film's 'graphic violence' (including lingering close-ups of chopped fingers and limbs, and blood squirting from bullet wounds), Zhou dismissed the criticism: 'These days we have too many *naiyou* (a derogatory term for "handsome young men lacking in macho masculinity"), and not enough *gangtie* (iron) men.' The violent scenes, he argued, promote a desirable martial masculinity model for young viewers (Ren 2018; see also Wang and Li 2018).

In *Operation Red Sea*, the endorsement of this masculinity model is reinforced through the portrayal of female figures. The PLAN elite task force consists of eight men who rescue Chinese embassy staff, including men, women and children. While the film depicts a female Chinese-French journalist as a tough investigative reporter with a key role in uncovering a plan to build a dirty bomb, the journalist also requires saving by the heroic all-male squad.

In the *Wolf Warrior* series, the main female characters – Leng Fang's commander, Long Xiaoyun in the first film, and medical doctor Rachel Smith in the second – are portrayed as intelligent, brave and capable, but they are not as strong or capable as the male hero. In *Wolf Warrior* II, Rachel – notably a Chinese-American – is portrayed as selfless, humanitarian and courageous. She even manages to cure the hero when he becomes infected with a deadly disease. But she does not take care of patients after a gun battle with Big Daddy and his group, and is portrayed as naïve. In one scene, she refuses to leave with the helicopter, saying that her medical knowledge is needed and that here 'she is not a woman but a doctor'. Leng Feng reacts by tossing her into the vehicle, telling her to not 'make any more trouble for me'. Indeed, throughout the film, Rachel is repeatedly rescued by

Leng Feng, implying that gender equality has its limits (Y. Cai 2018; P. Liu 2018; Wang 2018).²

As noted by several scholars, the gendered dimension in *Wolf Warrior II* also carries racial and ethnic characteristics (Cai 2018). All mainland Chinese characters in the movie are male. The African characters include a boy who calls the Chinese protagonist 'godfather', a mother named Pasha, factory workers who are rescued by the Chinese (men), and savage rebels, most of whom are male. The film does include brief images of local women with punk haircuts and AK-47s, but these women die in the skirmishes. The African characters saved by Leng Feng are invariably defenceless women or children. *Wolf Warrior II* constructs the African continent and its people as 'feminised' and 'infantilized' and in need of a Chinese 'macho-type hero' (Guan and Hu 2021, 850; P. Liu 2018).

The macho man is a prominent trope in the show *Takes a Real Man*, as the title clearly implies. Through the comparison between the soldiers and the celebrities, audiences are meant to recognise the positive qualities of the former and the admiration of the latter. These qualities include a sense of honour, responsibility, patriotism and self-improvement. In the show, these features are explicitly gendered, especially in Season Two, which casts both men and women.

In media interviews, the show's producer, Zhou Minyi, explained that the second season aimed for a younger target audience, with the women celebrities meant to 'represent the perspective of ordinary audiences' who may be 'less familiar' with military life (Sohu 2016; Xu 2016). When asked whether the inclusion of women in the second season contradicted the show's basic premise (or title), Zhou replied that 'manhood' refers to a 'spirit' and 'a state of mind' rather than a 'gender distinction' (Yang 2016).

The female participants undergo the same physical trials as their male counterparts, including live ammunition training and push-ups, but the show underscores the positive value of traits associated with martial masculinity, contrasting these characteristics with the 'physically unfit' or 'softer' behaviour of some of the male celebrities and female guest stars. Season Two begins with the women entering the military base wearing fashionable clothes and high-heeled shoes. Told that they must part not only with their civilian outfits but also with most of their beauty products, the women balk. Throughout the season, the production highlights women's naivety and unfamiliarity with military life, demonstrating their squeamishness in the face of difficult scenarios compared to the more stoic reactions of the men.

For instance, when actor and singer, Yang Mi, is shown a real bullet for the first time, she touches it, remarking that the bullet is very 'pointy'. None of the male participants are shown making similar statements. All participants undergo wilderness training, including having to eat raw meat in imitation of the harsh training conditions of the Airforce Special Forces. But encountering animals interested in their meal, the women scream in fear while the male soldiers remain calm and collected, and offer to protect them from harm. Throughout the season, the women chat about the (male) soldiers and express admiration for their 'strong physique' and 'passionate' spirit, with some women describing the squad leader, team leader and training instructors as 'handsome (*shuaige*)' or as 'men of steel/iron men' (*yinghan*) while talking flirtatiously about the soldiers' 'warm smiles'. The soldiers are portrayed as objects of female desire, conveying the appeal of a martial masculinity model embodied by the figure of the soldier.

Conclusion

This chapter examined how PLA-backed commercial productions present images of war and the military to contemporary audiences. The discussion identified several key themes. First, the three blockbuster films take pains to justify the use of armed force by Chinese soldiers as acts of self-defence waged by a government whose only concern is protecting its citizens against unchecked foreign aggression or an unscrupulous and/or 'inhumane enemy' terrorising innocent civilians, including women and children. The *Wolf Warrior* series and *Operation Red Sea* promote the message that China and its military 'abide by international law, strive to maintain the peace and will not attack unless provoked' (Guan and Hu 2021, 846).

Simultaneously, the films convey the implicit meaning that, despite its profound economic expansion worldwide, China's overseas involvements are not aimed at 'seeking hegemonism, reshaping the world order or challenging the established powers' (Guan and Hu 2021, 847). In each of the films, China is forced to intervene in international affairs by the 'rational and righteous incentive' of protecting its people and assets. The message meets Chinese citizens' expectation that their government is 'powerful and responsible' enough to protect its people and interests, even abroad (Ibid., 847).

This message and the depiction of confrontations (some physical), in which Chinese soldiers always and inevitably beat foreign combatants, evokes an image of 'a rising China'. In contrast to previous Main Melody productions, the PLA-backed films of the Xi Jinping era do not depict 'a historical China during its so-called Century of Humiliation'. They are about a potent China today and a powerful China 'in an imagined future'. Accordingly, the message of the three films reviewed here – and of comparable films like the more recent blockbuster *Born to Fly* – is no longer about 'grievance'. The message is about 'taking revenge' (Sun 2021, 128).

While the films create an image of a peaceful China, they also send the message that China operates in a hostile international environment. Such a message can reinforce public perceptions of the need to maintain a strong, battle-ready military, a perception reinforced by the films' display of China's technologically advanced military and the spectacular fighting scenes showing this technology in action. These sequences are crucial for the films' ability to thrill and entertain, and the entertainment values are reinforced by the inclusion of superhero-like action scenes which overlay the master narratives of fighting, sequences that render military combat as a fantasy detached from the realities of war and international relations. These sequences may also contribute to the creation of a 'pleasure culture of war', in which conflict is reconstructed as 'a fantasy game', and 'entertaining escapism' functions as a distraction and displacement from real-life concerns (Crowe 2011, 130). The entertainment allows audiences to resolve any moral uncertainties they may feel about the use of military violence (Maartens 2021, 216).

The market logic which has driven the production of these war-action films can nonetheless interfere with their political function of increasing public support for the Party and the military. By placing Chinese soldiers into a 'superhero' role, the blockbuster spectacles create a false expectation among domestic audiences about China's might. Such expectations will not always be met, which could cause a legitimacy problem for the Chinese government and the military should a real Leng Feng be needed to conduct a rescue mission (Guan and Hu 2021, 853). Despite the appearance of verisimilitude, reality TV shows like *Takes a Real Man* often use scripts. Naïve or inexperienced audience members may nonetheless assume that what they are seeing on the screen is 'authentic'. When they learn otherwise – as was the case during the second season of *Takes a Real Man* (W. Xu 2016), the program's messaging about the transformative nature of military training and army service might also lose credibility.

Another key theme observed in the three blockbuster films and the TV show *Takes a Real Man* is the display of militarised male heroes. The Xi-era productions aestheticise, romanticise and celebrate 'a culture of military masculinity' (Crowe 2011, 126), a move which can naturalise the use of political violence. To counter the threat of the 'delicate masculinity' model embraced by young audiences, the war-themed films and the reality show promote 'martial qualities (*wu*)' at the expense of other traditional aspects of masculinity, such as 'scholarly attainment (*wen*)'. This move is reminiscent of earlier periods in modern Chinese history, such as the late Qing Dynasty and the Republican era (1912–49), when China's elite sought to align with a robust macho masculinity to discard the image of the 'sick man of Asia' while fending off foreign invaders (P. Liu 2018). The celebration of military masculinity also recalls Maoist China, particularly the 1960s, when the country was beset by real (and imaginary) enemies within and without. Like those earlier periods, the promotion of a military masculinity in the media productions of the Xi era reflects the growing concern of the country's political elite about the strength and stability of the national collectivity amid increasing domestic and external threats.

To what extent are these sentiments shared by contemporary Chinese youth? How do young people perceive the imagery of war and the military in the PLA-backed productions? And how do they relate this imagery to the images found in the alternative media products they consume or to the messages they receive through school textbooks, Patriotic Education and National Defence Education activities? The following chapters address these questions by drawing on the results of field interviews with Chinese high school students of different backgrounds.

Notes

1. The term 'little fresh meat' was originally used by Chinese fans in 2014 to label South Korean pop idols. In its original usage, the expression was 'imbued with sexual innuendo' and as a subversion of 'a cannibalistic metaphor more usually used to refer to women'. Over the past decade or so, the meaning of the term has been extended to include young male celebrities (actors, singers, models) in China and other East Asian countries, who present 'exquisite make-up, delicate skin and exaggerated elegance' (Zhang and Nagus 2020, 495). In some instances, however, the expression has been adopted as a derogatory term for 'effeminate' male celebrities.

2. Some scholars (e.g. Y. Cai 2018; Xiang 2018) suggest that it is not a coincidence that Rachel's character is Chinese-American, and that her mixed nationality reflects the film's message about the complicated nature of contemporary Sino-American relations. In one notable scene, for instance, Leng Feng takes Rachel's guns and says: 'your role is to save people, not kill people'. By extension the message here may be that Chinese Americans can serve as a bridge between these two world powers who should cooperate rather than fight. Alternatively, the scene could be read as further assertion that women are 'naturally' suited for the role of life-givers and healers rather than lethal fighters – a role that is best left to male (super) hero Leng Feng.

CHAPTER 5

Youth Notions of Armed Conflict: 'If Peace Is Our Goal, Why Use War to Attain It?'

In a 2020 televised speech commemorating the seventieth anniversary of China's entry into the Korean War (known in China as the mission to 'Resist American Aggression and Aid Korea' [*Kang Mei yuan Chao*]), China's president and Communist Party leader Xi Jinping, described the significance of the conflict and elaborated on the relevance of the 'great spirit' of the Chinese fighters of the 1950s. 'We Chinese know well we must speak to invaders with the language they understand: so we use war to stop war; we use military might to stop hostility; we win peace and respect with victory,' Xi said (Xinhua News Agency 2020). While the speech also expressed assurance that China 'has always pursued a defensive military policy', and 'will never seek hegemony or expansion', foreign commentators focused on the more belligerent elements of Xi's address, noting China's unprecedented barrage of commemorative events, exhibitions, television documentaries and feature films marking the outbreak of a 70-year-old war (Bandow 2020; Shih 2020; Tiezzi 2020).

But how much do the Party's propaganda efforts shape young people's perceptions of the country's historical military conflicts? And to what extent is China's education system able to 'manoeuvre' (Enloe 2000) students into supporting or taking for granted war as a legitimate means of addressing China's contemporary disputes? This chapter explores these broader issues by drawing on the results of field interviews conducted over the past decade with Chinese high school students in Shanghai and Henan.

Scholarship on the militarisation of education has shown that even in non-conflict areas, children and youths can be affected by and connect to militarisation processes via the narratives they encounter in class and the messages they receive in activities related to patriotism and national defence education. Even in education systems that encourage peaceful practices by focusing on the horrors of war or promoting international cooperation, the absence of room for an exchange of ideas, often due to an emphasis on exam preparation, may result in a passive absorption of disseminated facts about historical struggles while preventing reflection on one's own position in conflict situations (Langager 2009; Gibson 2011). Teachers may sidestep contentious discussions about the international and structural dimensions of war, and opt instead to implement a limited form of 'peace education' as a strategy of conflict resolution in the classroom and the schoolyard, with the more modest aim of creating 'an orderly learning climate' and ensuring 'community safety' (Harris 2002; Cook 2008).

Studies in different national contexts have found that youths who object to war-related patriotic school messages may find their dissent stifled by peer pressure and by their subordinate position within the classroom (Solomon and Denov 2010). Family members can socialise some youth to accept (or reject) the use of force in international conflict. Media and popular culture products, including television, film, toys and video games, can be equally influential in propagating images of war and peace among youth with no firsthand experience of military conflict (Reagan 1994; Covell 1996; Power 2007; Frühstück 2017).

Building on these insights and on the observation that 'people's relations with their country's foreign policy are often incoherent and discursive' (Sun 2021, 104), this chapter considers how youth make sense of the messages they receive in and outside school about China's foreign policy and how they construct their own positions regarding the use of armed force to address the country's territorial disputes.

The analysis of data from interviews with Han (Chinese) high school students conduced in 2013 and in 2017–19, reveals several key findings. First, in contrast to the assumption that China's education system has advanced a bellicose message since the 1990s and particularly over the past two decades (e.g. Gries 2020; Suisheng Zhao 2021), informants in the present study – who received most of their basic education from the late 2000s to the late 2010s – stated that their schools had taught them to 'abhor war' and 'appreciate peace'. Moreover, most of the study participants expressed objection to the use of military force and preferred a conciliatory approach to China's territorial disputes. Second, among those who did express support for the use of the military, a majority chose to qualify their answers by listing specific conditions for such an intervention. Finally, the analysis also finds that young people in both camps provided divergent justifications for their views, ranging from moral reasoning to pragmatic calculations.

Overall, study informants of different genders and backgrounds exhibited a relatively thoughtful, circumspect approach rather than a bellicose attitude towards China's territorial disputes. These findings suggest that while the Chinese government is becoming more proactive and arguably more confrontational in its foreign relations approach, and while Chinese education may convey an ambiguous position about the use of military violence, the assumption that Chinese youth of the 2000s generation necessarily adhere to a 'militaristic' ethos – in the sense that they categorically endorse the use of force to resolve the country's territorial disputes – is debatable.

Nationalism and Chinese Public Attitudes Regarding the Use of Armed Force

Recent scholarship on China's international relations in the Xi era (2012–) has found that while Chinese diplomacy emphasises the country's 'peaceful intentions and efforts to promote mutually beneficial "win–win" solutions', China's claims to land and maritime territories it does not control complicate its efforts to reassure its neighbours (Saunders 2020, 189). Beijing's current territorial disputes include land border rows with India and Bhutan; claims to land features and waters in the South China Sea that are also claimed by Taiwan, Vietnam, Malaysia, Brunei and the Philippines; disputes over the Diaoyu/Senkaku Islands with Japan; and the unresolved issue of Taiwan's status, which as noted in previous chapters, the PRC regards as an inalienable part of Chinese territory (Saunders 2020, 189; Wang 2022, 14).

From 1998–2008, China improved relations with its Asian neighbours by employing a range of diplomatic, military and economic assurances. Exhibiting a patient approach to territorial disputes and restraint in the use of military force, the policy was predicated on China's rapid growth and increasing integration into the regional and global economy, a trend which made China the largest export market for almost all countries in Asia (Saunders 2020, 190). However, scholars generally agree that in 2009, a more assertive Chinese attitude emerged on a range of bilateral, regional and global issues (Shambaugh 2020; Suisheng Zhao 2021). In particular, the aggressive means used to advance Chinese maritime sovereignty claims in the South China Sea and East China Sea detracted from Beijing's efforts to persuade others that 'China's rise would be peaceful' (Saunders 2020, 190).

Since 2016, the deterioration of China's relations with the United States and other Western countries amid economic disagreements, Beijing's policies in Xinjiang and Hong Kong, and criticism of China's handling of the COVID-19 pandemic, along with rising tensions over Taiwan, have further undermined the Chinese government's peaceful stance. The Party leadership itself has amplified its nationalist rhetoric and the promotion of a narrative that describes the 'nation under siege'. Speaking at the hundredth anniversary of the CPC in July 2021, Xi Jinping warned for instance that 'foreign forces' who try to 'bully, coerce and enslave' China will 'break their heads on the steel Great Wall built with the blood and flesh of 1.4 billion Chinese people' (cited in Suisheng Zhao 2021, 157).

Notwithstanding the combative tone of this message and Beijing's policies, the attitudes of young Chinese regarding the use of military violence is a contested issue. Several large-scale survey studies have documented a relatively assertive position on foreign relations among young adults of the post-1990s and post-2000s generation (Weiss 2019). Linking the results of these studies with a documented rise in a hyper-nationalistic discourse on China's social media and periodic nationalist demonstrations on China's streets in the past two decades or so, some scholars postulate a causal link between young adults' 'hawkish position' and the promotion of 'nationalistic' and even 'aggressive' themes in the government's Patriotic Education (PE) campaign and the National Defence Education (NDE) curriculum (Z. Wang 2012; Yang and Zheng 2012; Weiss 2014; Wallace and Weiss 2015; Suisheng Zhao 2021).

The assumption that young Chinese tend to support a tougher foreign relation stance, including the use of armed force, and that this stance is a product of their stronger 'nationalistic' attitudes compared to those of older cohorts is disputed by the findings of other survey studies (Sinkkonen and Elovainio 2020; Qi, Zhang and Lin 2022). A survey by Tang and Darr (2012) found that the 'the most nationalistic' age group is those aged 59 and older. Another survey by Chubb (2014) found that urban Chinese adults of the 1990s generation who were subject to patriotic education throughout their school careers are 'more nationalistic' than their predecessors. However, the survey results also indicate that respondents of this age group are *less* likely to approve of the use of military force in the South and East China Sea disputes than older cohorts are.

Drawing on the results of another survey study conducted in 2013, researchers Zhong and Hwang (2020) documented 'strong support' for military action over the Diaoyu/Senkaku Islands dispute with Japan among urban adults. However, the study noted that this 'aggressive' attitude was more pronounced among 'older informants' than those of the 1990s generation. In a study which draws on the results of five surveys among urban adults in 2012–16, researcher Jessica Chen Weiss (2019) found that a large portion of respondents endorsed greater reliance on military strength, supported greater spending on national defence and expressed approval of sending troops to reclaim the disputed islands in the East and South China Seas. However, unlike the previous studies, the study by Weiss suggested that respondents who grew up with a 'patriotic education' (those born after 1978) were more 'hawkish' than their elders.

Moore and Primiano (2020), who conducted a 2017 survey among Chinese university students (aged 18 and above) majoring in international relations, political science or international law, found that the vast majority of respondents believed that China should *not* give in to international pressure regarding its policies in the South China Sea. But their study also found that participants displayed 'liberal, internationalist and flexible' attitudes, with 65 per cent of students saying that Chinese leaders should 'negotiate' with the leaders of other countries (Ibid., 340).

Similarly, surveys conducted in 2018 and 2019 among Chinese students enrolled in three Chinese top universities and Chinese students enrolled in over sixty US institutions indicate that while patriotic feelings are widespread among this elite population, they stop short of supporting actual war (Pan and Xu 2020; Mazzoco and Kennedy 2022). Most respondents supported maintaining or increasing China's military presence in the South China Sea yet support for military expansion declined significantly when it came at the cost of war (Mazzocco and Kennedy 2022).

Another large-scale survey conducted in 2019 among urban Chinese aged 18 and above documents that more than half the participants supported armed unification with Taiwan (Qi, Zhang and Lin 2022). Better-educated respondents were more likely to express this stance, but there were no significant differences between the different age groups. The researchers noted that the phrasing of the survey question did not allow a clear conclusion about whether respondents supported 'armed unification' with Taiwan 'at the earliest opportunity', 'as the last resort' and/or only 'under specific conditions'. As the authors observe, Beijing's official policy is closer to the latter: the CPC endorses 'peaceful unification but will enact armed unification under certain conditions' (Qi, Zhang and Lin 2022, 730). Meanwhile, a 2020–21 online survey of Chinese public attitudes towards 'non-peaceful unification' with Taiwan found that older respondents, rather than younger ones, tended to favour more aggressive policy choices (Liu and Li 2023).

Clearly, there is no scholarly consensus about young people's attitudes towards the use of armed force in China's various territorial disputes. Nor is there agreement about the relationship between these attitudes, respondents' socio-economic backgrounds and/or their place of residence within the country (Pan and Xu 2017; Pan and Xu 2020; Mazzoco and Kennedy 2022; Qi, Zhang and Lin 2022). The findings of these different surveys underscore the complex nature of young people's attitudes towards the use of military violence. However, they do not offer a systematic consideration of youth perceptions regarding the role of education in shaping these attitudes. Nor do they consider the type of reasoning young people employ to account for their positions.

This chapter attempts to address these issues. Building on the insights of a growing number of qualitative and quantitative studies which show that even in an authoritarian Party-state such as China, young people can still develop their own understandings – and may even be critical – of the messages they receive at school or through the state media (Law 2011; Liu 2012; Zhang and Fagan 2016; Qian, Xu and Chen 2017; Yan *et al.* 2021; Jackson and Du 2022), this chapter explores Chinese high school students' perspectives on armed conflict while paying particular attention to the question of how informants relate these perspectives to the messages they receive about the issue both within and outside the school.

Data and Research Questions

People's notions of war and peace may draw on different types of logic and argumentations. As several scholars have observed (e.g. Harris 2002; Cook 2008; Fiala 2018), opposition to warfare can be grounded in ethical considerations, the idea that war is morally repulsive, because it causes suffering and requires the systematic and deliberate killing of human beings. Opposition can also rest on pragmatic grounds, the notion that war is 'risky' because of its economic costs or because it may prove 'ineffective'. Opposition to war on ethical grounds may consist of a continuum from an absolute adherence to nonviolence to a more focused or minimal sort of anti-warism. Similarly, a pragmatic commitment to peace could be associated with the concept of a 'just war', a more controversial tradition of thought that holds that war can be a suitable way to bring peace under certain conditions. Building on these observations, the analysis in this chapter seeks to identify key themes in Chinese youth attitudes towards war and peace while noting the type of rationale (ethical, pragmatic or both) that youth employ to justify their views.

The data which forms the basis for the analysis was collected through semi-structured open-ended interviews with 155 Han (Chinese) high school students (aged 16–18; 51 per cent male; 49 per cent female) attending grades 10–12 in different high schools in the city of Shanghai on China's eastern coast, and in Henan province, which is set in the middle and lower reaches of the Yellow River. Interviews with students in both locations were conducted in 2013 and in 2017–19 by a Chinese research assistant (for more information about the study sample, see the book's Introduction).

During the interviews, which were conducted off campus, students in Henan (N = 85) and in Shanghai (N = 70) were asked the following questions:

(1) *'Do you feel your school encourages students to value war or peace?'*
(2) *'What do you think can be done to resolve disagreements between China and its neighbours over the control of territories and natural resource in the East and South China Sea?'*

Informants were asked to justify their responses to both questions. They were also encouraged to reflect on how their views related to school messages, to media products they consume and/or to their experiences in PE and NDE activities.

It should be noted that the purpose of the second question was not to ascertain students' position regarding a specific dispute (e.g. the Taiwan issue or the Diaoyu/Senkaku Islands). Rather, the aim was to elicit informants' general view of war and peace while prompting them to use freely chosen examples among China's current conflicts. In response to this question, some students mentioned the dispute with Japan over the Diaoyu/Senkaku Islands. Others referred to conflicts with countries in Southeast Asia. A few also brought up the issue of 'reunification' with Taiwan, linking it to a discussion of China's relations with the USA – an understandable link given that the latter never ruled out the possibility of defending Taiwan militarily in the event of a mainland attack (Liu and Li 2023, 1). As the discussion below will demonstrate, regardless of their position on the use of military force to resolve China's different disputes, young informants often evoked the US in contrast to their recommendation of a relatively 'peaceful' Chinese foreign policy.

Students' responses were analysed by drawing on both thematic analysis and basic content analysis. Content analysis of responses to the first question consisted of encoding students' replies into two main categories: (a) those who held that their schools taught them 'to value peace'; (b) those who held that their schools taught them 'to value war'. Those who were undecided were categorised under both (a) and (b). Content analysis of replies to the second question likewise consisted of encoding students' answers into two categories: (a) those who expressed opposition to the use of armed force in China's territorial disputes; (b) those who endorsed the use of armed force in China's territorial disputes. Those who were undecided were categorised under both (a) and (b).

Thematic analysis of students' responses to both questions was informed by the approach of constructivist grounded theory, which takes seriously informants' perceptions in constructing their social worlds (Charmaz 2008). Specifically, I sought to identify recurring patterns in students' responses while paying particular attention to the language informants used to make sense of the messages and information they received about war and peace in the classroom, in school activities, in the media or from friends and relatives. Thematic analysis of responses to the second question further sought to categorise the type of logic students employed to justify their position on the use of armed force in China's territorial disputes. If students were opposed to war, how did they frame their opposition? Did they employ moral or pragmatic reasoning, or both? If respondents expressed support for the use of armed force, how did they rationalise their position? Did they regard a military response to threat as both 'normal' and 'justified'? Did students frame warfare as a particularly 'effective solution' to international disputes? In other words, did informants' responses subscribe to what could be described as 'a militarised ethos?' (cf. Enloe 2004, 219; Pennell 2020, 384).

'Sovereignty Is Important, but We Shouldn't Bully Other Countries'

Content and thematic analysis of students' responses reveals several key findings. First, an overwhelming majority of informants of different genders, locales and educational backgrounds insisted that their schools rejected the use of military solutions to international conflicts. Second, despite this consensus, informants presented divergent views concerning the use of the military to settle China's territorial disputes. A majority (57 per cent) of participants opposed the use of military violence. The remaining 43 per cent endorsed such an intervention. Notably, there were no significant differences between informants of different genders, locations or type of schools among the two camps. Within the group who endorsed the use of military violence, many nonetheless qualified their responses in different ways while expressing complex and at times conflicted views regarding the usefulness and desirability of force as a way of solving China's disputes. In this section, I first examine the majority view – those who categorically objected to the use of military force – while noting the type of reasoning students used to defend their position. The next section will discuss the views and logic of those in the other camp.

Informants who objected to the use of military force to address territorial disputes employed different rationales, often simultaneously. Many relied on moral justifications. Students in both Shanghai and Henan claimed, for instance: 'We should resolve conflicts with other countries in a normal, peaceful way, without violence'; 'China should strive for harmonious coexistence. We should solve our problems without causing human suffering and a loss of life.' Or, as HY, a 17-year-old girl from Henan put it: 'In war, there is always loss. I mean, if peace is the goal, why use war to attain it? We should achieve peace through cooperation.' Another student from Henan related his view of war to stories he had heard at home:

> My great-grandfather and great-grandmother served in the military. They participated in the War of Resistance against Japan. They were very respected in their village. My great-grandfather told me about the war. He said that war is very cruel. He said that in a war, killing a person can be like trampling on an ant.

Students' empathy towards the suffering of war also extended to the plight of non-Chinese. CJ, a 16-year-old from Henan recalled that she had 'read an article about Syrian children fleeing from war, and how they were dying there every day'. In an interview conducted in 2017, she reflected: 'I feel that we are lucky compared to those children. We should appreciate that we live in peace now and do everything we can to maintain this peace.'

CJ's statement refers to an online article published in April 2017 by China's official news agency, *Xinhua*, under the title 'Cherish it! You were not born in a peaceful era, but in a peaceful country' (Xinhua News Agency 2017). The article contained multiple photos showing the misery of life in war-torn Syria, including numerous images of children of all ages (from small babies to teens) covered in blood, crying or in a state of shock. As noted in Chapter 2, China's high school history textbooks also include textual and visual references of conflict in Syria. CJ's words indicate the effect of these media and textbook images.

In another 2017 interview, LY, a Shanghai senior at a high school affiliated with one of the country's top universities, contemplates how school messages helped shape her anti-war position:

> We learnt about war in Chinese lessons but mostly in history classes. The history teachers' main point was that wars are caused by competition over resources. Countries struggle with each other to protect their interests . . . Some teachers also talked about how war makes people act inhumanely. It can destroy your humanity, just like what happened to the Japanese soldiers when they attacked China. I remember we watched a film in class about the War of Resistance against Japan. It was directed by Feng Xiaogang. I think it was called *Yijiusi'er*. The message of the film was that war is cruel and leads to unnecessary sacrifices.

The film LY mentions is a historical epic released in Chinese theatres in 2012.[1] Based on the novel *Remembering 1942* (*Wengu yijiusi'er*) by author Liu Zhenyun, the film (released internationally under the title *Back to 1942*), tells the story of a famine which took place during the Second Sino-Japanese War, driving millions of people from their homes in Henan province. Unlike the war-action blockbusters discussed in Chapter 4, *Back to 1942* centres on civilian suffering in wartime China. Focusing on the tale of two families, the film dwells on the impact of war and famine on the lives of children and youth, and highlights the indifference, corruption and cruelty of the KMT government whose actions exacerbated the disaster.

LY's response indicates that the screening of the film in her history class contributed to her opposition to war.

CJJ, a 16-year-old from Henan, also connected her views on war and foreign policy to a movie she had watched:

> I saw an American war film with my dad, called *Hacksaw Ridge*.[2] It's a very good movie about the Second World War. I can't recall the name of the protagonist right now, but he was a religious person who didn't want to go to the battlefield to kill people, so he served as an army medic. However, when his fellow soldiers died, he picked up a gun to protect his comrades. It's human nature. You pick up a gun when it comes to protecting your own life or those of your friends. I remember there was a final battle scene in which he fought on a cliff, and he not only saved American soldiers, but also the enemy soldiers while risking his own life. His spirit really surpassed national boundaries . . . Anyway, I felt this film was more realistic than most Anti-Japanese War dramas we have on TV, where one Chinese soldier can kill many people with just one gun, and Chinese soldiers never die. This is just distorted history (*waiqu lishi*).

The student added that watching *Hacksaw Ridge* changed her impression of the motivations of American soldiers. At school, she noted, she had learnt that the United States is driven by aggressive ambitions for foreign expansion. After watching *Hacksaw Ridge*, she came to realise that American soldiers 'did not voluntarily set out to conquer other countries. They acted on orders from above. They thought they were fighting for their country.'

CJJ's disdain for the anti-Japanese war drama screened on Chinese television matches the negative reaction to these shows observed in other studies. As noted in Chapter 4, some TV war dramas have won decent audience ratings and commercial profit. However, the overproduction of the dramas and the 'ridiculousness' of their content have angered some of the Chinese public. For instance, online commenters have mocked these war dramas for showing 'Chinese martial-arts warriors defeating Japanese soldiers using hand-to-hand combat against modern weaponry' (Wang and Chew 2021, 885). In a previous study I also found that adolescents criticised the excessive unrealism of some of these TV shows, with one student joking that 'if what you saw on the shows was actually true, then the war [with Japan] shouldn't have lasted so long!' (Naftali 2018, 714). Such criticism indicates the limited effect these anti-Japanese war dramas have on Chinese youth's views of armed conflict.

Among those who rejected the use of military violence in the study, some suggested that China employ alternative means to accomplish its strategic aims. In an interview conducted in 2017, FT, an 18-year-old boy who attended a vocational school in Shanghai observed:

> Peace should be the sincerest goal in everyone's hearts. It's just like Xue Zhiqian [also known as Joker Xue, a Chinese singer-songwriter and record producer] said: we should all work for world peace ... For example, if other countries really need the resources in the South China Sea, we can give them something. If they really want it, let them buy it with money. The price should be based on the value of these resources.

Echoing this pragmatic approach, ZQ, a 17-year-old student at another Shanghai vocational school remarked:

> Our politics teacher talked about current affairs with us in class, including the Diaoyu Islands conflict with Japan. The teacher said that China shouldn't show an aggressive attitude in this case ... I agree. If we have conflicts with other countries, we should communicate more with them, deepen our contacts with these countries. That is the best way to address any disagreements.

YF, a 17-year-old from Henan suggested in a 2019 interview: 'We should just sit down with the [other countries] and take our time to talk things through in order to find the best solution that is mutually beneficial, a win–win cooperation (*huli gong ying*).' The term 'win–win' is a favourite phrase among Chinese policymakers of the Xi era used to indicate Beijing's peaceful intentions in dealing with other countries (Hirono 2019; Nathan and Zhang 2022). The student invokes this official phrase in support of her stance.

In advocating negotiation and compromise rather than the use of military force, students in both Shanghai and Henan contrasted the approach of other countries, specifically the United States. JY, who in 2018 was attending an academic high school in Shanghai, argued: 'China shouldn't try to grab resources from others, like the US has been doing in Iraq'. Other informants in both locations insisted that China should be 'different' from other countries and pursue a more virtuous path to achieve its interests, a path which does not involve bloodshed on either side of the conflict. Looking back at the messages he received at school, XZ, an 18-year-old senior in Henan, elaborated:

Our textbooks talk about all sort of wars. War has certainly been a focus of our history classes, but the final message has always been that we are a peace-loving country, and that Chinese are peace-loving people. The textbooks also say that China's relations with its neighbours have always been about cultural exchange rather than conflict... I think we should strive for peace. China shouldn't behave like the US. I recently saw on the news that the US has been bombing Syria along with other countries. Our politics teacher mentioned this in class and strongly criticized American actions.

As this quote illustrates, youth who rejected the use of violence in territorial disputes also linked their conviction to their perceptions of China's historical experiences and distinct policy stance, perceptions which according to their testimonies had been shaped by their textbooks, by statements of individual teachers and by the media they had consumed. An 18-year-old student from Henan reflected on the type of messages she had received during various stages of her school career, and the lessons she had divulged from these messages:

We learnt about war in modern history classes: The Opium Wars, World War I, World War II, the War of Resistance against Japan . . . You could say there is a lot of focus about the issue of war in our schoolbooks. I also remember how in junior high school the teacher told us the story of the Five Heroes of Langya Mountain (*Lang ya shan wu zhuangshi*): how they sacrificed their lives for the country.

The Five Heroes of Langya Mountain is a famous tale taught to generations of Chinese schoolchildren and celebrated in film, theatre and paintings. According to the official narrative, five Communist soldiers killed dozens of Japanese soldiers in 1941 before committing suicide by throwing themselves off the top of Mount Langya in Hebei Province to escape capture by the Japanese, while shouting, 'Long live the Communist Party!'

In 2016, a defamation suit was heard against Chinese historian Hong Zhenkuai involving details of this story. Three years earlier, Hong had published a series of articles questioning the number of Japanese soldiers killed in the incident and whether the five men – three died but two survived the fall – had slipped or jumped from the cliff. A Beijing court found Hong guilty of damaging 'the Chinese nation's spiritual values' and ordered him to issue a public apology to the plaintiffs for 'defaming' the heroes (K. Zhao 2016). As noted in Chapter 2, a couple of years later after the trial, the Chinse government promulgated a 'Law on the Protection of Heroes and Martyrs', making the act a criminal offence.

While the interview with the Henan student was conducted about a year after the Hong Zhenkuai case, she did not mention the incident, nor did she doubt the veracity of the original story. She simply noted that the 'heroic spirit' of war heroes 'deeply impressed her' as a junior high school student. She then added:

> After entering high school, it seemed our teachers paid more attention to the current world situation and talked more about world peace . . . To solve conflicts with other countries, we must first make China stronger so that we can have a say in the world. Then, we should have friendly exchanges, close contacts with other countries. We should jointly agree on corresponding solutions which are beneficial to both sides instead of blindly hurting each other or challenging others. We shouldn't start any wars.

In a 2019 interview, JY, a senior at a Shanghai academic high school also described the effects his school experience had had on his views of warfare:

> Our textbooks talk about many kinds of wars, not just China's wars but also wars in other parts of the world . . . The school also took us on visits to historical museums, and I remember most of them showed exhibits that have to do with war, mainly the War of Resistance against Japan. I think it is necessary to remember the war experiences of previous generations in China, but world peace is what is really important. Only peace can help people around the world make progress.

LQ, a 17-year-old girl in Henan drew a similar link between her opposition to warfare, the contents of her textbooks and the messages she had heard from individual teachers:

> Our textbooks tell us to love peace, of course they do. What else would they say? I mean everyone loves peace, right? Our teachers also tell us that we shouldn't get involved in any fights, like gang fights at school. They say that if we have any problems, we shouldn't solve them by using force . . . It's the same when it comes to dealing with other countries. We should stick to the Five Principles of Peaceful Coexistence (*Heping gongchu wu xiang yuanze*). Our sovereignty is important, but we shouldn't bully other countries.

Here, the student invokes a long-standing tenet of China's foreign policy codified back in the mid-1950s. As noted in Chapter 2, history textbooks published in the Hu Jintao and the Xi Jinping era highlight the Five Principles of Peaceful Coexistence, which include respect for each other's territorial integrity and sovereignty; mutual non-aggression; mutual non-interference in each other's internal affairs; equality and cooperation for mutual benefit; and peaceful coexistence. Other informants invoked these five principles in their answers, while noting China's tradition of 'non-intervention' to argue against the use of military means today. An 18-year-old Henan student explained:

> We should solve our issues with other countries according to the Five Principles of Peaceful Co-Existence. We should look for common ground while also respecting differences between countries. We should show the world that we are a country pursuing peace. We shouldn't lean too much to any side.[3] It's better to stand in the middle and maintain a neutral attitude.

A girl from Henan echoed this stance in a 2019 interview while referring to Xi Jinping's vision of the world order:

> Our teacher said that just because we happen to live in a peaceful country doesn't mean that our world is peaceful. It's sad to see that people in places like Africa, for example, can't lead a stable life because of wars ... President Xi talks about 'a community of shared future for mankind' (*Renlei mingyun gongtongti*).[4] I think this is a good symbol of peace and of how we should deal with other countries.

Another student from Henan interviewed in the same year held a less benign view of China's contemporary foreign policy, and questioned the benefits of the more assertive stance demonstrated under Xi Jinping:

> Force cannot solve our current problems with other countries. I think the joint development and prosperity (*gontong fuyu*) principle proposed by Deng Xiaoping is a better way. It's true that right now, other countries have become more afraid of us, but if our Chairman changes in the future, maybe in a few decades or so, we might face some serious problems. What we do now might lead to new conflicts between China and other countries down the line.

As this quote illustrates, students who objected to the use of military force in China's territorial disputes drew both on ethical considerations as well as on a cost-benefit analysis. Some recommended the use of economic pressure – rather than military violence – to achieve China's aims. This view was particularly prevalent among students in Shanghai. LY, the 18-year-old who attended an elite high school in the city, opined that:

> We shouldn't have a warlike attitude. If your own resources are insufficient, or your country has some defects, then you should do your best to improve and develop yourself rather than try to grab the resources of other countries through aggression or launching a war. We should maintain our sovereignty over our territory and our airspace, but if others oppose us, we should use economic sanctions, not military force. The countries in Southeast Asia, for example, are much smaller than us, and a large part of their capital comes from China! So economic sanctions could be quite effective. We should slowly assert our sovereignty over [the South China Sea] through economic as well as cultural means, for example by spreading the use of Chinese language, just like we dealt with other border countries in the past.

LW, a senior from another Shanghai academic high school explained why she thought economic sanctions would work best:

> Our neighbouring countries are making trouble unreasonably. How could they beat us? We are stronger than they are. You see what happened when South Korea wanted to deploy THAAD. Their economy was badly hurt as a result. Look at how much money the Korean companies lost because of this! Our government also banned Korean dramas and that was a big blow to the Korean economy.

The student's reply alludes to China's reaction to the South Korean government's agreement in 2016 to deploy the US-made Terminal High Altitude Area Defence (or THAAD) system. Although presented as protection against the growing military capacity of North Korea, the Chinese government perceived THAAD as a threat to Chinese military operations, armed forces and weapon systems, and responded with economic sanctions. One result was the cancellation of concerts and tours by Korean musicians, removing Korean celebrities from adverts, and refusing to allow Korean actors and musicians to appear on talent shows and TV series in China. Korean-produced films and contributions by Korean workers to film production in China were also halted. Restrictions were imposed on all music shows funded and produced by Korean companies (Zhang and Nagus 2020, 500).

While the move may not have pleased the K-Pop fandom communities in China, the Chinese government argued that 'the economic difficulties' experienced by Korean companies reflected the 'strong feelings in the general public in China' (cited in Lim 2019). Indeed, in 2016–17, there were calls on the Chinese Internet to boycott South Korean Lotte department stores that operated in China because the company had given some of its land to the Korean government for the deployment of the THAAD system (Zhong and Hwang 2020, 61). Chinese tourism to South Korea also plummeted (Gries 2020, 71). According to some estimates, the Korean entertainment industry lost the equivalent of $USD54 million in revenue, and tourism, confectionary and direct investment declined by the equivalent of $USD11 billion (cited in Zhang and Nagus 2020, 500). From the official Chinese perspective, the use of economic sanctions was effective,[5] and the statement of the Shanghai student cited here demonstrates support for Beijing's retaliatory actions.

Several other students in the present study opposed the use of military means on the grounds that China was not strong enough to engage in warfare, and that war could further hurt China's economic development. An 18-year-old at a Shanghai academic school remarked in an interview in 2013: 'Right now, people in China care more about what they eat and wear. The government also pays attention to this aspect. War would not be good for China's economy.' A 2019 interview with an eleventh grader from Henan reflects a similar notion:

> At school they teach us to cherish peace because peace is hard-won. Our history teacher in junior high school also said that a country must be strong enough to not be bullied by others . . . I think China is not that strong right now, so we cannot use force. In fact, if the US wants to fight us, for example, if Taiwan wants independence, then we would be in serious trouble.

In short, students who negated the use of violence in China's disputes provided different rationales for their responses, ranging from pragmatic to moral. Nonetheless, most respondents in both locations noted the tragic costs of war in terms of human lives and suffering. Many related this view to the messages they had read in textbooks or heard from teachers. Conversations with several teachers in Shanghai and Henan revealed a similar view on the basic messages of Chinese education. A Henan history teacher interviewed in 2017 said:

> I think our education promotes peace. To say that Chinese textbooks are militaristic or that military training promotes militarism is totally wrong. We focus on the destructive effects of war on the national economy and culture. We tell students that peace is hard to come by, that it's precious . . . When talking about the cruel nature of war, for example in relation to the War of Resistance against Japan, we shouldn't tell students that the Japanese were cruel. We should teach them that soldiers of every nation and country might become cruel as a result of war. War inevitably turns a kind-hearted person into a cruel person, no matter what nationality they are.

The teacher's words notably recall those of LY, the Shanghai student cited earlier. Echoing this view, another Henan teacher maintained: 'Our school encourages students to cherish peace, because war will bring huge disasters, and peace is hard-won. We teach children that people are happiest when there is peace.'

In a 2013 interview, a teacher at a vocational school in Shanghai further contrasted Chinese attitudes to peace education to that of Japan and the USA. 'China', she noted, has 'always emphasised the idea of peaceful rise. We are not competing for hegemony like the US or Japan . . . Our education is accordingly not militaristic. Japan's schoolbooks on the other hand deny war crimes. They also enshrine war criminals in Japan. We are not like them.' Teachers interviewed at Shanghai academic schools expressed a similar view. As the discussion in Chapter 2 has shown, this view glosses over the ambiguous messages of China's history textbooks regarding the role of armed conflict in modern Chinese history. History teachers in China are strictly constrained when it comes to critiquing the state-sanctioned narrative or departing from it in any way, not only because of political considerations but also because of examination pressures (Yan *et al.* 2021, 82). It is difficult therefore to determine whether the teacher interviewees did not detect the ambiguity or simply preferred not to raise the point in the interview setting. Nonetheless, it is important to note that the teachers saw fit to emphasise the peaceful themes in the history curriculum when talking to the Chinese interviewer.

Students formed their views on warfare not only from what they heard from teachers or read in textbooks but also on the media they consumed. As the next section discusses, some media products led students to form a more belligerent view.

'We Love Peace, but Are Not Afraid of War'

Although most of the study participants espoused a policy of cooperation and compromise, a considerable minority (more than 40 per cent) of students did support the use of force in China's territorial disputes. Within this group, however, a very small number of students (fourteen respondents: eight in Shanghai and six in Henan) endorsed the use of military force unequivocally. In an interview conducted in 2017, ZM, a senior at a Shanghai vocational school, criticised what he viewed as China's weak stance when dealing with other countries:

> The territorial disputes we now have with other countries are actually the result of our own policies. For example, look at the Japanese grabbing our Diaoyu Islands. They can do that because our country has been acting too peacefully. We can't be too soft, otherwise other countries will exploit us. I think our government should act tougher.

YJH, a vocational school student in Shanghai interviewed in the same year explained why he endorsed an aggressive course of action:

> What is war actually? War is a way for high-level officials to compete for benefits. War can also bring benefits. You think that the US is fighting Afghanistan for any other reason than resources? If the US starts a war, the American arms dealers are the ones who are most profitable, right? ... But at the same time, how should I put it ... Excessive peace is not a good thing either. If you have a period of peace that is too long, then people might relax too much, they will lower their vigilance and become too lazy. So, we need war to stimulate the country and our society, to make people more competitive.

The idea that war might have positive effects for the country and for people's characters was not expressed by any other informant. Instead, youth who supported warfare often underscored the importance of protecting 'national honour'. In a discussion of China's territorial disputes in the East and South China Sea, a 16-year-old student in Henan asserted that 'China is China, they can't take away what's ours!' Acknowledging that her school textbooks and teachers promoted a more peaceful stance, the student, whose interview took place in 2019, observed that her foreign policy views were informed by war-action films which depict Chinese military operations on foreign soil. In particular, she mentioned the two *Wolf Warrior* (*Zhan lang*) films released in 2015 and 2017, and *Operation Red Sea* (*Honghai xingdong*) which came out in 2018.

As discussed in Chapter 4, the three blockbuster films were strongly backed by the PLA in the hope that they would foster a spirit of assertive patriotism among Chinese audiences, especially young viewers. Indeed, several students interviewed in Shanghai in 2019 noted that they had watched these films as part of their military training. Testimonies of informants who supported military action attest to the impact the films had on some students.

HY, a student at a Shanghai elite school who endorsed the use of armed force in China's current conflicts noted for instance that *Wolf Warrior II* had left 'a particularly strong impact' on his views. The student said that the film demonstrated 'the glorious honour' of the Chinese military and that he was impressed by its message that 'although you may be far away from home, the motherland is always there to protect you'. Another Shanghai student mentioned that *Wolf Warrior II* was the kind of film that 'made you want to fight'.

One Shanghai high school teacher commented on the effects of media representation on youth belligerence by saying:

> Our children have been living in peaceful times for quite a long time. They have no concept of war. It's not like when we were children, in the 1980s and 1990s. Back then, our elders would tell stories about their war experiences, their hardships. Children nowadays are different. They were born after the era of Reform and Opening Up. Their ideological outlook is different. They don't pay too much attention to textbooks . . . They are much more influenced by the media and the entertainment industry.

Despite this teacher's observation, it is worth noting that even among students who supported the use of force in China's disputes, a majority exhibited a relatively prudent stance, with many maintaining that the Chinese government should only use force as a 'defensive measure'. Typical responses included statements such as: 'if the US attacks China directly, then we must fight, of course'; 'If Japan blows up all our fishing boats and kills our people in the Diaoyu Islands, what can we do? We have to fight!' A student at a Shanghai academic school reflected: 'We should use force only if we are invaded. If China ends up attacking another country, I don't know if I would support that. Maybe it's because the history of China's invasion by others is too deep-rooted in my mind.'

In an interview conducted in 2017, CJ, an 18-year-old at a Shanghai vocational school alluded to the tagline of the *Wolf Warrior* film series while qualifying his support for military action:

> Because previous generations experienced brutal wars, I believe we should cherish peace. Wars are too costly for a country: there are always many innocent victims. But at the same time, we must make sure that those who violate China's interests are punished even if they are far away. If others infringe on our territory for profit, we must not back down and just be peaceful. If they reach our doorstep, we will have to get involved in a war, but we should use as little force as possible.

Others maintained that the Chinese government must first attempt 'peaceful negotiations' and only if those fail, resort to force. WJ, a 17-year-old student at a Shanghai vocational school elaborated on what she thought was the best course of action:

> What we need to do first is make sure our own country is managed well, in a harmonious way. We shouldn't take the initiative and act aggressively. At the same time, we should make sure we are not too weak so that other countries look down on us. If others want to invade us, there must be an appropriate counterattack, just to let them know that we cannot be bullied. But we shouldn't initiate anything ourselves.

ZM, who in 2013 was attending a Shanghai academic high school, similarly advocated a cautious strategy:

> First, we should take care of our domestic affairs. If you have no power, what can you do? Don't mess around if you don't have the ability. If the country is strong enough, then we could use force, but I think war is necessary only if negotiations fail or if the violation is serious, for example if another country invades us. Because fighting is also very expensive.

Commenting on foreign perceptions of the 'China threat', JH, a 17-year-old at a Shanghai elite high school made the following observation in his 2013 interview:

Other countries think that China is overly ambitious, and that it has risen too rapidly in the past two decades. They think we are aggressive. The US is particularly afraid of us because the US was the number one power after the fall of the Soviet Union, and now with China's rise, the US is unsure of itself. They want to suppress us. That's why they interfere in the Taiwan issue. And they say that we are unstable and that we are going to provoke an international war or something . . . But in fact, I don't think China is threatening others, not to the point of invading other countries. We are relatively peaceful compared to other countries. At the same time, I don't think China should use only peaceful means if it is oppressed by others. For example, if Japan has a strong desire to possess the Diaoyu Islands, then China should maintain a firm stand. In that case, we might need to get involved in a war.

In a 2019 interview, WH, a student at another Shanghai academic high school commented on the relations between her views on war and peace, and the messages she had received at school:

I think everyone should hate war and desire peace. China has always had friendly ties with its neighbouring countries. Our textbooks say that we should be kind and create partnerships with our neighbours. However, if other countries are repeatedly aggressive and have disputes with us, then we shouldn't make any concessions. We should warn them first, and after we warn them, we should use force.

A Henan student interviewed in the same year agreed, again highlighting a perceived discrepancy between the peaceful messages he had heard at school and his personal views:

Our teachers encourage peace, but I support our military's message: 'We love peace but are not afraid of war.' I think we should first negotiate, and if the negotiation fails, we must use force to defend our territory. Sovereignty is nonnegotiable. We should not actively start a war, but we will not hesitate to use our own strength to protect ourselves.

Another Henan student interviewed in 2019 expressed a more conflicted stance:

Our textbooks talk about the importance of peace, but I also read about current affairs in the media and have my own views . . . China stands for peace, but we must fight back if we are bullied. Sometimes, if you have no choice, you must go to war! I think war is kind of exciting . . . at the same time, whoever wants to start a war must know that it can also bring death. What if going to war one day hurts your own family and friends?

As illustrated in this quote and in those cited earlier, students who supported the use of force in China's territorial disputes were not entirely aggressive. Some employed careful calculations and thoughtful reasoning. Others brought up China's past humiliations and 'bullying' by foreign forces – topics they had learnt about in class, through PE and NDE activities, and through media products – to justify their strong approach.

While passionately arguing for the defence of China's 'national honour', informants of different genders and social backgrounds nonetheless insisted that it is precisely because of the country's historical war experiences and its victimisation by others that China should never rush into – or instigate – military violence. As noted, youths who endorsed military force mostly subscribed to the notion of a 'just war', a theme which as Chapter 2 has shown, features prominently in their history textbooks. The small minority who expressed an unqualified belligerent attitude acknowledged that this approach contrasted with the messages they had received at school. Based on the students' testimonies, exposure to recent blockbuster war-action films such as *Operation Red Sea* and *Wolf Warrior* may have contributed to their pro-war attitudes.

Conclusion

This chapter examined youth notions of war and peace and the view young people held regarding the use of military means in China's territorial disputes in the East and South China Sea. The analysis focused on the type of logic informants employed to justify their positions as well as students' insights into the role of school and media messages in shaping their views. The data presented here indicate that youth participants in both locations held a broad range of views, which cannot be easily confined by the restrictive binaries of 'militaristic/anti-militaristic' or 'nationalist/internationalist' attitudes. Youth of different locales and different types of schools employed diverse rhetoric and reasoning to justify their positions. Some cited official messages circulating in Chinese media or in their textbooks. Others referred to their teachers' views or offered thoughtful interpretations of these messages. Yet others highlighted the role of news media and popular culture products in shaping their views.

Overall, students' responses indicated their opinion that their schoolteachers and textbooks emphasise the role of war in shaping modern history while highlighting the suffering of Chinese people as a result of war. The lessons youth took from these messages was not one of constant vigilance, however. A vast majority of informants in both Henan and Shanghai were convinced that their textbooks and teachers promoted peacekeeping as a virtue and rejected military violence. While a considerable minority endorsed the use of force to address China's territorial conflicts, most even in this group appealed to the logic of 'just war' for defensive purposes while remaining skeptical of armed conflict as an effective means of attaining China's goals.

Arguably, students' statements (made to a Chinese interviewer) may represent what they perceived as model answers. There is no guarantee that informants professed positions which accurately reflected their value systems. Moreover, youth attitudes may change in response to domestic and international developments or as they grow older and gain additional knowledge and experience. That said, the findings of this chapter are significant in that they challenge the assumption that Chinese schools of the 2000s and 2010s promote a 'militant' worldview. Like other education systems worldwide, schools in China assign priority to the study of wars as turning points in national history, a fact that informants picked up on. As the students' testimonies noted, and as demonstrated in the analysis in Chapter 2, Chinese history textbooks legitimise the notion of defensive warfare as it applies to China. However, many participants strongly rejected acts of war regardless of the circumstances.

The students demonstrated their ability to empathise not only with the war suffering of previous generations in China, but also with the contemporary war experience of people in other countries. Informants learnt about these experiences not only from textbooks but also from Chinese media. Reports about war suffering in other parts of the world, such as the 2017 *Xinhua* article on the plight of Syrian children cited earlier, may be seen as a form of nationalist propaganda in that they explicitly invite Chinese readers to 'cherish' the fact that unlike people in war-torn areas abroad they are 'lucky' to have been born in a 'peaceful country' and should be grateful to the CPC for their peace (cf. Zhang and Ma 2023, 904).

But the informants' comments suggest that for some youths, the key lesson from these official media stories was opposition to war. Youth informants also exhibited the ability to organise the meaning of China's historical conflicts around what they 'deem worthy of remembering' (Bellino 2017, 8; Jackson and Du 2022). They drew on images and narratives of past conflicts to draw their own view on the use of armed force in China's contemporary disputes.

Overall, a large majority of participants in the study did not exhibit the belief that the world is 'a dangerous place' or that war is 'inevitable' (Enloe 2007, 4) – notions commonly associated with a 'militaristic attitude'. Instead, they exhibited a relatively prudent attitude towards military solutions while drawing on both ethical and pragmatic considerations. As the next chapter will discuss, informants exhibited a similar circumspect attitude about the role and functions of the Chinese military in general and about army service in particular.

Notes

1. Produced by two Chinese commercial companies, Huayi Brothers Media Group and Chongqing Film Group, *Back to 1942* was a box office hit in China. While foreign critics and international social media websites gave the film mixed reviews, it received a relatively high score on the Chinese website *Douban*, where more than 300,000 reviewers awarded it an average grade of four out of five stars (or 8.1 of 10). The film also won several awards in Chinese and international film festivals and was selected as the Chinese entry for the Best Foreign Language Film at the 86th Academy Awards but was not nominated.
2. Directed by Mel Gibson, *Hacksaw Ridge* is a 2016 American war film based on the documentary *The Conscientious Objector* (2004). The film focuses on the World War II experiences of Desmond Doss, an American pacifist combat medic who, as a Seventh-Day Adventist Christian, refused to carry or use a weapon or firearm of any kind. Doss became the first conscientious objector to be awarded the Medal of Honour, for service above and beyond the call of duty during the 1945 Battle of Okinawa.
3. The phrase 'lean to one side' (*yibian dao*) alludes to a principle of China's foreign policy in the first five years of socialist rule. As Mao Zedong explained, this meant that 'whoever is not with us'–the socialist–communist camp–'is against us'. From 1955–57, however, China pursued a much more accommodative policy based on the principle of non-Alignment (for more on this topic, see Chapter 2).
4. The canonical full phrase 'A Shared Future for Mankind' emerged for the first time in a speech Xi Jinping delivered on 18 January 2017 at the United Nations in Geneva. One of the key themes of Xi's address was that international issues should be settled not by war but 'through dialogue and consultation' (*duihua*

xieshang). For further discussion of the phrase, its meanings and its implications for China's foreign policy, see Nathan and Zhang (2022).
5. In October 2017, after the completion of the THAAD system, South Korea declared the 'three noes' (no additional THAAD batteries, no participation in any US regional missile defence system and no trilateral alliance with the US and Japan). By the end of that month, the two countries agreed to restore relations to the 'normal development track', and following this agreement many of the difficulties Korean firms and industries faced in China gradually began to ease (Lim 2019).

CHAPTER 6

Youth Views of the PLA: 'You Can Serve the Country in More Than One Way'

In August 2022, the state-run magazine, *China Youth Daily* [*Zhongguo qingnian bao*], published a curious news story. Entitled, 'Conscription in the farmyard', the story described the efforts of a Chinese farmer called Wu Fengbiao to convince young people in his area to join the military. According to the piece, Farmer Wu, whose own son had enlisted in 2007, had been conducting 'voluntary conscription propaganda work' since 2020 from the backyard of his small farmhouse in Xuji Village in the eastern province of Shandong.

One afternoon, Farmer Wu gathered 'five recent college graduates' from the area to tell them about the benefits of military service. He began his motivational speech by explaining that the 'development and construction of the army requires highly educated and high-quality talents', and that 'as college graduates', joining the army was a most 'suitable career choice' for youths such as them. The recent launch of China's 'third aircraft carrier' was 'a source of national pride', Wu declared, and then raised a different rationale for enlistment. 'Now is a good time to serve the country', he reportedly told his small audience. 'If you enlist, you will definitely have a stage to display your talents on.' Serving in the military, he continued, 'is equivalent to having a job experience on your resume', and 'veterans enjoy clear advantages' when applying for civil service positions and when starting private businesses. According to the report, the young men were immediately persuaded by Wu's speech and 'all five of them' expressed a willingness to sign up. The article adds that under the influence of Farmer Wu's voluntary propaganda work, 'more than ten graduates' from his village and surrounding areas had signed up for military service in the past two years (H. Li 2022).

Despite the optimistic message of the report, its publication (timed with the PLA's annual recruitment and conscription period in August) raises few questions. Why did the speech dwell on the material and personal benefits of army service? Do recruiters consider 'patriotism' and 'fulfilment of national duty' insufficient incentives to convince young audiences? And why does the PLA need to rely on veterans' families to perform unpaid propaganda work at all? What does this tactic tell us about the effectiveness of the Chinese military's efforts to improve its image through NDE activities such as military training or through investment in commercial popular culture products as described in previous chapters? This chapter sheds light on these issues by drawing on data from interviews with students in Shanghai and Henan conducted over the past decade.

Previous studies have noted the PLA's mounting conscription challenges in recent decades following the Chinese government's economic reform and Open-Door policy, the demographic outcomes of the One-Child policy (1979–2015), and the growing influence of individualistic and materialistic values among youth of the post-1990s and 2000s generation. Due to the political sensitivity of the topic, many of these studies draw on media reports. Empirical data on Chinese youth perceptions of the army and military service, and how the educational and propaganda efforts of the Party-state and the PLA have shaped these perceptions is lacking.

The present chapter illuminates this issue while drawing on data from interviews with 155 Han Chinese students (aged 16–18; 51 per cent male; 49 per cent female) attending academic and vocational high schools in Shanghai and Henan.[1] The discussion begins with an overview of the PLA's conscription challenges in the twenty-first century and the army's efforts to overcome them. I then move on to present the results of interviews conducted in 2013 and 2017–19 regarding youth notions of the military, soldierhood, and army service.

As the analysis will show, an overwhelming majority of study participants in both locations profess a generally positive image of the PLA. Even so, only a minority of informants in Shanghai and Henan stated their willingness to join the military. The discussion identifies key themes in students' impressions and their accounts of the reasons for their willingness and/or reluctance to enlist. It further highlights differences and commonalities in the positions of youth of different genders, locations, and types of schools. The concluding section accounts for these findings and discusses their implications for our understanding of the militarisation of education and youth in contemporary China.

The PLA's Conscription Challenges in the Twenty-First Century

According to recent estimates, China has approximately 2–2.2 million service personnel, with 975,000 active in PLA combat units, which makes the Chinese military the largest armed force in the world (Clay and Blasko 2020; US Department of Defense 2022).[2] China's Military Service Law (adopted in 1984, and amended in 1998, 2007, 2011, 2021, 2023) states that all male citizens must perform military service, that China 'practices a military service system which combines conscripts with volunteers', and that the duration of service is two years.[3] Women are not required to register for military service but may do so providing they are at least eighteen years of age (PRC State Council 2021).[4] According to the 2021 revision, citizens who are not enlisted at the age of 18 may still be enlisted for active service until the age of 22. The revision further raises the age limit on new recruits to 24 for college graduates and to 26 for postgraduates, from 22 previously. Chinese law stipulates that students in full-time higher education institutes can postpone their conscription but should still perform military service and undergo national defence education (PRC State Council 2021).

In practice though, China's military recruitment system is selective. Though the PLA does not publish the percentage of 'volunteers' and 'involuntary conscripts' it recruits, a recent report reckons that most enlisted troops volunteer, though can be forced to join to meet quotas. After their mandatory two-year service, troops can serve another two years, return to civilian life, volunteer as Non-Commissioned Officers (NCOs) or take exams to become officers. NCOs, officers, and civilian staff are all volunteers (The Economist 2023b). According to estimates, each year, between 10 million and 11 million Chinese males turn eighteen. Yet the country needs only about 3 per cent of them to enlist in the military to meet its annual quota of 300,000–400,000 recruits (Johnson et al. 2009, 26, 34; Clay and Blasko 2020). As noted in Chapter 3, the growth of the economic sector and the liberalisation of government controls over job assignments since the late 1990s has made attracting the best talent the PLA's main challenge. The obstacles the Chinese military faces then are similar to those of military establishments in capitalist democracies with non-mandatory conscription.

Studies on the factors shaping military enrolment rates in Western liberal democracies without mandatory conscription indicate that economic factors, in particular unemployment rates and civilian income, have a greater impact on variations in recruitment rates than influences such as exposure to military PR campaigns (Maartens 2021, 214). While the military's public relations and propaganda efforts may produce 'more favourable beliefs' regarding army service, recent scholarship suggests that these beliefs do not necessarily translate into increased interest in service or indeed the likelihood of individuals serving. In countries such as the USA and Germany, the attitudes of significant others, including parents, tend to play a more important role in shaping youth decisions to enlist (cited in Maartens 2021, 215).

As a result, military establishments in capitalist democracies without mandatory conscription negotiate their recruitment needs with the dreams and aspirations of individual youths and their families. Recruiters link military service with the values of 'self-fulfilment' and 'personal development', aligning young people's quest for self-actualisation with the political project of the neo-liberal state (Strand and Berndtsson 2015, 245).

The applicability of these insights to China remains unclear, however, and is an understudied topic in academic scholarship, not least because of the high secrecy regarding the military in China's authoritarian environment. While public survey data is missing, studies and reports published since the 2000s point to several structural, economic and sociocultural factors which shape Chinese youth motivations to enlist.

As noted, one key factor relates to changes in China's economic environment and social values in the post-1978 era, particularly from the 1990s onwards. Under Maoist ideology, soldiers were cast as one of the three 'purest proletarian classes' alongside workers and peasants. As Chapter 1 discusses, PLA soldiers were portrayed in official media and cultural works as role models, regardless of age, gender, or social background. This notion has faded since the beginning of economic reform and the Open-Door policy in 1978 (Zhang 2014, 5; Cliff 2015, 11) and values among Chinese born after the 1980s and particularly the 1990s have separated from the values of the state.

Studies suggest that some contemporary Chinese youths are eager to enlist because of a sense of patriotism or because they are attracted to the challenges and lifestyle. Others volunteer because of a family tradition, for future educational and financial benefits, or because they are looking for a stable job to improve their economic conditions. Still others regard military service as a means of expediting their path in becoming members of the Communist Party of China, which may help them secure better career opportunities after they leave the military (Clay and Blasko 2020). There are indications, however, that the desire to join the PLA is diminishing for several reasons.

As a key institution of the Party-state's sovereignty, the military is dominated by a collective mind-set and the legacy of Maoist thinking. In post-socialist China, however, these ideologies have been eclipsed by an emphasis on economic development and the increasing pursuit of individual interests in social and economic life (Lin 2021, 1096; see also Li 2021). Amid this crucial value shift, in recent decades, most low-ranking demobilised PLA members have suffered from low social status. Labelled as 'losers' for their lack of vocational training and any higher educational degree (Diamant 2010), a recent study documents a generally negative image of ex-PLA servicemen among private entrepreneurs and white-collar, urbanite informants. The latter described ex-servicemen as 'brainwashed by communist ideology', 'uneducated', and 'violent and not gentlemanly-like' (Lin 2021). Echoing Diamant's earlier findings, Lin's study argues that the negative stereotypes assigned to ex-servicemen of the PLA are often related to their marital struggles; a difficulty marrying or maintaining marital relationships is common among PLA veterans (Lin 2021, 1096).[5] Service in the PLA involves danger, high-intensity training, strict discipline, and often a remote, hardship posting. Chinese soldiers often struggle to find wives and those who are married may experience family difficulties (Wang and Brady 2012, 135; Wang 2015, 16).

These challenges have generated expressions of widespread dissatisfaction among active and retired personnel regarding their (anticipated or actual) post-service employment and benefits (Chase et al. 2015, 53–54; Diamant 2008).[6] Recent studies document that despite official media messages proclaiming army veterans to be the nation's pride, many never received the benefits they were promised and felt degraded, humiliated and neglected by society (Diamant and O'Brien 2015; O'Brien and Diamant 2015). The grievances of millions of veterans who have demanded better living conditions and social and political recognition of their contribution have produced frequent protests (Wang 2022, 254–55).

Amid these issues, studies suggest that high school graduates in China, particularly in urban areas, prefer to pursue higher education than join the military. Since the early 2000s, an increasing number of Chinese high school students have gone on to further education: during the 1990s, only about 8 per cent of high school graduates attended college, but this rose to 26.2 per cent in 2013 and 54.4 per cent by 2020. Rates of college attendance are higher in urban areas (cited in Allen et al. 2022). Youth who fail college entrance exams (or cannot enrol due to financial reasons) usually opt to work in factories or companies instead (Wang 2015, 16).

From the 1950s to the late 2000s, China maintained mandatory quotas of specifically rural conscripts to reflect the demographic distribution of the population. This system remained as the foundation until 2013. It was largely abolished when the military recognised that conscripts from urban areas were the most likely to possess the educational and technical skills it needed (Allen et al. 2022, 24). Yet, military service in China continues to be more attractive to poor rural residents or to children of migrant workers whose parents come from the countryside than to wealthier urban youth (Cheng 2007; Yan 2009; Cockain 2012; Sinkkonen 2013; Pun and Qiu 2020).

University students can postpone being drafted until after they graduate, and until the 2021 amendment, the delay usually put them past the age requirement, exempting them from compulsory service. Current provisions allow university graduates to enlist if they want, but few young Chinese with a degree from a good university are willing to consider joining the army (Wang 2017). Indeed, in recent years the PLA has publicly recognised problems in bribery and quota manipulation during conscription periods, practices which allow some youths to avoid enlistment and give others a place in the military even if they fail to meet the criteria (Cheng 2007, 241; Naftali 2014b, 14; Allen et al. 2022; Corbett, O'Dowd, and Chen 2008; Hundman 2023).

A recent study by Hundman (2023) documents a marked increase in Chinese state media and academic reports regarding instances of refusal to serve. One such report, published in 2017 in the magazine *Sixth Tone* (a state-run English publication in China), noted wide differences in enlistment rates among China's provinces. Quoting a retired military officer, the article observes that in China's affluent eastern regions (where the city of Shanghai is located), 'few are willing to accept the hardships of military life'. But even youth in less developed central and western regions have in recent years shown a growing reluctance to join the military. Meanwhile, in provinces with large populations that are home to relatively many service personnel, 'enthusiasm for being a soldier is high, and you need connections to enlist' (Wang 2017).

In the past several decades, the PLA has sought to attract high school and college graduates, especially those with science, technology, engineering, and mathematics (STEM) backgrounds. But rural recruits – who are the most enthusiastic about joining – often have only nine or twelve years of education, limited training, and insufficient exposure to advanced technologies to master and maintain complicated equipment. For an army that seeks to become a world-class force that can fight wars under 'conditions of informatisation', this lack of knowledge constitutes a severe problem (Cliff 2015, 104–5; Wang 2015, 14–16; Li 2022, 98). The pace of the army's modernisation efforts exacerbates the challenge. A 2023 report in the PLA's official newspaper suggests, for instance, that 'the navy did not have enough fully trained personnel to operate all of its new warships – dubbing the phenomenon 'equipment awaiting talent' (cited in The Economist 2023b).

Demographic factors pose another obstacle for the PLA's conscriptions goals. China's One-Child policy (launched in 1979) ended in 2015, when it was replaced by a two-child policy which was further amended in 2021 to a three-child policy. Even after these changes, few couples – just 5–6 per cent – have opted for a second child, citing inadequate childcare and increased living costs in big cities like Beijing and Shanghai (Liu 2023). Amid decreasing birth rates in China, the policy may continue to evolve and could soon be abolished altogether (Reuters 2023). Nonetheless, the government's former stringent population policy has had – and will continue to have – a lingering effect on recruitment. Most male recruits born under the policy, have no siblings. This is particularly true in urban areas: the policy was implemented more strictly in cities than in the countryside where rural families were allowed to have more than one child if the first (or even second) is a girl.

But as China's level of urbanisation has grown (rising from 36 per cent in 2002 to 65 per cent in 2022), recruits increasingly need to be drawn from cities. Urban parents are reluctant to allow their only child to choose a non-lucrative path requiring prolonged family separation and possibly even harm to their child's safety and, as noted earlier, their marriage prospects (Wood 2017, 2; Cheng 2007). The latter issue has become particularly salient amid recent developments in China's marriage market. Due to the lingering preference for sons in Chinese society, the One-Child policy has led to a widespread practice of sex-selective abortions, which has in turn produced a skewed gender balance. There are currently more men than women of marriageable age in China, and the marriage rate among men of fewer means is diminishing (Greenhalgh 2012). This trend has made military service a less attractive option for young men and their families, particularly in urban areas where there is a larger selection of more profitable, high-status jobs.

A related problem concerns the distinct characteristics of the One-Child generation. As noted in previous chapters, Chinese media and academic publications have suggested that the One-Child policy and the improved standards of living in cities have created a 'culture of entitlement' among urban youths of the post-1990s and post-2000s generation (Wood 2013, 15). Urban youth may uphold strong patriotic sentiments but increasingly subscribe to the ideals of self-fulfilment, personal development, and the pursuit of a comfortable lifestyle (Li 2020; Liu 2020). The PLA's focus on political education and the austerity of military life deter this generation of digital natives; enlisted troops live in barracks far from home,[7] where internet access is tightly restricted (Allen et al. 2022, 31; The Economist 2023b). Potential recruits reportedly suffer from poor physical fitness, including high BMI and short-sightedness, issues that have become prevalent among city youth with sedentary lifestyles.[8] Other issues include a 'refusal to take orders from superiors ... lack of mental preparation for hardship, inability to deal with frustration, lack of real-life experience, self-centeredness, unwillingness to sacrifice themselves for national defense, and poor discipline' (Cheng 2007, 237–8; Cliff 2015, 112; The Economist 2023b). Chinese media reports, for instance, have described military instructors in recent years arguing with recruits about the need to fold bed quilts neatly, and complaints against encroachments on soldiers' 'right to privacy' (Naftali 2014b, 3–4). In one published case, recruits even offered to pay for their own rooms during basic training (Wood 2013, 16).

In recent decades, the Party-state and the military have employed both sticks and carrots to address these challenges. Those who refuse to serve in the army and are unable to secure an official exemption are subjected to a range of legal sanctions, ranging from prison sentences to steep fines, bans on starting new businesses or receiving bank loans, exclusion from government benefits, revocation of university acceptance, and travel restrictions. Recent years have also witnessed an increase in instances of public 'naming and shaming', and in some localities in China, those who refuse military service have been included in blacklists linked to the country's emerging social credit systems (Hundman 2023, 564, 570–1).

At the same time, authorities have taken a series of steps to attract and retain well-educated youth, especially graduates of colleges and universities (Xinhua News Agency 2019a). Measures have included a reduction of service from four to two years (Blasko 2012, 49), and raising the age limit to twenty-four (in some military units: twenty-six) to allow college graduates to enlist. Other measures include a reduction of the physical examination criteria; adjusting the timing of the conscription intake to coincide with college graduation; and a system of preferential treatment, according to which student conscripts have their tuition fees paid, among other benefits (Cliff 2015, 112; Wang 2015; China Daily 2019; Zhang and Liu 2019). To encourage more university students to enlist, the central government has increased the basic annual salaries of college graduates and the central government has offered graduates a financial bonus after they complete their two years of service (Wang 2017; Allen et al. 2022). Recent revisions to the Military Service Law, effective from May 2023, focus on recruiting tech-savvy science and engineering students to prepare for warfare in new domains such as space and cyber, and allow universities to handle drafting students. As part of these new measures, Chinese universities can now draft students at the site of their family registers or the locations of the schools. Another provision makes it easier for the military to draft people in case of an emergency, and allows retired service people to re-enlist. The latter measure is regarded as essential considering China's dwindling, ageing population. In 2022, the population fell, year on year, for the first time in sixty-one years (Tajima 2023).

The Chinese government has also attempted to address the plight of PLA veterans. In 2017, for instance, Xi Jinping announced the creation of a Ministry of Veterans Affairs to protect veterans' rights and 'make the military a respected career in Chinese society'. The ministry was formally established in 2018. Two years later, China published a Veterans Law (adopted November 2020, and effective January 2021) (National People's Congress 2020b) to 'improve the handling of veterans' affairs, better safeguard their rights and interests, and boost the attractiveness of military careers' (Zhao 2020). In June 2021, the government adopted another new law to protect the public image of

China's armed forces. Adding to existing legislation which already prohibits the slandering of 'Heroes and Martyrs', the 2021 law bans 'the defamation of military personnel', stipulating that 'no organization or individual may in any way slander or derogate the honor' of servicemen (or women) (Xinhua News Agency 2021).[9]

It is hard to ascertain the effectiveness of this raft of measures. A 2019 report published by China's official News Agency, *Xinhua*, states that 'the number of college students joining the army has continued to increase since 2009', and that in the period of 2009–19, the PLA has been able to recruit 'more than 1.5 million college students' (Xinhua News Agency 2019a; see also Gao and Allen 2023). A national census in 2020 showed the proportion of PLA personnel (of all types) with higher education had increased to 57 per cent from just over half in 2010. Yet, the figure was well short of the PLA's target of around 70 per cent (cited in The Economist 2023b). In the absence of large-scale independent survey data, it is difficult to verify these reports or to assess the precise role of the PLA's recruitment policies and other factors in shaping enlistment motivations.

Due to the relatively small sample size of the present study, the discussion in this chapter does not seek to break down these different factors. Rather, it sheds light on key themes in youth perceptions of the PLA and military service, and the factors that the young report as influential in shaping these perceptions. Specifically, the discussion considers students' replies to the following open-ended questions:

(1) What is your general impression of the People's Liberation Army (PLA) and/ or of PLA soldiers?
(2) Would you be willing to enlist in the military? Why or why not?
(3) Which sources of information have shaped your impression of the military and your attitude toward military service?

When replying to Question (3) students were given room to mention any source of information they deemed applicable and were asked to explain how that source had impacted their views. Informants were then prompted to address the potential effects of school lessons and textbooks; Patriotic Education activities; National Defence Education activities, including military training courses; news and social media; popular media products (e.g. books, TV shows, films); as well as the views of teachers, peers, and family members. Informants were also asked whether they knew anyone who had served in the army, and whether and how this person may have affected their attitudes towards the military and army service.

The review of interview data employed basic content analysis followed by a thematic analysis of students' replies to each question. The aim was to identify key patterns across the sample while noting any differences in the responses of students of different genders, locations, and types of schools. Below I begin with a discussion of students' sources of knowledge about the military followed by a description of their common impressions of the PLA based on these sources. I then move on to students' attitudes towards military service and the reasons informants provided for their readiness or reluctance to enlist.

'The PLA Is the Backbone of the Country'

Informants drew their knowledge of the military from a number of different sources: information supplied by textbooks and teachers; the military training courses they attended as part of NDE; organised school visits to history museums, national memorials, and other PE or NDE sites; popular culture products such as films and TV shows; and news and social media. A small share (28 per cent) of informants reported having a family member and/or a member of their immediate social circle who had served in the military, and with whom they had talked about the experience. Informants in Henan, that is, those of rural backgrounds, formed a majority of those respondents. The rest of the students reported coming into physical contact with a veteran only during their week-long military training course at the school.

Informants in both locations (regardless of gender and type of school) stated having a generally favourable image of the PLA and its functions. Responses frequently associated military soldiers with positive qualities such as 'bravery', 'passion', 'willingness to withstand hardship' (in Chinese, *chiku*, literally 'eat bitterness'), and 'selfless dedication' to the country. Some used the phrase the 'backbone of the country' to describe the PLA's role. Others called soldiers' mission 'sacred (*shensheng*)'. A senior in Henan (who also expressed a willingness to join the military) mentioned 'getting goosebumps' when he saw 'PLA soldiers raising the national flag at Tiananmen Square' during a family trip to the capital.

Informants reported forming this positive impression from their textbooks, NDE activities, the general media, or on social media. ZQ, a 16-year-old vocational school student in Shanghai whose parents had migrated to the city from the countryside and who had no relatives in the military, related that she had learnt about army life through social media posts. Chatting with 'some soldiers online' left her with the impression that their lives are 'fulfilling and exciting'. Students in both locations also mentioned the influence of popular culture products, including war-themed TV shows like *Drawing Sword* (2005), the reality show *Takes a Real Man* (2015–17) discussed in Chapter 4, or *The Founding of an Army* (2017), a historical drama about the establishment of the PLA. Informants also mentioned blockbuster films such as *Wolf Warrior* and *Wolf Warrior II* (2015, 2017 respectively) and *Operation Red Sea* (2018),[10] noting that they viewed these films during their military training course as part of NDE.

A 16-year-old from Henan stated that after watching *Wolf Warrior II*, she felt that 'Chinese soldiers are really great compared to soldiers in foreign countries'. A classmate added that watching *Operation Red Sea*, a film inspired by the true story of the evacuation of Chinese civilians from Yemen, left him 'deeply impressed' with PLA soldiers' 'superhuman determination' and their 'willingness to sacrifice themselves to save Chinese hostages'. An eleventh grader in Henan said that watching *Wolf Warrior II* had 'increased his love for the country' and left him impressed with 'China's military might'. Shanghai students made similar statements about the impact of the film on their positive image of the PLA.

The responses of youth in both locations attested to the contribution of such blockbusters to students' notion of the army as a site in which a person gains 'maturity' and attains 'true manhood'. Youth of different genders, locations, and social backgrounds related soldiering to qualities such as 'male friendship and camaraderie', being 'masculine (*yanggang*)', and 'physical strength', and described PLA fighters as 'handsome (*shuai*) men' (a phrase mentioned by both girls and boys). In some cases, the close association between the army and masculinity was also a product of the notions and expectations of students' family members. HY, who attended a Shanghai academic school affiliated with one of China's elite universities noted:

> My mother wants me to be a soldier . . . she said that after serving in the military for two years, your personality becomes different . . . she thinks it would be good for me because she says boys are particularly

spoiled by their families these days, no one lets them do anything on their own.

XM, a senior from Henan, likewise linked soldiering with 'true masculinity' when explaining his motivation for enlisting. 'Of course I want to join the army', he said. 'A good man (*hao nan'er*) has to consider it! Many boys in my school want to be soldiers too. It's their dream. Being a soldier would make them very proud'.

Students' positive impression of the PLA also involved an appreciation for the military's functions and contributions to the country. Informants of different backgrounds mentioned the army's crucial role in guarding China's borders and ensuring that they 'don't become too chaotic' due to 'ethnic unrest'. Students also mentioned that the army plays a key part in guarding China's 'national dignity' and protecting the country's interests. Or, as one Henan senior put it: 'It's important that we have a strong military, so we are no longer bullied by other countries'. One student mentioned reading a news report about injured Chinese soldiers during 'peacekeeping missions in the Middle East'. A Henan informant whose uncle was an army veteran noted how impressed she was with the PLA's rescue efforts during a recent flood disaster. 'The soldiers stayed up for days and nights. They have done so much for the victims and helped them get out of danger . . . they are really heroic and selfless.' Many others noted the PLA's historical role in the War of Resistance against Japan, a topic they noted that they had learnt about at school and through the media they consumed.

'The Most Beloved People'?

References to the PLA's historical role were also evident in some informants' use of the phrase 'China's most beloved people' ('*Jiefangjun Zhongguo zui ke'ai de ren*') to refer to soldiers. As noted in Chapter 1, the phrase alludes to the title of a famous 1951 *People's Daily* article which praises the role of the Chinese People's Volunteer Army (PVA) in the Korean War. The term 'most beloved people (*zui ke'ai de ren*)' has long since become synonymous with admiration for the PLA, so it is not surprising that study participants were familiar with it and chose to invoke it when asked about their impressions of the PLA.[11]

Several students also connected the PLA to the slogan 'never taking any property from the masses (*bu na qunzhong yizhen yixian*)'.

Informants employed the phrase to contrast it with the 'corrupt' and 'cruel' behaviour of KMT soldiers before 1949: a topic they had learnt about in school and through the media. The relevance of the slogan to the behaviour of contemporary soldiers has been questioned in the past two decades or so, as reports in Chinese state media reveal instances in which PLA soldiers were accused of inappropriate behaviour. The existing literature on the Chinese military (e.g. Li 2020, 18–19; Li 2022, 96–7; Wang 2016) has documented how the PLA's growing commercialisation in the 1980s and 1990s led to an explosion of corruption and smuggling, as well as to practices of buying and selling of military positions. Some of these corruption scandals have been reported in Chinese media. For instance, during the deployment of the PLA after the 2008 Sichuan earthquake, personnel of some military units were reported taking away livestock belonging to locals in the earthquake-affected villages. Chinese media also revealed that some soldiers had diverted the relief material to sell for personal gain (Coutaz 2019, 57). Under Xi Jinping, the party has engaged in an extensive anticorruption campaign, including in the military, yet recent reports suggest that so far, these efforts have not been entirely successful (e.g. Wuthnow 2023). A 2017 interview with JZ, an 18-year-old science major at a Shanghai academic school, alludes to these illegal practices:

> I think in general the PLA has a positive image in our society. There have been some negative media stories about corruption scandals in the military, but these are a bit one-sided . . . If the world was truly peaceful, there would be no need for soldiers or national defence, but that is not the case, so the army is still a necessary part of the country. Soldiers who can fight are indispensable to the country, and the military's fighting strength is very important.

Like JZ, most participants in both locations stated they had a highly favourable notion of the military and its role. There was one noted exception, however. A vocational school student in Shanghai interviewed in 2017 spoke at length about how his view of the PLA had soured after reading a foreign media report about the military's involvement in the Tiananmen crackdown:

> People used to think that being a soldier was a sacred (*shensheng*) thing, but that's changed. Maybe it's because we have had peace for so long. Now all people see is that being a soldier gives you priority treatment, for example you can jump the queue at the hospital . . .

I also read about the PLA's role in the *Liusi shijian* ['June 4 incident,' a Chinese term referring to the date of the violent crackdown]. I read two versions of what happened that night: An early version published in China and a foreign version. If you want to read the foreign one, you have 'to scale the wall (*fanqiang*)' [A slang term referring to overcoming the government's Internet censorship system, known as the Great Firewall of China]. Anyway, the Chinese version said that the army only killed five people that night, and that these people were rioting. But the foreign report said that nearly a thousand people disappeared, and that the PLA shot the masses. One mother was quoted saying that her son never came back that night . . .

After reading the foreign report, I wondered: is the New China any different than what came before? I can't really tell. We still have to believe in the party and the country, right? In terms of democracy, we are definitely better than North Korea, so we should thank the party. I don't know . . . Anyway, our generation is not that bad. We can still search for alternative information. But the state's brainwashing work (*women guojia xinao de gongzuo*) is getting better and better, so the next generation may know nothing about June 4.

No other informant mentioned the military's involvement in the 1989 crackdown. It is hard to say whether this omission stems from young people's lack of knowledge about the incident or a reluctance to raise the topic considering the Party-state's official position on the issue. While the events of June 4 have captured the attention of the global media and have been widely discussed in academic scholarship outside China (Ibrahim 2016, 585), in mainland Chinese public discourse, the topic remains a political taboo. The party's official narrative has consistently emphasised the riotous nature of the youth-led demonstrations to justify the use of lethal force against civilians, and presented the crackdown as necessary for China's subsequent growth and prosperity. To date, the Chinese leadership has not redressed this characterisation (Chung and Fu 2022, 322). Any attempt to publicly honour the dead on the Chinese mainland has been suppressed by the authorities. While Chinese netizens continue to create commemorative posts on social media during the anniversary period, these attempts are routinely crushed by a censorship system that promptly deletes any related content. Chinese citizens who publicly dare to challenge the official version of the event face dire personal consequences (Chung and Fu 2022, 322).

Several other Shanghai informants, however, voiced criticism of the Party-state's educational and propaganda efforts. When discussing the influence of media and popular culture products on her notions of the military, ZL, a student at an academic high school in Shanghai commented: 'If the media is always controlled by some people, you never know the truth. It is impossible to understand the truth'. LM, an 18-year-old who had attended an elite academic high school in Shanghai, also reflected on the impact of PE and NDE activities:

> It's all just a formality. I don't know, maybe the more you force something down, the more it will stick ... Some students are more willing to play a leading role in these [Patriotic Education] activities because they believe they might benefit from it somehow ... but even some teachers don't attach too much importance to these activities. I have a Chinese teacher who mocks these rituals ... She has read a lot and has formed her own value judgment. It's obvious that she finds these [PE] activities very boring and treats them as nothing more than a performance. There is no way to avoid it altogether because someone will come for her, but I don't know if the person in charge of the inspection work takes it very seriously either ... Anyway, our Chinese teacher just goes through the motions (*fuyan*). She clearly doesn't agree with this in her heart. So, when the Head Teacher tells her to organize a patriotic activity, she just tells us to go and study something on our own (*zixiu*).

The student's candid testimony suggests that he himself did not put much stock in the school's PE and NDE activities. His account could also be read as a criticism of the underlying messages these activities were trying to impart, and of students who either took these messages to heart or pretended to do so to please their teachers. The criticism was nonetheless extremely rare among informants in the study and was only voiced by a minority of students in Shanghai. Indeed, Shanghai students were generally more willing to criticise NDE activities, including the military training course they undertook before their entry into high school. Compared to youths in Henan, Shanghai students grumbled more openly about the physical hardship and poor conditions at their courses. Some also complained about the harshness of army veteran instructors who, according to students' accounts, had insulted the trainees and meted out physical punishments (cited in Naftali, 2021c).

The training courses Shanghai students reported attending appear to have contained 'heavier' military content than those attended by students in Henan. In Shanghai, the courses took place in a secluded, off-school site and included guns. The youths in Henan (all of whom attended boarding schools as is common in China's rural areas where long distances make commuting unrealistic) reported that their course was conducted on campus. Unlike the Shanghai courses, Henan informants did not take part in any training with live ammunition. Despite the Shanghai students' more immersive and 'military-intensive' experience, when asked about the effects of the courses on their notion of the military, they professed indifference and sometimes even resentment toward the programme. The only benefits they saw were social and personal, such as helping them befriend future classmates or training them to become more 'self-disciplined' (see Naftali 2021c).

The view of the social benefits of the military training programme was also shared by students in Henan. Yet for youth in both locations, the weeklong experience did not seem to have played a decisive factor in shaping their motivation to enlist. As the next section will discuss, students' testimonies reveal that their attitudes toward army service were shaped by the views of family members, teachers, and peers rather than their short military training experience, the contents of their textbooks or the images circulating in war- and military-themed media products.

'The PLA Is Great, but I Would Rather Go to University'

Content analysis of students' responses to the question *'Would you be willing to enlist in the military? Why or why not?'* reveals several key findings. First, of the 155 students in the entire sample, only a minority (21 per cent) affirmed a willingness to enlist. A slightly larger share (32 per cent) stated a reluctance to do so, while 12 per cent said they were 'undecided'. The remainder (35 per cent) preferred not to answer the question. Students in this group did not specify a reason for avoiding the topic, but their reluctance could be related to the sensitivity of the question.

A second key finding is that among those who stated their readiness to enlist, the share of informants in Henan, that is, those with a rural background, was higher than those with an urban Shanghai background. While a quarter of all Henan students (both boys and girls) said they would be willing to join the army, only 15 per cent of the Shanghai sample – the majority attending vocational schools – made a similar statement. Among boys, who are legally required to enlist, only about a quarter of students in the entire sample stated their willingness to fulfil their obligation. Here too there was a difference between urban and rural informants, however: a third of boys in Henan compared to a fifth of boys in Shanghai expressed their readiness to join up.

Finally, among Shanghai boys, there was a gap between academic and vocational school students. Thirty per cent of boys in the vocational schools but just 15 per cent of boys in the academic schools were willing to join the military. Among girls, for whom military service is optional, the share of those willing to enlist was much lower than the boys and stood at 14.2 per cent of all girl respondents, most in Henan.

In short, it was mostly Henan informants who asserted a readiness to join the military but students offered more than one rationale for their willingness or reluctance to enlist. In what follows I note the key themes mentioned by students in all three groups (those who were willing to enlist; those who were reluctant; and the undecided).

Common among the reasons for enlisting were 'love for the country' and a 'sense of national duty'. Students also mentioned the contribution of military service to personal development, in either a mental and/or physical sense. Students stated their belief that military service could help them acquire a stronger sense of 'discipline', learn 'perseverance', or allow them to get 'in shape'. For boys, army service was also associated with a desirable masculine ideal though the association between manhood and military service was prevalent among girl respondents as well, including those who professed a desire to join the military. A small number of boys in Henan said that army service could help them secure a good job in the future. LJ, a senior in Henan, described his motivations for wanting to enlist:

> I'm interested in military affairs. I like modern technology and high technology. I like watching all the military parades . . . You could also say that my interest in military issues was influenced by my family. My uncle has served in the army since I was a kid, he joined when I was born . . . I think being in the military can improve your personal qualities and help you maintain good physical fitness . . . I don't mind the discipline. I'll adapt. Being a soldier can help you exercise your will and make your stronger. It can also help you get a job later. You can develop personal connections in the military. A lot of other kids in my school want to enlist because of the so-called *'tie fanwan'* (literally, 'iron rice bowl', a Chinese term for an occupation with guaranteed job security). After I leave the army, I can find a relatively stable job. That's why my family is quite supportive. Doesn't every parent want their children to have a good job?

XM, another senior from Henan, made a similar reference to material considerations when explaining his desire to enlist:

> After all, our starting point in life is relatively low. Our area is considered a national-level impoverished county, so if we want to get more social resources, there are fewer channels compared to kids in places like Shanghai. People here think that if you can work hard and have the ability, being a soldier can be a good way to get somewhere . . . In cities like Shanghai, some students may be afraid of hardship, but we are used to it. I help my family with some farm work. During mid-Autumn festival I help with the harvest.

AJ, another Henan senior also commented on the difference between boys in Henan and Shanghai regarding military service:

> My uncle was in the army. Now he is discharged, and the army has helped him find a job and buy a house . . . My classmates and I want to join the military because it matches what we want in life. It might be different for students in Shanghai though . . . Shanghai's economy is developed, and people there mainly engage in business. So, young people there may be more interested in making money than going to the military.

The responses of Shanghai informants largely confirmed the assumptions of rural youths. Asked to explain why they were reluctant to enlist, Shanghai students mentioned a range of reasons, including the 'strict discipline' and 'lack of freedom' associated with army life; fear of 'loneliness' and 'boredom'; and an unwillingness to serve in 'remote, desolate areas'. Another common reason was the belief that military service would hinder their chances of finding a high-earning job. Boys in Shanghai academic high schools emphasised that because they were singletons, their parents did not want them to join the military but steered them toward higher education in the hope that a university degree would help their only child attain a lucrative career.

JZ, the Shanghai science major at an academic high school cited earlier for stating that the military was 'indispensable for the country', admitted that he himself did not want to join because he was 'an only child', and therefore carried the load of his parents' hopes and expectations. Other informants in Shanghai academic schools offered similar reasons for their reluctance. Military service was not an option they wanted to pursue; they would rather go to university in China or abroad. WJ, an 18-year-old from a Shanghai academic school, said: 'The PLA is really great. I saw a documentary about how the army guards the borders'. The *Wolf Warrior* films also made WJ 'want to join the military', he added, but after he thought about it 'some more', he decided he would rather go to university. Military life is too 'difficult' and 'lonely', and he 'didn't know anyone who wanted to join the military'. After all, he observed, 'our lives are too comfortable to want to enlist. Most of the boys in Shanghai are only children now, they are kind of spoiled.'

Compared to their peers in the academic schools, vocational students in the city were more willing to enlist. More students in vocational schools noted they had family members who served in the military, and some mentioned that their parents encouraged them to consider the option. Overall, however, vocational school students in Shanghai held ambiguous views about military service. As the cost of living in a city like Shanghai was much higher than in Henan, the vocational school informants also mentioned financial concerns and their future mobility aspirations as reasons *not* to enlist.

FT, a Shanghai senior who in 2017 was majoring in electronics and computers at a vocational school in the city, said that while some of his classmates were going to enlist, and he himself had been planning to join them, he eventually changed his mind.

> I don't like army life very much. Being a soldier is too tiring, and I'm not in great shape . . . Also, to be honest, I want different things than people who want to enlist. Maybe it's a shortcoming on my part or maybe my thinking is a bit twisted, but I just want to make money, lots of money . . . Some people say that you can also make money as a soldier, but it's only about 100,000 RMB a year! As soon as I heard this figure, which isn't even enough to buy a good car, I changed my mind about wanting to enlist. I'd rather start my own business.

While FT criticised himself for putting material gains above his duty to the country, he was not alone in voicing such an attitude. Other vocational students in Shanghai raised similar concerns. DQ, an 18-year-old who had migrated to Shanghai from a village in Shandong province at the age of seven, praised PLA soldiers for their willingness to 'sacrifice their life for a noble cause (*sheshengquyi*)', described soldiers as very 'strong' and 'manly (*hen yemen er*)' and said they formed 'deep friendship' with their comrades-in-arms. These reasons initially attracted DQ to the military and he considered enlisting, but both his teacher and his parents had 'talked him out of it'. They had told him 'there are no prospects in joining the military', and that he should continue his studies if he wants to find a lucrative job.

ZX, another 18-year-old student at a Shanghai vocational school mentioned his positive image of soldiers as 'tall, strong men who fight for justice'. However, he himself was not going to enlist:

> Like all boys, I yearn for military life... Those who have experienced the military come out differently. Their personality is different. You become more integrated into the collective. I thought about enlisting, but I can't meet the physical criteria. I'm shortsighted and have flat feet, which means I get very tired if I have to stand for a long time... If the country enters a state of war and they need soldiers, then I would definitely join, but now that we are at peace, I plan to become a technical talent. You can serve the country in more than one way, not only through military service.

Other Shanghai students in both the vocational and academic schools mentioned material considerations as a factor in their unwillingness to enlist. One informant explained: 'I have heard that veterans receive preferential treatment, but I don't want to be a soldier so much because I live in a big city and have a little more education than people in rural areas.'

Indeed, more boys in Henan voiced readiness to enlist compared to the boys in Shanghai but even the Henan respondents were ambivalent about military service, noting that they saw few benefits to their future mobility. As they prepared for their university entrance examination (*gao kao*), higher education appeared a much better choice than military service. As one rural student put it: 'I dream of a job in which I can make money. I want to go to university so I can get out of here'. XZ, a Henan student, elaborated on his conflicted views on military service:

> Sometimes I think I want to join the military, other times I don't. As a regular conscript, the conditions are not very good. You're not allowed to go home for two years, and I don't think I would make such an important contribution anyway... I would rather gain professional knowledge. Anyway, my main ambition is to apply to Tsinghua [one of China's top universities] to study engineering.

FG, another senior in Henan, said:

> I have thought about joining the army and know of a boy in my dorm who has applied, but my family objects . . . They say it's because I am the only boy in my family. My father is also the sole male heir in his family; he only has sisters. My parents are worried about my future and don't want me to enlist. So, I'm going to apply to a technical vocational college instead.

Gender expectations also played a role in students' ambivalent attitudes about military service. ZB, a 17-year-old Henan student explained that he did not want to join the military because he 'liked' his 'freedom too much'. He would rather take the university entrance examination (*gao kao*), 'study abroad, if possible, maybe go to America, or open a business and make money'. However, 'if a war broke out', he would 'definitely enlist, because after all, I'm a man'.

The association between military service and the performance of ideal masculinity was also evident in an interview with YX, a liberal arts major in Henan, who said that he did not want to enlist even though he knew boys are 'supposed to like the military'. He personally did not, and was 'not interested in guns, and the like'.

Female respondents also invoked gender expectation to explain their reluctance to enlist. 'I am a girl. I don't want to be a soldier' and 'few girls do it' were common responses.

Several girls noted that army life is 'too restrictive' and not much 'fun'. They don't 'let you use a mobile phone, and the hairstyle is too uniform'. Those who wanted to enlist noted a conflict between their desire and the predominant femininity ideals. HH, a senior in Henan said: '*Although I'm a girl*, I yearn for military life. The army protects our homes, our country. I would have liked to join the military, but I will not be able to meet the physical criteria. Also, my parents don't really want me to go to the army. They feel it's not suitable for a girl'.

HM, another Henan senior who stated her desire to enlist, explained her motivations and how they conflicted with her family's gendered expectations:

> I don't have any relatives in the military, so if I pass the criteria, I will be the first in my family. There is a boy in my class who wants to enlist. He knows a lot about the army. He told me some famous battle stories . . . My mother is a bit worried, however, because she knows someone whose son is in the military and she heard they have limited vacation time and that military life might be too hard for

a girl. My sister also says that it's a dangerous profession . . . I have read some online posts, and people said that you might be assigned to a remote area when you are a soldier, but I don't mind . . . I want to go into a medical military profession. China was invaded because of its weak national power, so if I go to a military academy to do scientific research, this can help enhance the strength of our country's national defence and protect our people.

Noting that she had wanted to be a soldier since she was a 'child', another 17-year-old from Henan said that she would like to enlist so that she could 'do something for the country', 'temper' herself, and become 'stronger'. Her father was supportive because he thought military service could improve her physical ability, but her mother objected and wanted her to study accounting instead.

The clashing views of this girl's parents demonstrate the tension between the ethos of serving the country and the importance of self-development and social mobility. This crucial tension was evident in the ambivalent attitudes of a considerable number of students of different genders and social backgrounds.

Conclusion

This chapter set out to explore how Han Chinese youths of different genders, locations, and types of schools perceive the PLA and military service. The analysis also considered how these perceptions were shaped by teachers and textbooks, PE and NDE activities, media and popular culture products and the opinions of peers and family members.

The discussion reveals several noteworthy findings. First, the responses of youth participants demonstrated a generally positive image of the PLA's historical and current contribution to the China's strength, stability and prosperity. Young people professed a largely favourable image of PLA soldiers whom they regarded as the embodiment of 'true masculinity' and of admirable qualities such as heroism and selfless devotion to the country.

Students' statements mirrored the messages in their textbooks, PE and NDE activities, news media, and popular media. It's possible that such statements reflected informants' awareness of the 'politically correct response' to questions about the PLA and its functions. Only a very small minority, all in Shanghai, challenged the positive image of the PLA in their responses.

One explanation for this finding is that for young people in Henan – from rural communities symbolically as well as geographically peripheral in China – a patriotic attitude constitutes 'a cultural asset' (Naftali 2021a, 64; for a similar point, see Fong 2007). For young people in Shanghai – one of China's central, globalised metropolises – detachment from the nation can be a sign of social distinction and cultural refinement in line with a coveted 'cosmopolitan' identity (see Henningsen 2012; Farrer 2014; Naftali 2021a).

A second notable finding was that despite the Henan participants' more overt patriotism, neither group was enthusiastic about joining the military. Only a minority of informants and a small share of the boys (who are required to enlist unless given an exemption) expressed a willingness to serve. A considerable share of the informants was either undecided or reluctant. While aversion to military service was observed among youths of different school types, genders, and locations, the analysis showed that this rejectionism was more evident among Shanghai youth, especially those in academic high schools and from higher socio-economic backgrounds.

The relatively small sample size and the focus on Henan and on Shanghai – China's most global city and one which may not be representative of other urban locations in the country – limits the generalizability of this study's findings. But the findings match that of existing scholarship on the conscription challenges of the PLA in contemporary China, which as noted earlier, are similar to those of militaries in capitalist democracies. The analysis in this study demonstrates that army service may be a more attractive option for youths with rural and/or lower socio-economic backgrounds. Enlistment was also a slightly more attractive option to vocational school informants in Shanghai; most vocational school informants in the present study came from a lower socio-economic background than their peers in academic schools.

As noted by other studies (Hansen and Woronov 2013; Pun and Koo 2019), since their schools do not prepare them for the *gao kao*, Chinese students in vocational schools have little prospect of entering a higher education institute. That they are more likely to enter lower-paying professions may explain why they expressed a higher willingness to enlist than students in the city's academic high schools. Overall, however, even vocational school students held at best an ambivalent attitude toward enlistment.

The Henan informants were similarly ambivalent. Though more of them expressed a willingness to enlist than their Shanghai counterparts, Henan youth overall did *not* regard military service as the best option for future socio-economic mobility. Unlike vocational students, the rural students in this study attended academic high schools and believed their best prospects were to pass the *gao kao* and attend university.

A third and final finding of the chapter relates to students' perceptions of the messages they received about the army and military service in school textbooks, PE and NDE activities, news media and military-backed popular culture products. Informants' testimonies indicate that the Party-state's and the military's educational and propaganda efforts have had only partial success in forming youth attitudes toward the military.

The efforts appear to have induced strong support for the military and a generally favourable image of the PLA among youth informants. Official messages may have helped foster patriotic feelings and (a professed) sense of gratitude and esteem towards military soldiers whom informants associated with the attainment of a martial masculinity ideal. And yet, these government and military-backed messages had a limited effect on students' attitudes toward enlistment. Informants' testimonies suggest that the opinions of teachers, family members, and peers – some of whom steered them away from military service – may have played a more crucial role in shaping enlistment motivations. Ultimately, youth views of military service drew on pragmatic calculations of personal cost and benefit rather than on a sense of collective duty or an unfettered admiration for soldierly qualities.

Notes

1. For more information about the study sample, see the book's Introduction.
2. According to recent estimates, the PLA consists of approximately 450,000 officers and civilian cadres, 850,000 Non-Commissioned officers (NCOs), and 700,000 two-year conscripts (Allen et al. 2022, 8; Clay and Blasko 2020).
3. In addition to the Han Chinese majority, the PLA both conscripts and recruits ethnic minorities, who currently constitute 8.5 per cent of the total population. According to census data, the number of ethnic minorities in active service in the PLA has gone up by nearly one-third, from 101,686 to 135,055 between 2010 and 2020 (from 4.4% of personnel to 6.75%) (cited in Allen et. al 2022, 30).
4. In the past several decades, women have constituted approximately 5 per cent or less of the PLA, and until relatively recently, there were only limited positions open to female officers and enlisted personnel. The majority had served in support roles, such as administrative personnel, medical personnel,

communications specialists, and political and propaganda workers, including the PLA's performing arts troupes. Since the mid-1990s, however, some women have taken on various combat roles in the Army, Navy, Air Force, and Rocket Force (Kania 2016).

5. Because a soldier's marriage is regulated by Criminal Law, the divorce rate of PLA couples during a period of service is artificially low. Applications for divorce raised by the wife of a PLA member have to be approved by the military and any behaviour harming a military marriage could be deemed criminal (Lin 2021, 1096).
6. Since the 1980s, there have been several rounds of army demobilisation resulting in substantial numbers of veterans. Between the mid-1980s and mid-1990s, approximately 1.1 million soldiers were either demobilised or repurposed. An additional wave of demobilisation occurred in the late 1990s, when the PLA removed some half a million troops from its ranks. Between 2003 and 2005, 200,000 soldiers were demobilised. The most recent round of demobilisation, which was announced by Xi Jinping during a major speech in 2015, reportedly trimmed another 300,000 uniformed personnel from the PLA (Scobell 2022, 358).
7. As a rule, since the June 1989 Tiananmen crackdown in Beijing, during which nearby units made up primarily of native Beijing residents refused to follow orders to crack down on the local population, the PLA does not allow enlisted personnel to serve near their hometowns (Allen et al. 2022, 31).
8. In 2016, PLA medical experts reportedly found that Chinese infantry recruits 'suffered stress fractures almost twice as frequently as their American counterparts' (cited in The Economist 2023b).
9. It is this law which made comedian Li Haoshi's army-related joke described in the Introduction a potential criminal offence.
10. For an in-depth discussion of the images promoted in these blockbusters, see Chapter 4.
11. As Chapter 2 notes, the essay was omitted from the Chinese curriculum in 2001 due to directives from the Party leadership but was reinstated to the seventh-grade Chinese curriculum in 2021 – after the study's informants already graduated high school.

CONCLUSION

Rethinking the Militarisation of Chinese Youth in the Xi Era

This book set out to explore how the Chinese Party-state presents the tropes of war and the military to the country's youngest citizens, and how these official representations contribute to what could be described as the militarisation of youth and their education in twenty-first century China. Drawing on the notion that militarisation is best understood as a discursive process through which the army's goals and priorities extend into civilian life, the discussion traced the spread of the Chinese military's practices and attitudes into the educational sphere, and considered whether this process has socialised Chinese youth to show unconditional admiration for the military and army service, to regard the world as 'a dangerous place', and to see war-waging as an effective means to address this threat. In this concluding chapter, I address these broader questions and summarise the book's findings, while pointing out potential directions for future research.

The Militarisation of Education in the PRC: Continuity in Change

A key argument of the book is that we are witnessing the growing militarisation of education in contemporary China. However, this trend represents a continuity rather than an entirely new occurrence of the Xi Jinping era. As the historical overview in Chapter 1 makes clear, the introduction of martial pedagogy in modern Chinese education can be traced back to the acute national crisis China suffered after repeated foreign incursions from the mid nineteenth century onwards. Successive military defeats to imperial powers led the country's cultural and political elite to reconceptualise the role of the military in the construction of a modern, strong nation-state, and to recast soldiers (rather than scholar-officials) as ideal role models for the population. At the same time, the introduction of new ideas about nationhood and martial citizenship imported from Europe and Japan from the late nineteenth century onward added to the prioritisation of war education. The militarisation of childhood during this period was further grounded in the rise of a modern conceptualisation of youth, especially boys, as social and political agents rather than as mere appendages to their families.

The militarisation of youth education persisted after the socialist revolution and the establishment of the People's Republic in 1949. For the next twenty years, Chinese education continued to foster a war mentality among students of all ages, though in contrast to earlier periods, this process also applied to girls. The CPC, at least in this area, was keen to advance the principle of gender equality. While a growing militarisation of education was also observed in other countries during the Cold War – on both sides of the political divide – in China, this process reached a peak in the late 1950s and early 1960s when Mao Zedong called upon the entire population, in particular children and youth, to emulate the PLA. Young Chinese responded enthusiastically and during the early years of Cultural Revolution (1966–76) participated in violent conflict against domestic enemies of Mao and the revolution. It was the PLA though, that ultimately suppressed a youth-led rebellion that had become chaotic. Though the army had acted on Mao's orders, the success of the PLA attested to the key role of the military in maintaining the strength and stability of the regime.

The emphasis on war education and the promotion of soldierly models among China's youngest students diminished in the 1980s amid a shift in the CPC's development policy and in China's security environment. But the 1989 youth-led protest movement in Tiananmen, suppressed again by the military on the orders of the CPC leadership, generated a new surge of militarisation in Chinese youth education. Coupled with strategic shifts in China's geopolitical environment after the collapse of the Soviet Union, the protests motivated the government to launch a systematic Patriotic Eduction campaign and to intensify student military training at the college level. Even as the country became more integrated with the global market economy, a process which led to growing socioeconomic disparities and the rise of a new consumer culture especially among the urban population, the Chinese government increased its emphasis on national defence values and fostered patriotic vigilance among youths to address domestic and external challenges to China's social and political stability.

Although the PRC has not taken part in any wide-scale military conflict since 1979, and the CPC has consistently promoted the country's image as a non-aggressive power, the 2000s saw the consolidation and expansion of student military training as part of National Defence Education (NDE). As the analysis in the previous chapters showed, both history curriculum materials and visual media productions created with the backing of the PLA in the 2010s promote the narrative of China's peaceful intentions without categorically sanctioning the use of military force to address international conflict. However, the educational materials reviewed in the book clearly espouse the idea of a 'just' war and promote a notion of war conducive to the development of a modern Chinese national collectivity. They also stress the importance of a strong military for the continued prosperity of the nation.

While this message isn't new in the history of PRC education, the emphasis on the military's role in guarding Chinese citizens' safety both at home and abroad – a key trope in Xi-era blockbuster films such as *Wolf Warrior II* and *Operation Red Sea* – marks a shift in the conceptualisation of the military's mission. This change coincides with China's growing economic interests in different global regions and the transition of the PLA from a force limited to the defence of China's immediate territorial and sovereign interests to a force that could assume a global role. The implementation of an expanded NDE programme in Chinese schools of the 2000s and 2010s facilitates this growing responsibility. It might also help address the PLA's recruitment challenges.

Despite obligatory conscription, the Chinese military has been forced to employ tactics similar to those of military establishments in capitalist democracies. China now uses commercial propaganda products that repackage war and military service as exciting experiences that help youth achieve maturity and personal development. As Chapters 3 and 4 discussed, this marketing effort has been accompanied by an idea of 'martial masculinity'. The circulation of this ideal in academic and media discourse in the Xi Jinping era is meant to address a 'crisis of masculinity' thought to afflict a present generation of young men, a trend cast as a national peril undermining the ability of China's citizenry to fend off external threats. This model of manliness is circulated not only through visual media productions sponsored by the PLA, but also through student military training undertaken as part of NDE, which seek to foster a patriotic spirit and improve the physical, mental, and moral capacities of all youths. As we saw, however, urban boys of the One Child generation are a special target of these interventions. Girls – as well as boys who fail to master the required physcial and/or mental 'soldierly qualities' – are relegated to relatively minor, auxilary roles in the exercise of this 'martial citizenship' ideal.

The roots of this martial ideal stretch back to the early decades of the twentieth century, a time when China was facing numerous external and domestic threats. Unlike the failing court of the late Qing Dynasty, or the ineffectual Chiang Kai-shek regime in the Republican period, or even the Maoist administration in the first decades of socialist rule, the Chinese Party-state now possesses both the *desire* and the *means* to effectively propagate national defence values across all the country's youth. Compared to the 2000s, the Xi Jinping era has also seen the exercise of stricter control over the media and educational spheres, measures which have considerably diminished the space for alternative accounts of the military's past (or present) functions. In this sense then, the evidence presented in the book does indicate that we are witnessing a growing militarisation of youth education in China, one that has leaked from history books, courses and movies into broader society.

This spread is evident in public reactions to the proliferation of military-style methods in educational and care facilities catering to young people. As noted in Chapter 3, Chinese media reports suggest that some urban middle class parents have welcomed these military methods and have even sent their children to commercial 'boot camps' hoping that the experience would teach their offspring discipline and self-management skills, and give their only-child a competitive edge in the education and job markets. Others have embraced military-style interventions as a potential cure for their children's psychological and moral 'deficiencies'. These trends can be viewed as an indication of the successful penetration of the army's logic and techniques into civilian realms that have no direct relation to the military. These sites – which include privately run summer camps and commercial psychiatric clinics for children – arguably exercise disciplinary, bio-political forms of power that seek to produce normative, obedient subjects who can then govern themselves.

And yet, the book's findings demonstrate potential challenges to this process of militarisation. As the discussion in Chapter 3 showed, the universalisation of the state-mandated military training course and the propagation of martial-style therapeutics in educational and care settings over the past two decades has met growing public criticism. Some media and academic writers, as well as netizens, have highlighted the abuses in these programmes or even negated their underlying logic. The criticism derives from shifts in public sensibilities about the nature of childhood and the social and political roles of children. In some cases, the comments also draw on the contradiction between the values military training is supposed to foster, such as discipline and respect for hierarchy, and the stress in China's education system on the importance of individual innovation and creativity, values which the government has promoted in recent decades alongside patriotism and collective duty.

In short, public criticism of the military training programmes suggest that these are controversial issues in China and underscore the tensions between the military ethos and the (neo)liberal elements within contemporary Chinese education. The recurrent reports in the Chinese press and social media about student insubordination during the government-mandated training courses attest to the partial ineffectiveness of these courses to instil military-style values. As I elaborate in the next section, this finding was also corroborated by the data from interviews.

Youth Reactions: Embracing and Challenging the Official Narrative

The interviews with high school students presented in Chapters 5 and 6 suggest that the young subjects of these militarist messages do not necessarily embrace the teachings they receive about war both inside and outside school. Rather than being 'interpellated' into 'the subjectivity of a soldier and the attendant readiness to take life' (MacMillan 2011, 66), informants who undertook compulsory military training courses prior to junior and senior high school generally viewed these courses as inconsequential. They were too short, or a physical nuisance, and at best, an opportunity to make new friends before the beginning of the school year. Students' testimonies suggest that the mandatory training did not necessarily produce an admiration for soldierly qualities or military life. Cynicism towards both was a more common result. At least among the student populations examined in this book, it is doubtful that the mandatory military training courses at the basic education level have achieved their intended effect of producing 'docile' bodies.

The interview data also suggests that informants held complex, non-uniform views about armed conflict. While many informants professed their love for the country and their positive impression of the PLA, these statements did not necessarily translate to an overtly belligerent attitude toward the use of military force in China's international disputes. Rather, youth in both Shanghai and Henan demonstrated their preference for a non-confrontational approach and a circumspect attitude toward the use of military force in addressing China's territorial disputes. When prompted, some young people were able to critically reflect on the messages they received both inside and outside school to form their own judgements of the issue.

A similar picture emerges in regard to youth attitudes about enlistment. As noted throughout the discussion, the Chinese military struggles to enlist well-educated young men, particularly from urban areas. Like military establishments in capitalist democracies, the Party-state and the PLA have responded not only by reforming recruitment policies, but by devising more sophisticated PR methods and strategies, including the sponsoring of commercial military entertainment products to attract and encourage (urban) well-educated youths to join the military. The interview data presented in the book suggests that these latter strategies have not been entirely effective. Most study participants, including boys who are legally obliged to serve, stated that they preferred to enter university and find well-paid jobs. Informants were sceptical about the benefits of army service for their personal development or their social mobility chances.

This position was most evident among Shanghai students attending academic high schools who were also more willing to challenge official narratives about war and the military. As the discussion in Chapter 6 suggests, this attitude is linked to the rise of an individualised, pragmatic ethos among city students. Their reluctance to enlist may also be the product of a cosmopolitan worldview and shifting conceptions of masculinity and military violence among youth in this globalised metropolis.

At the very least, the findings highlight the key role pragmatic calculations play for young people and their families facing a decision to enlist. Although values such as 'love for the country' and 'love for the military' are heavily featured in school textbooks, PE and NDE activities, and in mainstream media and popular culture products that young people are exposed to, material considerations were of primary importance across different backgrounds. Henan boys attending academic high school in a rural, relatively impoverished region also expressed ambivalence about military service, even if more of them stated their willingness to enlist. While drawing on a relatively small sample, this finding notably matches the observations of other studies regarding the sort of demographic the PLA can expect to attract: uneducated youths with few prospects.

Ultimately, the interview data with Chinese high school students of different backgrounds paints a complex picture regarding students' notions of war and the military, and the sources of information which they believe have shaped their ideas. While the type of school, socioeconomic background, and location within the country appear to affect informants' attitudes toward military service and their willingness to criticise the official narrative on war and the military, the analysis did not detect an 'unquestioning admiration of a masculinised military institution', an attitude commonly associated with militarisation (cf. Enloe 2015, 7). Likewise, informants' views on the use of armed force in China's territorial disputes cannot be easily subsumed to restrictive binaries of 'militaristic/anti-militaristic' or 'nationalist/internationalist' attitudes.

Study Limitations and Future Research Directions

The sample size examined in the present study does not allow for causal claims about the effects of schooling, military training courses, or the PLA's increasingly sophisticated propaganda work on the attitudes of Chinese youth of different backgrounds. Subsequent studies could explore this issue in a larger sample while employing quantitative analysis to tease out the relative importance of each variable in shaping the views of young people about war and the military. Future studies should also consider additional factors that may shape ideas of war and the military beyond the school curriculum.

As students' testimonies in the study suggest, such factors may include but are not limited to messages on social media or in alternative popular culture products, including those originating outside mainland China that students are able to access by bypassing the government censorship system. They may also include the views and behaviours of individual schoolteachers. The evaluation of teachers may further require participant-observation within and outside the classroom to appreciate how teachers and school staff engage with the contents of textbooks and the dictates of official guidelines in their day-to-day practices, and the extent to which teachers' performance of their duties shapes the views and practice of students.

The attitudes of family members are another key issue mentioned by informants in the study. Future research could explore this issue by interviewing students' relatives. Such an inquiry should also consider the importance of residence in a particular region in shaping the attitudes of youth and their families. Beyond factors such as economic development and interactions with the world, regional histories in China, including the extent to which an area was under Japanese occupation during the 1930s and 1940s or witnessed intense fighting during the Chinese Civil War can play a role in shaping the notions of youth and their families toward armed conflict. Residence in a region with a traditionally high conscription rate in China according to informants' testimonies or other forms of public data may also be an influential factor in shaping youth information sources on military service and their motivation to enlist.

As noted in the introductory chapter, due to political limitations, the present study focused on the views of youth from the Han majority. Future studies may want to expand the inquiry to consider how students of different ethnicities in China engage with the messages of the PE campaign and the NDE programme to form their notion of war and the military, and how these engagements interact with students' sense of belonging to a 'national Chinese collective', and/or their geographically and symbolically marginalised position within the country.

The data presented in the study draws on interviews conducted with youth in 2013, and 2017–19. Several months after the completion of the last round of interviews, the COVID-19 epidemic broke out in Wuhan, China. The resulting pandemic has been catastrophic, causing over 100 million infections, millions of deaths, and trillions of dollars of economic loss. There have been serious disputes between Beijing and the rest of the world, notably the United States and Australia, over the origin of the virus, the responsibility for controlling its initial spread, and China's contributions to contain the epidemic both at domestic and international levels. National leaders in the United States and Brazil, in particular, have overtly blamed China for causing the coronavirus crisis (Ho 2022). This development – together with the heightening tension around the Taiwan issue – may have shifted Chinese youths' views on war and the military. Future research should address this issue. Longitudinal-type studies could also seek to capture whether and how notions of war and the military change as youths of different social backgrounds come of age, and reveal the extent to which exposure to messages about war and the military during adolescence influence the attitudes of the post-2000s generation later in life.

More recently, the outbreak of the Russo-Ukraine war in 2022 also highlighted the tensions between the Party-state's sometimes ambiguous militarised messaging and the response of citizens. The Chinese government sided with Russia diplomatically yet refused to send the country weapons. Several days after the invasion began, a few lone activists could be spotted in Chinese cities with banners calling for peace in Ukraine, according to photos shared on social media. Among them was a 24-year-old Chinese university student who brought a banner that read 'Bullets have no turning back, but you can put down your guns' to a crowded shopping district in the eastern city of Hangzhou. The student was taken to a police station but after his release, continued his vigil for several hours at a quieter spot. According to a media report, the student received sympathetic reactions from passers-by. He was again summoned by the police and warned that he was 'disturbing the public order', but the media quotes the student as saying that he planned 'to carry on the activism' (Zhou 2022).

The limitations of the present study notwithstanding, the data presented in this book suggests that at the very least, we should be 'energetically wary of simplistic descriptions and facile explanations' (cf. Enloe 2015, 7) when evaluating the nature of militarisation processes in an authoritarian political context such as China. The interview data presented in the book prompts us to think in more complex ways about resisting war and militarisation, specifically by 'moving away from such binaries of military/civilian, co-option/subversion, and militarisation/demilitarisation' (Basham and Bulmer 2017, 67). Rather than looking for indications of an 'anti-war' movement of the sort found in democratic countries – apart from the occasional lone protestor – or assuming that the absence of this kind of movement and the proliferation of hyper-nationalistic messages on China's tightly controlled Internet implies that youth are becoming more 'militarised', we should examine how young Chinese creatively engage with the messages they receive within and outside the school to form their own judgements of war and the military.

REFERENCES

Abajian, Suzie M. 2016. 'Documenting Militarism: Challenges of Researching Highly Contested Practices within Urban Schools'. *Anthropology & Education Quarterly* 47, no. 1 (March): 25–41. https://doi.org:10.1111/aeq.12133

Abebe, Tatek, Anandini Dar, and Ida M. Lyså. 2022. 'Southern Theories and Decolonial Childhood Studies'. *Childhood* 29, no. 3 (July): 255–75. https://doi.org/10.1177/09075682221111690

Allen, Kenneth W., Thomas Corbett, Taylor A. Lee, and Ma Xiu. 2022. 'Personnel of the People's Liberation Army'. Report prepared for the U.S.-China Economic and Security Review Commission by BluePath Labs, 3 November 2022. https://www.uscc.gov/sites/default/files/2022-11/Personnel_Peoples_Liberation_Army.pdf

Amar, Paul. 2018. '"Thank you, Godfather": Love and Rejuvenation, Mercenaries and Biomedicine Forge Africa and China into One Family in Wolf Warrior II'. In *Wolf Warrior II: The Rise of China and Gender/Sexual Politics*, edited by Petrus Liu and Lisa Rofel. Columbus, Ohio: MCLC Resource Center, The Ohio State University. http://u.osu.edu/mclc/online-series/liu-rofel/

Anagnost, Ann. 1997. 'Children and National Transcendence in China'. In *Constructing China: The Interaction of Culture and Economics*, edited by Kenneth G. Lieberthal, Lin, Shuen-fu and Ernest P. Young, 195–222. Ann Arbor: Center for Chinese Studies, The University of Michigan Press.

Anderson, Benedict. 2006 [1983]. *Imagined Communities: Reflections on the Origin and Spread of Nationalism*. Revised edition. London: Verso.

Bailey, Beth. 2007. 'The Army in the Marketplace: Recruiting an All-Volunteer Force'. *Journal of American History* 94, no. 1 (June): 47–74. https://doi.org/10.2307/25094776

Bandow, Doug. 2020. 'Xi Jinping Doubles Down on Korean War Propaganda'. *Foreign Policy*, 18 November 2020. https://foreignpolicy.com/2020/11/18/xi-jinping-korean-war-propaganda-chinese-intervention-nationalism/

Bandurski, David. 2022. 'Honoring China's Heroes'. *China Media Project*, 10 May 2022. https://chinamediaproject.org/2022/05/10/honoring-chinas-heroes./

Bao, Hongwei. 2019. 'Performing Gender in Chinese Cinema.' In *Routledge Handbook of East Asian Gender Studies*, edited by Jieyu Liu and Junko Yamashita, 285–300. London: Routledge.

Bao, Limin. 2009. '"Huai" haizi huoshi huai jiaoyu?' ['"Bad" kids or bad education?']. *Zhongguo qingnian bao [China Youth Daily]*, 2 September 2009.

Barrett, Martyn D. 2007. *Children's Knowledge, Beliefs and Feelings about Nations and National Groups*. New York: Psychology Press.

Basham, Victoria M. 2011. 'Kids with Guns: Militarization, Masculinities, Moral Panic, and (Dis)Orgnanized Violence'. In *The Militarization of Childhood*, edited by J. Marshall Beier, 175–93. NYC: Palgrave Macmillan.

Basham, Victoria M. 2013. *War, Identity and the Liberal State*. London: Routledge.

Basham, Victoria M. 2015. 'Waiting for War: Soldiering, Temporality and the Gendered Politics of Boredom and Joy in Military Spaces'. In *Emotions, Politics, and War*, edited by Linda Åhäll and Thomas Gregory, 128–40. London: Routledge.

Basham, Victoria M. 2016. 'Raising an Army: The Geopolitics of Militarizing the Lives of Working-Class Boys in an Age of Austerity'. *International Political Sociology* 10, no. 3 (September): 258–74. https://doi.org/10.1093/ips/olw013

Basham, Victoria M., and Sarah Bulmer. 2017. 'Critical Military Studies as Method: An Approach to Studying Gender and the Military'. In *The Palgrave International Handbook of Gender and the Military*, edited by R. Woodward, C. Duncanson, 59–71. London: Palgrave Macmillan.

Bax, Trent. 2014. 'Internet Addiction in China: The Battle for the Hearts and Minds of Youth'. *Deviant Behavior* 35, no. 9 (May): 687–702. https://doi.org/10.1080/01639625.2013.878576

Bax, Trent. 2016. '"Internet Gaming Disorder" in China: Biomedical Sickness or Sociological Badness?' *Games and Culture* 11, no. 3 (January): 233–55. https://doi.org/10.1177/1555412014568188

Beier, Marshall J. 2011. 'Introduction: Everyday Zones of Militarization'. In *The Militarization of Childhood: Thinking beyond the Global South*, edited by Marshall J. Beier, 1–11. New York: Palgrave Macmillan.

Beier, Marshall, and Jana Tabak. 2020. 'Children, Childhoods, and Everyday Militarisms'. *Childhood* 27, no. 3 (July): 281–93. https://doi.org/10.1177/0907568220923902

Beijing Youth Daily [Beijing qingnian bao]. 2018. 'Jinri sheping: Bingqi "niang pao" zhi feng jianshe yanggang shehui' ['Editorial: Abandon the "niang pao" trend and build a masculine society']. *Beijing qingnian bao [Beijing Youth Daily]*, 8 September 2018. https://www.chinanews.com.cn/m/sh/2018/09-08/8621771.shtml

Bellino, Michelle J. 2017. *Youth in Postwar Guatemala: Education and Civic Identity in Transition*. New Brunswick: Rutgers University Press.

Berlowitz, Marvin J., and Nathan A. Long. 2011 [2003]. 'The Proliferation of JROTC: Educational Reform or Militarization'. In *Education as Enforcement: The Militarization and Corporatization of Schools*, edited by Kenneth J. Saltman and David A. Gabbard, 181–91. NYC: Routledge.

Billig, Michael. 1995. *Banal Nationalism*. London: Sage.

Blair, Elizabeth E., Rebecca B. Miller, and Mara Casey Tieken. 2009. 'Editors' Introduction'. In *Education and War*, edited by Elizabeth E. Blair, Rebecca B. Miller, and Mara Casey Tieken, 1–6. Cambridge: Harvard Educational Review.

Blanchette, Jude. 2022. 'The Edge of an Abyss: Xi Jinping's Overall National Security Outlook'. *China Leadership Monitor*, 1 September 2022, 1–11. https://www.prcleader.org/post/the-edge-of-an-abyss-xi-jinping-s-overall-national-security-outlook

Blasko, Dennis J. 2007. 'People's War in the Twenty-First Century: The Militia and the Reserves'. In *Civil-Military Relations in Today's China: Swimming in a New Sea*, edited by David M. Finkelstein, and Kristen Gunness, 270–303. Armonk, NY: Routledge.

Blasko, Dennis J. 2012. *The Chinese Army Today: Tradition and Transformation for the 21st Century*. London: Routledge.

Boyatzis, Richard E. 1998. *Transforming Qualitative Information: Thematic Analysis and Code Development*. Thousand Oaks, CA: Sage.

Boyd, Alexander. 2022. 'Luo Changping Sentenced as Party Warns of "Historical Nihilism".' *China Digital Times.* 6 May 2022. https://chinadigitaltimes.net/2022/05/luo-changping-sentenced-as-party-warns-of-historical-nihilism/.

Boyd, Alexander. 2023. 'Word(S) of the Week: $2 Million Army Joke "Forge Exemplary Conduct, Fight to Win".' *China Digital Times.* 18 May 2023. https://web.archive.org/web/20230516204103/

Brady, Ann-Marie. 2008. *Marketing Dictatorship: Propaganda and Thought Work in Contemporary China.* Plymouth: Rowman & Littlefield Publishers.

Brzycki, Melissa. 2019. 'Revolutionary Successors: Deviant Children and Youth in the PRC, 1959–1964'. In *Children's Voices from the Past,* edited by Kristine Moruzi, Nell Musgrove, and Carla Pascoe Leahy, 285–304. Cham, Switzerland: Palgrave Macmillan.

Büttner, Clemens. 2023. 'The National Protection War and the Intellectual Foundations of Chinese Warlordism'. *Modern China* 49, no. 6 (April): 679–708. https://doi.org/10.1177/00977004231153331

Cai, Rong. 2018. 'Screening War in Contemporary China: The Case of The Assembly'. *Journal of Contemporary China* 27, no. 113 (April): 780–93. https://doi.org/10.1080/10670564.2018.1458064

Cai, Yiping. 2018. 'New Superheroes Have Arrived: Made in China, for Domestic Consumption Only'. In *Wolf Warrior II: The Rise of China and Gender/Sexual Politics,* edited by Petrus Liu and Lisa Rofel. Columbus, Ohio: MCLC Resource Center, The Ohio State University. http://u.osu.edu/mclc/online-series/liu-rofel/

Callahan, William A. 2010. *China: The Pessoptimist Nation.* Oxford: Oxford University Press.

Callahan, William A. 2017. 'Dreaming as a Critical Discourse of National Belonging: China Dream, American Dream and World Dream'. *Nations and Nationalism* 23, no. 2 (March): 248–70. https://doi.org/10.1111/nana.12296

Carlson, Marie, and Tuba Kanci. 2017. 'The Nationalised and Gendered Citizen in a Global World: Examples from Textbooks, Policy and Steering Documents in Turkey and Sweden'. *Gender and Education* 29, no. 3 (February): 313–31. https://doi.org/10.1080/09540253.2016.1143917

Chan, Anita. 1985. *Children of Mao:Personality Development and Political Activism in the Red Guard Generation.* London: Macmillan.

Chan, Wai-keung. 2007. 'Contending Memories of the Nation: History Education in Wartime China, 1937–1945'. In *The Politics of Historical Production in Late Qing and Republican China*, edited by Tze-ki Hon Hon and Robert Culp, 169–210 Leiden: Brill.

Chang, Vincent K. L. 2021. 'Recalling Victory, Recounting Greatness: Second World War Remembrance in Xi Jinping's China'. *The China Quarterly* 248, no. 1 (June): 1152–73. https://doi: 10.1017/S0305741021000497

Chang, Vincent K. L. 2022. 'Exemplifying National Unity and Victory in Local State Museums: Chongqing and the New Paradigm of World War II Memory in China'. *Journal of Contemporary China* 31, no. 138 (January): 977–92. https://doi.org/10.1080/10670564.2022.2031004

Charmaz, Kathy. 2008. 'Constructionism and the Grounded Theory Method'. In *Handbook of Constructionist Research*, edited by James A. Holstein and Jaber F. Gubrium, 397–412. London: Guilford Press.

Chase, Michael, Jeffrey Engstrom, Tai Ming Cheung, Kristen A. Gunness, Scott Warren Harold, Susan Puska, and Samuel K. Berkowitz. 2015. 'Weaknesses in People's Liberation Army Organization and Human Capital'. In *China's Incomplete Military Transformation: Assessing the Weaknesses of the People's Liberation Army (PLA)*, 43–68, RAND Corporation.

Che, Chang, and Olivia Wang. 2023. 'No Joke: China Fines a Comedy Firm $2 Million for "Insulting" the Military'. *The New York Times*, 17 May 2023. https://www.nytimes.com/2023/05/17/world/asia/china-comedy-2-million-fine.html

Chen, Jian. 1996. *China's Road to the Korean War*. New York: Columbia University Press.

Chen, Jingkun. 1989. 'Minguo shiqi de xuesheng junxun' ['Student Military Training during the Republic of China']. *Guofang [National Defense]* 5: 31–2.

Chen, Longchang, and Jingru Hu. 2017. 'Zhuoyan sheng junqu xitong zhineng renwu goujian xuesheng junshi xunlian xin geju' ['Focusing on the Functional Tasks of the Provincial Military Region to Build a New Pattern of Military Training for Students']. *Guofang [National Defense]* 12: 64–8.

Chen, Minjie. 2016. *The Sino-Japanese War and Youth Literature: Friends and Foes on the Battlefield*. London: Routledge.

Chen, Qin, and Guangcheng Song. 2016. 'Woguo xuexiao junxun de bainian huimou yu tiyu xiaoneng' ['A Review of Sports Performance and School Military Training in the Past Century']. *Wuhan Tiyu Xueyuan Xuebao [Journal of Wuhan Institute of Physical Education]* 50, no. 1: 21–6.

Chen, Rou-Lan. 2020. 'Trends in Economic Inequality and Its Impact on Chinese Nationalism'. *Journal of Contemporary China* 29, no. 121 (May): 75–91. https://doi.org/10.1080/10670564.2019.1621531

Chen, Tina Mai. 2001. 'Dressing for the Party: Clothing, Citizenship, and Gender-formation in Mao's China'. *Fashion Theory* 5, no. 2 (April): 143–71. https://doi.org/10.2752/136270401779108590

Chen, Yigong. 2019. 'Guofang daxue jiaoshou wei "Zhenzheng nanzihan" dian zan, liyou shi . . . [National Defense University Professor Likes "Takes a Real Man" Because . . .]'. *China Military Network*, 23 January 2019. http://www.xinhuanet.com/mil/2019-01/23/c_1210038956.htm

Chen, Yunfang, and Jianquan Zhang. 2023. 'Xin shidai shaoxiandui guofang jiaoyu de tansuo yu Shijian [Exploration and Practice of Young Pioneers' National Defense Education in the New Era]'. Shaoxiandui huodong [Young Pioneers Activities] 9: 18–19.

Cheney, Kristen E. 2005. '"Our Children Have Only Known War": Children's Experiences and the Uses of Childhood in Northern Uganda'. *Children's Geographies* 3, no. 1 (January): 23–45. https://doi.org/10.1080/14733280500037133

Cheng, Sijin. 2007. 'The Challenge of Conscription in an Era of Social Change'. In *Civil-Military Relations in Today's China: Swimming in a New Sea*, edited by David M. Finkelstein, and Kristen Gunness, 235–54. Armonk, NY: Routledge.

Cheng, Yanlong. 1998. 'Qian tan gaoxiao xuesheng junxun zhong de sixiang zhengzhi gongzuo' ['On the Ideological and Political Work in the Military Training of College Students']. *Suzhou sichou gong xueyuan xue bao [Journal of Suzhou Institute of Silk Textile Technology]* 18, no. 4: 100–1.

Cheung, Tai Ming. 2011. 'Engineering Human Souls: The Development of Chinese Military Journalism and the Emerging Defense Media Market'. In *Changing Media, Changing China*, edited by Susan L. Shirk, 128–49. Oxford: Oxford University Press.

Chew, Ming-Tak, and Yi Wang. 2021. 'How Propagames Work as a Part of Digital Authoritarianism: An Analysis of a Popular Chinese Propagame'. *Media, Culture & Society*, 43, no. 8 (November): 1431–1448. https://doi.org/10.1177/01634437211029846

Chicharro-Saito, Gladys. 2008. 'Physical Education and Embodiment of Morality in Primary Schools of the People's Republic of China'. *China Perspectives* 1 (January): 29–39. https://doi.org/10.4000/chinaperspectives.3273

Chin, Sei Jeong. 2023. 'The Korean War, Anti-US Propaganda, and the Marginalization of Dissent in China, 1950–1953'. *Twentieth-Century China* 48, no. 1 (January): 23–47. https://doi.org/10.1353/tcc.2023.0002

China Daily. 2019. 'Chinese Military to Open Online Enlisting Service'. *China Daily*. 9 January 2019. https://www.xinhuanet.com/english/2019-01/09/c_137730915.htm

Chongqing University. 1987. 'Zai junxun zhong nuli tigao xuesheng de sixiang juewu' ['Make an effort to improve students' ideological awareness in military training']. *Zhongguo gaodeng jiaoyu [Higher Education in China]* 5: 34–5.

Chu, Stephen Yiu-Wai. 2022. *Main Melody Films: Hong Kong Directors in Mainland China.* Edinburgh: Edinburgh University Press.

Chu, Yin. 2014. 'Bu ying yi guli shijian fouding junxun zhidu de heli xing' ('The Rationality of the Military Training System Should Not Be Denied Based on Isolated Incidents'). *Zhongguo qingnian bao* (*China Youth Daily*). 27 August, 1. https://zqb.cyol.com/html/2014-08/27/nw.D110000zgqnb_20140827_6-01.htm

Chubb, Andrew. 2014. *Exploring China's 'Maritime Consciousness': Public Opinion on the South and East China Sea Disputes.* Crawley: Perth USAsia Centre Report. https://perthusasia.edu.au/getattachment/fdba7508-e152-46b8-b770-a0aa34f27559/2014_Exploring_Chinas_Maritime_Consciousness_Final.pdf

Chung, Regina Wai-man, and King-wa Fu. 2022. 'Tweets and Memories: Chinese Censors Come after Me: Forbidden Voices of the 1989 Tiananmen Square Massacre on Sina Weibo, 2012–2018'. *Journal of Contemporary China* 31, no. 134 (June): 319–34. https://doi.org/10.1080/10670564.2021.1945742

Clay, Marcus, and Dennis J. Blasko. 2020. 'People Win Wars: The PLA Enlisted Force, and Other Related Matters'. *War on the Rocks*, 31 July 2020. https://warontherocks.com/2020/07/people-win-wars-the-pla-enlisted-force-and-other-related-matters./

Cliff, Roger. 2015. *China's Military Power: Assessing Current and Future Capabilities.* Cambridge: Cambridge University Press.

Cockain, Alex. 2012. *Young Chinese in Urban China.* London: Routledge.

Connell, R. W. 1987. *Gender and Power.* Sydney, Australia: Allen and Unwin.

Connell, R. W, and James W. Messerschmidt. 2005. 'Hegemonic Masculinity: Rethinking the Concept'. *Gender and Society* 19, no. 6 (December): 829–56. https://doi.org/10.1177/0891243205278639

Cook, Sharon Anne. 2008. 'Give Peace a Chance: The Diminution of Peace Education in Global Education in the United States, United Kingdom, and Canada'. *Canadian Journal of Education* 31, no. 4: 889–913. http://www.jstor.org/stable/20466733

Corbett, John F. Jr., Edward C. O'Dowd, and David D. Chen. 2008. 'Building the Fighting Strength: PLA Officer Accession, Education, Training, and Utilization'. In *The 'People' in the PLA: Recruitment, Training, and Education in China's Military*, edited by Roy Kamphausen, Andrew Scobell and Travis Tanner, 139–90. Strategic Studies Institute, US Army.

Costigan, Johanna M. 2022. 'China's War on History is Growing'. *Foreign Policy*, 23 September 2022. https://foreignpolicy.com/2022/09/23/china-historical-nihilism-li-jiaqi-ccp/

Coutaz, Gregory. 2019. 'Image-Building as Impetus for the Growth of the People's Liberation Army (PLA)'s Engagement in International Humanitarian Assistance and Disaster Relief (HA/DR) Operations' *European Journal of East Asian Studies* 18, no. 1 (July): 36–65. https://doi.org/10.1163/15700615-01801006

Covell, Katherine. 1996. 'National and Gender Differences in Adolescents' War Attitudes'. *International Journal of Behavioral Development* 19, no. 4 (December): 871–83. https://doi.org/10.1177/016502549601900411

Crowe, Lori A. 2011. 'Superheroes or Super-Soliders? The Militarization of our Modern-Day Heroes'. In *The Militarization of Childhood: Thinking beyond the Global South*, edited by Marshall J. Beier, 111–32. New York: Palgrave Macmillan.

CSIS. 2023. 'What Does China Really Spend on Its Military?' China Power Project. Washington DC: Center for Strategic and International Studies (CSIS). https://chinapower.csis.org/military-spending/

Culp, Robert. 2006. 'Rethinking Governmentality: Training, Cultivation, and Cultural Citizenship in Nationalist China'. *Journal of Asian Studies* 65, no. 3 (March): 529–54. https://doi.org/10.1017/S0021911806001124

Culp, Robert. 2007. *Articulating Citizenship: Civic Education and Student Politics in Southeastern China, 1912–1940*. Cambridge: Harvard University Press.

Dai, Jinhua. 1995. 'Invisible Women: Contemporary Chinese Cinema and Women's Film'. *Positions* 3, no. 1 (February): 255–80. https://doi.org/10.1215/10679847-3-1-255

Dauncey, Sarah. 2017. 'Gentlemen, Heroes, Real Men, Disabled Men: Explorations at the Intersections of Disability and Masculinity in Contemporary China'. *Nan Nü* 19, no. 2 (January): 357–84. https://doi.org/10.1163/15685268-00192P05

David, Kyle E. 2018. 'The Poster Child of the "Second" Cultural Revolution: Huang Shuai and Shifts in Age Consciousness, 1973–1979'. *Modern China* 44, no. 5 (January): 497–524. https://doi.org/10.1177/0097700417753354

Davies, Lynn. 2005. 'Schools and War: Urgent Agendas for Comparative and International Education'. *Compare: A Journal of Comparative and International Education* 35, no. 4 (August): 357–71. https://doi.org/10.1080/03057920500331561

Davis, Becky. 2014. 'Violence at Chinese High School Raises Questions about Mandatory Military Training'. *New York Times*, 28 August 2014. https://archive.nytimes.com/sinosphere.blogs.nytimes.com/2014/08/28/chinese-high-schoolers-harsh-military-training-leads-to-internet-firestorm/

de Giorgi, Laura. 2014. 'Little Friends at War: Childhood in the Chinese Anti-Japanese War Propaganda Magazine Kangzhan Ertong (The Resistance Child)'. *Oriens Extremus* 53: 61–84. https://www.jstor.org/stable/26372424

Deng, Xiaoqing. 2021. 'Lüse junying, rexue shaonian: shiqianju feng yingdi junshi zhuti yanxue ying' ['Green Barracks, Hot-blooded Youth: Military Theme Research Camp at Jufeng Camp in Shiqian']. *Xin kecheng dao xue [New Curriculum Guidance]* 24: 13–16.

Denton, Kirk A. 2007. 'Horror and Atrocity: Memory of Japanese Imperialism in Chinese Museums'. In *Re-envisioning the Chinese Revolution: The Politics and Poetics of Collective Memories in Reform China*, edited by Ching Kwan Lee and Guobin Yang, 245–286. Stanford: Stanford University Press; Washington DC: Woodrow Wilson Center Press.

Denton, Kirk. 2014. *Exhibiting the Past: Historical Memory and the Politics of Museums in Postsocialist China*. Honolulu: University of Hawaii Press.

Der Derian, James. 2009 [2001]. *Virtuous War: Mapping the Military-Industrial-Media-Entertainment Network*. 2nd edition. NYC: Routledge.

Diamant, Neil J. 2008. 'Veterans, Organization, and the Politics of Martial Citizenship in China'. *Journal of East Asian Studies* 8, no. 1 (March): 119–58. https://doi.org/10.1017/S1598240800005117

Diamant, Neil J. 2010. *Embattled Glory: Veterans, Military Families, and the Politics of Patriotism in China, 1949–2007*. Lanham: Rowman & Littlefield Publishers.

Diamant, Neil, and Kevin O'Brien. 2015. 'Veterans' Political Activism in China'. *Modern China* 41, no. 3 (May): 278–312. https://doi.org/10.1177/0097700414533631

Dikötter, Frank. 1995. *Sex, Culture and Modernity in China*. Hong Kong: Hong Kong University Press.

Dreyer, June Teufel. 1982. 'The Chinese Militia: Citizen-Soldiers and Civil-Military Relations in the People's Republic of China'. *Armed Forces and Society* 9, no. 1 (Fall): 63–82. https://doi.org/10.1177/0095327X820090010

Drinhausen, Katja, and Helena Legarda. 2022. '"Comprehensive National Security" Unleashed: How Xi's Approach Shapes China's Policies at Home and Abroad'. *MERICS China Monitor*, 15 September 2022. Berlin: Mercator Institute for China Studies (MERICS). https://www.merics.org/en/report/comprehensive-national-security-unleashed-how-xis-approach-shapes-chinas-policies-home-and

Du, Xinyu, and Qi'an Chen. 2021. 'China Wants to Mitigate Male "Feminization" with More Gym Class'. *Sixth Tone*, 29 January 2021. https://www.sixthtone.com/news/1006779

Edwards, Louise. 2010. 'Transformations of the Woman Warrior Hua Mulan: From Defender of the Family to Servant of the State'. *Nan Nü* 12, no. 2 (January): 175–214. https://doi.org/10.1163/156852610X545840

Edwards, Louise. 2016. *Women Warriors and Wartime Spies of China*. Cambridge: Cambridge University Press.

Edwards, Louise, and Lili Zhou. 2011. 'Gender and the "Virtue of Violence": Creating a New Vision of Political Engagement through the 1911 Revolution'. *Frontiers of History in China* 6, no. 4 (December): 485–504. https://doi.org/10.1007/s11462-011-0138-8

Ehs, Tamara. 2013. 'Steeling the Body for War in Austrofacist Education'. In *War and the Body: Militarisation, Practice and Experience*, edited by Kevin McSorley, 51–61. New York: Routledge.

Enloe, Cynthia. 1983. *Does Khaki Become You? The Militarization of Women's Lives*. London: Pluto Press.

Enloe, Cynthia. 1990. *Bananas, Beaches, and Bases*. Berkeley, CA: University of California Press.

Enloe, Cynthia. 2000. *Maneuvers: The International Politics of Militarizing Women's Lives.* Berkeley, CA: University of California Press.

Enloe, Cynthia. 2004. *The Curious Feminist: Searching for Women in a New Age of Empire.* Berkeley, CA: University of California Press.

Enloe, Cynthia. 2007. *Globalization and Militarism: Feminists Make the Link.* Lanham, MD: Rowman and Littlefield.

Enloe, Cynthia. 2015. 'The Recruiter and the Sceptic: A Critical Feminist Approach to Military Studies'. *Critical Military Studies* 1, no. 1 (October): 3–10. https://doi.org/10.1080/23337486.2014.961746

Evans, Harriet. 2008. 'Sexed Bodies, Sexualized Identities, and the Limits of Gender'. *China Information* 22, no. 2 (July): 361–86. https://doi.org/10.1177/0920203X08091550

Evans, Harriet. 2021. '"Patchy Patriarchy" and the Shifting Fortunes of the CCP's Promise of Gender Equality since 1921'. *The China Quarterly* 248, no. S1 (August): 95–115. https://doi.org/10.1017/S0305741021000709

Fairbrother, Gregory P. 2003. *Toward Critical Patriotism: Students' Resistance to Political Education in Hong Kong and China.* Hong Kong: Hong Kong University Press.

Fang, Zhun. 1951. 'Cheng Yong zhuo tewu' ['Chen Yong Catches a Spy']. *Xiao pengyou [Little Friends]*, 25 June 1951, 4–5.

Farquhar, Mary Ann. 1999. *Children's Literature in China.* Armonk: M. E. Sharpe.

Farrer, James. 2014. 'Foreigner Street: Urban Citizenship in Multicultural Shanghai'. In *Multicultural Challenges and Redefining Identity in East Asia*, edited by Nam-kook Kim, 17–44. London: Ashgate.

Fiala, Andrew. 2018. 'Pacifism'. *The Stanford Encyclopedia of Philosophy*, edited by Edward N. Zalta. Stanford: Stanford University Press. https://plato.stanford.edu/archives/fall2018/entries/pacifism/

Finnane, Antonia. 2008. *Changing Clothes in China: Fashion, History, Nation.* New York: Columbia University Press.

Fish, Eric. 2015. *China's Millennials: The New Generation.* Lanham: Rowman & Littlefield.

Flath, James, and Norman Smith. 2011. 'Introduction'. In *Beyond Suffering: Recounting War in Modern China*, edited by Norman Smith and James A. Flath, 1–10. Vancouver: University of British Columbia Press.

Fong, Sau-yi. 2022. 'Militarization as Personal Cultivation: Student Military Training in Guomindang China, 1927–1937'.

Modern China 49, no. 4 (December): 480–514. https://doi.org/10.1177/00977004221134211

Fong, Vanessa L. 2004. 'Filial Nationalism among Chinese Teenagers with Global Identities'. *American Ethnologist* 31, no. 4 (November): 631–48. https://doi.org/10.1525/ae.2004.31.4.631

Fong, Vanessa L. 2007. 'Morality, Cosmopolitanism, or Academic Attainment? Discourses on "Quality" and Urban Chinese-Only-Children's Claims to Ideal Personhood'. *City & Society* 19, no. 1 (June): 86–113. https://doi.org/10.1525/city.2007.19.1.86

Foster, Stuart, and Jason Nicholls. 2005. 'America in World War II: An Analysis of History Textbooks from England, Japan, Sweden, and the United States'. *Journal of Curriculum and Supervision* 20, no. 3 (Spring): 214–33.

Foucault, Michel. 1974[1970]. *The Order of Things: An Archaelogy of the Human Sciences.* London: Tavistock. Publications.

Foucault, Michel. 1977. *Discipline and Punish.* London: Penguin.

Foucault, Michel. 1978. *The History of Sexuality, Vol. 1, An Introduction.* Translated by Robert Hurley. New York: Random House.

Foucault, Michel. 1982. *The Archaeology of Knowledge and the Discourse on Languages.* Translated by A. M. Sheridan Smith. New York: Pantheon Books.

Foucault, Michel. 2008. *The Birth of Biopolitics: Lectures at the Collège de France, 1978–79*, edited by M. Senellart, translated by Graham Burchell. Basingstoke: Palgrave Macmillan.

Frühstück, Sabine. 2007. *Uneasy Warriors: Gender, Memory, and Popular Culture in the Japanese Army.* Berkeley: University of California Press.

Frühstück, Sabine. 2017. *Playing War: Children and the Paradoxes of Modern Militarism in Japan.* Oakland, CA: University of California Press.

Frühstück, Sabine. 2020. 'Protect Someone, Become Yourself: How the Japanese Military Reinvents Childhood for the 21st Century'. *Childhood* 3, no. 27 (May): 399–412. https://doi.org/10.1177/0907568220908632

Fu, Jun. 2018. 'Chinese Youth Performing Identities and Navigating Belonging Online'. *Journal of Youth Studies* 21, no. 2: 129–143. https://doi.org/10.1080/13676261.2017.1355444

Fu, Yan, and Fan Yang. 2018. 'Xuesheng yu jiaoyuan zhengzhi bei kongzhi shi zhixi siwang' ['Student Suffocated to Death in Dispute with Teacher']. *Beijing qingnian bao [Beijing Youth Daily]*, 19 April 2018.

Galaviz, Brian, *et al*. 2011. 'The Militarization and the Privatization of Public Schools'. *Berkeley Review of Education* 2, no. 1: 27–45. http://dx.doi.org/10.5070/B82110029

Gao, James Z. 2001. 'War Culture, Nationalism, and Political Campaigns, 1950–1953'. In *Chinese Nationalism in Perspective: Historical and Recent Cases*, edited by C. X. George Wei and Xiaoyuan Liu, 179–203. London: Greenwood Press.

Gao, Jie, and Kenneth Allen. 2023. 'PLA Officer Cadet Recruitment: Part 1'. China Brief 23, no. 21 (November): 5–14. https://jamestown.org/program/pla-officer-cadet-recruitment-part-1/

Ge, Quan.1987. 'Dui gaodeng xuexiao xuesheng junxun de jidian kanfa' ['Views on Military Training of Students in Colleges and Universities']. *Shanghai gaojiao yanjiu [Shanghai Higher Education Research]* 94, no. 4: 66–7.

Genevaz, Juliette. 2019. 'Defense Education in Chinese Universities: Drilling Elite Youth'. *Journal of Contemporary China* 28, no. 117 (November): 453–67. https://doi.org/10.1080/10670564.2018.1542224

Gerth, Carl. 2020 [2003]. *China Made*. Leiden, The Netherlands: Brill; Harvard University Asia Center.

Gibson, Ian. 2011. 'Flowers in the Cracks: War, Peace and Japan's Education System'. *Journal of Peace Education* 8, no. 2 (July): 101–26. https://doi.org/10.1080/17400201.2011.589249

Giroux, Henry A. 2004. 'War on Terror: The Militarising of Public Space and Culture in the United States'. *Third Text* 18, no. 4 (May): 211–21. https://doi.org/10.1080/0952882042000229827

Gittings, John. 1964. 'China's Militia'. *The China Quarterly* 18 (June): 100–17. https://doi.org/10.1017/S0305741000041904

Global Times. 2022. 'Chinese Minors' Addiction to Online Games Has Been Largely Solved: Industry Study'. 24 November 2022. https://www.globaltimes.cn/page/202211/1280323.shtml

Gor, Haggith. 2010. 'Education for War in Israel: Preparing Children to Accept War as a Natural Factor of Life'. In *Education as Enforcement: The Militarization and Corporatization of Schools*, edited by Kenneth J. Saltman and David A. Gabbard, 175–84. New York: RoutledgeFalmer.

Green, Colin. 2011. 'Turning Bad Iron into Polished Steel: Whampoa and the Rehabilitation of the Chinese Soldier'. In *Beyond Suffering : Recounting War in Modern China*, edited by Norman Smith and James A. Flath, 153–85. Vancouver: University of British Columbia Press.

Greenhalgh, Susan. 2012. 'Patriarchal Demographics? China's Sex Ratio Reconsidered'. *Population and Development Review* 38, no. 1 (February): 130–49. https://doi.org/10.1111/j.1728-4457.2013.00556.x

Gries, Peter Hays. 2004. *China's New Nationalism: Pride, Politics and Diplomacy*. Berkeley, CA: University of California Press.

Gries, Peter. 2020. 'Nationalism, Social Influences, and Chinese Foreign Policy'. In *China and the World*, edited by David Shambaugh, 63–84. Oxford: Oxford University Press.

Guan, Tianru, and Tingting Hu. 2021. 'Re-Narrating Non-Intervention Policy in China's Military-Action Genre Films'. *Journal of Contemporary China* 30, no. 131 (March: 841–54. https://doi.org/10.1080/10670564.2021.1884963

Guo, Hongmin. 2015. 'Dangnian naxie gujun yuanzheng de "wawa bing"' ['The "Child Soldiers" Who Went on an Expedition on Their Own']. *Yunnan dang'an [Yunnan Archives]* 8: 27–30.

Guojia guangbo dianshi zongjiu [State Administration of Radio and Television]. 2021. 'Guojia guangbo dianshi zongju bangong ting guanyu jinyibu jiaqiang wenyi jiemu ji qi renyuan guanli de tongzhi, guangdian ban fa [2021] 267 hao' ['Notice of the General Office of the State Administration of Radio and Television on Further Strengthening the Management of Literary and Artistic Programs and their Personnel, Radio, Film and Television (2021) No. 267']. September 2. http://www.nrta.gov.cn/art/2021/9/2/art_113_57756.html

Han, Meijia. 2013. 'Junxun dui gaozhongsheng zili yishi yu yingdui fangshi yinxiang de yanjiu' ['Research on the Effects of Military Training on Senior High School Students' Self-Reliance Consciousness and Coping Styles']. *Zhongguo Xiaoyi [Chinese Journal of School Doctors]* 27, no. 8: 578–83.

Han, Woori, Claire Shinhea Lee, and Ji Hoon Park. 2017. 'Gendering the Authenticity of the Military Experience: Male Audience Responses to the Korean Reality Show Real Men'. *Media, Culture & Society* 39, no. 1 (October): 62–76. https://doi.org/10.1177/0163443716673895

Hansen, Mette Halskov. 2013. 'Learning Individualism: Hesse, Confucius, and Pep-Rallies in a Chinese Rural High School'. *The China Quarterly* 213 (February): 60–77. https://doi.org/10.1017/S0305741013000015

Hansen, Mette Halskov. 2015. *Educating the Chinese Individual: Life in a Rural Boarding School*. Seattle: University of Washington Press.

Hansen, Mette Halskov, and T. E. Woronov. 2013. 'Demanding and Resisting Vocational Education: A Comparative Study of Schools in Rural and Urban China'. *Comparative Education* 49, no. 2 (December): 242–59. https://doi.org/10.1080/03050068.2012.733848

Hao, Xiaoyang. 2020. 'What Is Criminal and What Is Not: Prosecuting Wartime Japanese Sex Crimes in the People's Republic of China'. *The China Quarterly* 242 (June): 529–549. https://doi.org/10.1017/S0305741019001085

Harris, Ian. 2002. 'Challenges for Peace Educators at the Beginning of the 21st Century'. *Social Alternatives* 21, no. 1 (January): 28–31.

Hass, Ryan. 2022. 'From Strategic Reassurance to Running Over Roadblocks: A Review of Xi Jinping's Foreign Policy Record'. *China Leadership Monitor*, 1 September 2022, 1–15. https://www.prcleader.org/post/from-strategic-reassurance-to-running-over-roadblocks-a-review-of-xi-jinping-s-foreign-policy-recor

He, Dongchang. 1985. 'Xuesheng junshi xunlian shi shishi bingyifa de yi xiang yansu gongzuo' ['Military Training of Students Is a Serious Task in the Implementation of the Military Service Law']. *Renmin jiaoyu [People's Education]* 9: 5.

He, Yi. 1952. 'Zhongguo de ertong geng duo geng hao de duwu' ['Give Children in New China More Books of Better Quality']. *Renmin ribao [People's Daily]* 2 June: 3.

He, Yinan. 2007. 'History, Chinese Nationalism and the Emerging Sino–Japanese Conflict'. *Journal of Contemporary China* 16, no. 50 (February): 1–24. https://doi.org/10.1080/10670560601026710

Heilmann, Sebastian. 2017. *China's Political System*. Lanham: Rowman & Littlefield.

Hein, Laura, and Mark Selden. 2000. 'The Lessons of War, Global Power, and Social Change'. In *Censoring History: Citizenship and Memory in Japan, Germany, and the United States*, edited by Laura Hein and Mark Selden, 3–50. Armonk, NY: ME Sharpe.

Hemment, Julie. 2015. *Youth Politics in Putin's Russia: Producing Patriots and Entrepreneurs*. Bloomington: Indiana University Press.

Henningsen, Lena. 2012. 'Individualism for the Masses? Coffee Consumption and the Chinese Middle Class' Search for Authenticity'. *Inter-Asia Cultural Studies* 13, no. 3 (June): 408–427. https://doi.org/10.1080/14649373.2012.689709

Higate Paul, and John Hopton. 2005. 'War, Militarism, and Masculinities'. In *Handbook of Studies on Men and Masculinities*, edited by Michael S. Kimmel, Jeff Hearn and Robert W. Connell, 432–47. Thousand Oaks: Sage.

Hill, Malcolm. 2010. 'Ethical Considerations in Researching Children's Experiences'. In *Researching Children's Experience*, edited by Sheila Greene and Diane Hogan, 61–86. London: Sage.

Hird, Derek. 2019. 'Masculinities in China'. In *Routledge Handbook of East Asian Gender Studies*, edited by Jieyu Liu and Junko Yamashita, 350–66. London: Routledge.

Hirono, Miwa. 2019. 'China and Peacekeeping'. *Oxford Bibliographies*. https://doi.org/10.1093/OBO/9780199920082-0168

Ho, Wing-Chung. 2022. 'The Surge of Nationalist Sentiment among Chinese Youth during the COVID-19 Pandemic'. *China: An International Journal* 20, no. 4 (November): 1–22. https://doi.org/10.1353/chn.2022.0032

Honig, Emily. 2002. 'Maoist Mappings of Gender: Reassessing the Red Guards'. In *Chinese Femininities, Chinese Masculinities: A Reader*, edited by Susan Brownell and Jeffrey N. Wasserstrom, 255–68. Berkeley, CA: University of California Press.

Hong, Xiaoyin. 2019. 'Chongshang yingxiong, laoji fendou' ['Advocate Heroes, Remember Struggle']. *Nanfang wang [Southern Network]*, 12 November 2019.

Hope, Arran. 2023. 'MSS WeChat Sets the Tone for the National Security State.' *China Brief* 23, no. 17: 2–4. https://jamestown.org/program/mss-wechat-sets-the-tone-for-the-national-security-state/

Hughes, Christopher R. 2017. 'Militarism and the China Model: The Case of National Defense Education'. *Journal of Contemporary China* 26, no. 103 (September): 54–67. https://doi.org/10.1080/10670564.2016.1206280

Hundman, Eric. 2023. 'Fearing Hardships and Fatigue? Refusals to Serve in China's Military, 2009–2018'. *Journal of Contemporary China* 31, no. 142: 559–85. https://doi.org/10.1080/10670564.2022.2109797

Ibrahim, Yasmin. 2016. 'Tank Man, Media Memory and Yellow Duck Patrol: Remembering Tiananmen on Social Media'. *Digital Journalism* 4, no. 5 (July): 582–96. https://doi.org/10.1080/21670811.2015.1063076

Information Office of the State Council of the People's Republic of China. 2011. 'China's Peaceful Development'. 6 September 2011. http://www.china.org.cn/government/whitepaper/node_7126562.htm

Jackson, Isabella, and Siyi Du. 2022. 'The Impact of History Textbooks on Young Chinese People's Understanding of the Past: A Social Media Analysis'. *Journal of Current Chinese Affairs* 51, no. 2 (August): 194–218. https://doi.org/10.1177/18681026221105525

Jiang, Delong, Guoping Tang, Tingting Li, Hongying Wu, and Jian Li. 2010. 'Woguo xuexiao junxun yu xuexiao tiyu fazhan xianzhuang yanjiu' ['Research on Development Condition of School Military Training and Physical Education in China (sic)']. *Tiyu keji wenxian tongbao [Bulletin of Sport Science and Technology]* 18, no. 5 (May): 28–31.

Jiang, Haofeng. 2022. 'Zenyang rang xuesheng aishang junxun?' ['How to Make Students Love Military Training']. *Xinmin Zhoukan [Xinmin Weekly]*, 11 August 2022. https://m.xinminweekly.com.cn/content/4466.html

Jiao, Lin. 2022. 'Reconciling Femininities and Female Masculinities: Women's Premarital Experiences of Breast-Binding in the Maoist Era'. *Modern China* 48, no. 2 (February): 321–52. https://doi.org/10.1177/0097700421992314

Jin, Tao. 2018. 'Honghai xingdong' zui congming zhi chu, shi meiyou chengwei 'Zhan lang 3' [The Smartest Thing about 'Operation Red Sea' Is That It Didn't Become 'Wolf Warrior 3']. *Wenhui bao (Wenhui daily)*. 25 February 2018.

Joffe, Ellis. 2008. 'Shaping China's Next Generation of Military Leaders: For What Kind of Army'. In *The 'People' in the PLA: Recruitment, Training, and Education in China's Military*, edited by Roy Kamphausen, Andrew Scobell and Travis Tanner, 353–88. Carlisle, PA: US Army War College, The Strategic Studies Institute.

Johnson, David, Jennifer D. P. Moroney, Roger Cliff, M. Wade Markel, Laurence Smallman and Michael Spirtas. 2009. *Preparing and Training for the Full Spectrum of Military Challenges: Insights from the Experiences of China, France, the United Kingdom, India, and Israel*. RAND Corporation.

Johnston, Alastair Iain. 2017. 'Is Chinese Nationalism Rising? Evidence from Beijing'. *International Security* 41, no. 3 (Winter): 7–43. https://doi.org/10.1162/ISEC_a_00265

Jones, Alisa.. 2005. 'Changing the Past to Serve the Present: History Education in Mainland China'. In *History Education and National Identity in East Asia*, edited by Edward Vickers and Alisa Jones, 65–100. London: Routledge.

Jones, Andrew. 2002. 'The Child as History in Republican China: A Discourse on Development'. *Positions* 10, no. 3 (Winter): 695–727 muse.jhu.edu/article/37043

Judge, Joan. 2002. 'Citizens or Mothers of Citizens? Gender and the Meaning of Modern Chinese Citizenship'. In *Citizenship in Modern China*, edited by Elizabeth Perry and Merle Goldman, 23–43. Cambridge: Harvard University Press.

Kang, Fashun, and Jun Wang. 2021. '2021 nian quanmin guofang jiaoyu wan ying jihua: yong dianying jiangshu guofang gushi' ['National Defense Education 10,000 Screening Program: Telling National Defense Stories through Film']. *People's Liberation Army Daily [Jiefangjun bao]*, 13 November 2021. http://www.mod.gov.cn/gfbw/gfjy_index/zyhd/4898815.html

Kania, Elsa. 2016. 'Holding Up Half the Sky? (Part 1)—The Evolution of Women's Roles in the PLA'. *China Brief* 16, no. 15, 4 October 2016. https://jamestown.org/program/holding-half-sky-part-1-evolution-womens-roles-pla/

Kao, Ying-Chao. 2017. 'Weapons of the Weak Soldiers: Military Masculinity and Embodied Resistance in Taiwanese Conscription'. In *East Asian Men: Masculinity, Sexuality, and Desire*, edited by Xiaodong Lin, Chris Haywood and Mairtin Mac an Ghaill, 199–218. London: Palgrave Macmillan.

Kauffman, Andrew. 2020. 'Imagining the New Socialist Child: The Cultural Afterlife of the Child Martyr Wang Erxiao'. *Cross-Currents: East Asian History and Culture Review* 9, no. 1 (May): 269–96. https://doi.org/10.1353/ach.2020.0006

Keane, Michael, and Joy Danjing Zhang. 2017. 'Where Are We Going? Parent–Child Television Reality Programmes in China'. *Media, Culture & Society* 39, no.5 (August): 630–43. https://doi.org/10.1177/0163443716663641

Kelly, Catriona. 2007. *Children's World: Growing Up in Russia 1890–1991*. New Haven: Yale University Press.

Kipnis, Andrew. 2007. '*Suzhi*: A Keyword Approach'. *The China Quarterly* 186 (July): 295–313. https://doi.org/10.1017/S0305741006000166

Langager, Mark. 2009. 'Elements of War and Peace in History Education in the US and Japan: A Case Study Comparison'. *Journal of Peace Education* 6, no. 1 (February):119–136. https://doi.org/10.1080/17400200802677985

Lanza, Fabio. 2012. 'Springtime and Morning Suns: "Youth" as a Political Category in Twentieth-Century China'. *Journal of the History of Childhood and Youth* 5, no. 1 (Winter): 31–51. https://doi.org/10.1353/hcy.2012.0014

Lässig, Simone. 2013. 'Introduction Part 1: Post-Conflict Reconciliation and Joint History Textbook Projects'. In *History Education* and *Post-Conflict Reconciliation: Reconsidering Joint Textbook Projects*, edited by Karina V. Korostelina and Simone Lässig, 1–18. New York: Routledge.

Law, Wing-Wah. 2011. *Citizenship and Citizenship Education in a Global Age: Politics, Policies, and Practices in China.* New York, NY: Peter Lang.

Lee, Haiyan. 2011. 'The Charisma of Power and the Military Sublime in Tiananmen Square'. *The Journal of Asian Studies* 70, no. 2 (June): 397–427. https://doi.org/10.1017/S0021911811000040

Li, Chunling. 2021. *China's Youth.* Washington, DC: Brookings Institution Press.

Li, Huaxi. 2022. 'Nongjia xiao yuan hua zhenbing' ['Conscription in the Small Farmyard']. *Zhongguo qingnian bao [China Youth Daily]*, 10 August 2022. https://edu.youth.cn/wzlb/202208/t20220810_13908337.htm

Li, Jian. 1994. 'Gaoxiao guofang jiaoyu shi zujin xuesheng quanmian fazhan de youxiao tujing' ['National Defense Education in Colleges and Universities Is an Effective Way to Promote Students' All-Round Development']. *Hebei shifan daxue xuebao (shehui kexue ban) [Journal of Hebei Normal University (Social Science Edition)]* S1: 17–18.

Li, Nan. 2020. *Civil-Military Relations in Post-Deng China: From Symbiosis to Quasi-Institutionalization.* Singapore: Palgrave Macmillan.

Li, Nan. 2022. 'The People's Liberation Army as a Party Army'. In *CPC Futures: The New Era of Socialism with Chinese Characteristics*, edited by Frank N. Pieke and Bert Hofman, 95–101. Singapore: National University of Singapore University Press.

Li, Wei, Hong Li, and Hua Yan. 2009. 'Qian xi dangqian junxun gongzuo cunzai wenti de genben yuanyin' ['Analysis of the Basic Cause of the Problems in Current Military Training']. *Gaoxiao Luntan [Higher Education Forum]* 9: 17–18.

Li, Weike. 2011. 'International Wars in Chinese Secondary School History Textbook, 1931–1951'. In *History Textbooks and the Wars in Asia: Divided Memories*, edited by Gi-Wook Shin and Daniel C. Sneider, 140–52. New York: Routledge.

Li, Xuan, and William Jankowiak. 2016. 'The Chinese Father: Masculinity, Conjugal Love, and Parental Involvement'. In *Changing Chinese Masculinities: From Imperial Pillars of State to Global Real Men*, edited by Kam Louie, 186–203. Hong Kong: Hong Kong University Press.

Lian, Hongping. 2014. 'The Post-1980s Generation in China: Exploring Its Theoretical Underpinning'. *Journal of Youth Studies*

17, no. 7 (January): 965–81. https://doi.org/10.1080/13676261.2013.878786
Liang, Shumei. 2020. 'Idol-Style War Drama Suspended amid Criticism for Misleading Young Audiences'. *Global Times*. 16 November 2020. https://www.globaltimes.cn/content/1207015.shtml
Liboriussen, Bjarke and Paul Martin. 2020. 'Honour of Kings as Chinese Popular Heritage: Contesting Authorized History in a Mobile Game'. *China Information* 34, no. 3 (March): 319–41. https://doi.org/10.1177/0920203X20908120
Lim, Darren J. 2019. 'Chinese Economic Coercion during the THAAD Dispute'. 28 December 2019. https://theasanforum.org/chinese-economic-coercion-during-the-thaad-dispute/#5
Lin, Jacqueline Zhenru. 2021. 'Remembering Forgotten Heroes and the Idealisation of True Love: Veteran Memorial Activism in Contemporary China'. *Memory Studies* 14, no. 5 (May): 1081–105. https://doi.org/10.1177/17506980211017952
Lin, Liza. 2020. 'Xi's China Crafts Campaign to Boost Youth Patriotism: Slick Videos on Social Media with a Nationalistic Message Are Notching Millions of Views'. *Wall Street Journal*, 30 December 2020. https://www.wsj.com/articles/xi-china-campaign-youth-patriotism-propaganda-11609343255
Lin, Xiaodong, and Mairtin Mac an Ghaill. 2019. 'Shifting Discourses from Boy Preference to Boy Crisis: Educating Boys and Nation Building in Neoliberal China'. *Discourse: Studies in the Cultural Politics of Education* 40, no. 3 (April): 281–93. https://doi.org/10.1080/01596306.2017.1312284
Lin, Xiaoyi. 2023. 'Spotlight on PLA Test Pilots, "Born To Fly" Sets Standard for Chinese Air Combat Films'. *Global Times*, 27 April 2023. https://www.globaltimes.cn/page/202304/1289891.shtml
Ling, Minhua. 2017. 'Returning to No Home: Educational Remigration and Displacement in Rural China'. *Anthropological Quarterly* 90, no. 3 (Summer): 715–42. https://doi.org/10.1353/anq.2017.0041
Liu, Adam, and Xiaojun Li. 2023. 'Assessing Public Support for (Non-)Peaceful Unification with Taiwan: Evidence from a Nationwide Survey in China'. *Journal of Contemporary China*, published online first (May): 1–13. https://doi.org/10.1080/10670564.2023.2209524
Liu, Baochang. 2005. 'Gaoxiao junxun gongzuo xianzhuang ji duice tanxi' ['Analysis of the Current Situation and Countermeasures

of Military Training in College']. *Weifang jiaoyu xueyuan xuebao [Journal of Weifang Educational College]* 18, no. 4: 5, 46–7.

Liu, Fengshu. 2008. 'Constructing the Autonomous Middle-Class Self in Today's China: The Case of Young-Adult Only-Children University Students'. *Journal of Youth Studies* 11, no. 2 (April): 193–212. https://doi.org/10.1080/13676260701800746

Liu, Fengshu. 2012. '"Politically Indifferent" Nationalists? Chinese Youth Negotiating Political Identity in the Internet Age'. *European Journal of Cultural Studies* 15, no. 1 (February): 53–69. https://doi.org/10.1177/1367549411424950

Liu, Fengshu. 2014. 'From Degendering to (Re)gendering the Self: Chinese Youth Negotiating Modern Womanhood'. *Gender and Education* 26, no. 1 (November): 18–34. https://doi.org/10.1080/09540253.2013.860432

Liu, Fengshu. 2018. 'Chinese Young Men's Construction of Exemplary Masculinity: The Hegemony of Chenggong'. *Men and Masculinities* 22, no. 2 (March): 294–316. https://doi.org/10.1177/1097184X17696911

Liu, Fengshu. 2019. 'Chinese Young Men's Construction of Exemplary Masculinity: The Hegemony of Chenggong'. Men and Masculinities 22, no. 2 (June): 294–316. https://doi.org/10.1177/1097184X17696911

Liu, Fengshu. 2020. *Modernization as Lived Experiences: Three Generations of Young Men and Women in China*. London: Routledge.

Liu, Fushui. 1987. 'Xuesheng junxun yao yi guofang jiaoyu zhongdian' ['Military Training for Students Should Focus on National Defense Education']. *Zhongguo bingmin [Chinese Militia]* 12: 18.

Liu, Jieyu. 2006. 'Researching Chinese Women's Lives: "Insider" Research and Life History Interviewing'. *Oral History* 34, no. 1 (Spring): 43–52. https://www.jstor.org/stable/40179843

Liu, Jieyu. 2022. 'Childhood in Urban China: A Three-Generation Portrait'. *Current Sociology* 70, no. 4 (April): 598–617. https://doi.org/10.1177/0011392120985861

Liu, Jieyu. 2023. 'Filial Piety, Love or Money? Foundation of Old-Age Support in Urban China'. *Journal of Aging Studies* 64 (March): 1–12. https://doi.org/10.1016/j.jaging.2023.101104

Liu, Min, and Wei Zhuang. 2010. 'Daxuesheng wangluo cheng yin yanjiu xianzhuang ji jiejue duice' ['Research Status and Countermeasures of Internet Addiction in College Students']. *Jiaoshu yu ren: gaojiao luntan [Teaching and Educating People: Higher Education Forum]* 12, no. 4: 102–4.

Liu, Petrus. 2018. 'Women and Children First: Jingoism, Ambivalence, and Crisis of Masculinity in Wolf Warrior II'. In *Wolf Warrior II: The Rise of China and Gender/Sexual Politics*, edited by Petrus Liu and Lisa Rofel. Columbus, Ohio: MCLC Resource Center, The Ohio State University. http://u.osu.edu/mclc/online-series/liu-rofel/

Liu, Petrus, and Lisa Rofel. 2018. 'Introduction'. In *Wolf Warrior II: The Rise of China and Gender/Sexual Politics*, edited by Petrus Liu and Lisa Rofel. Columbus, Ohio: MCLC Resource Center, The Ohio State University. http://u.osu.edu/mclc/online-series/liu-rofel/

Liu, Qiusheng. 2005. 'Jiaqiang gaoxiao guofang jiaoyu de ji dian sikao' ['Reflections on Strengthening National Defense Education in Colleges and Universities']. *Guangxi Daxue Xuebao [Journal of Guangxi University]* 3, no. 27: 99–101.

Liu, Xiulin, and Guoduo Huan. 2013. 'Songshan kengdao da baopo de lishi zhenxiang' ['The Historical Truth of the Songshan Tunnel Blasting']. *Guizhou Literature and History Series* 2: 50–2.

Lo, Joe Tin-yau. 2007. 'Nationalism and Globalism in the Junior Secondary History Curricula of Hong Kong and Shanghai'. *Compare: A Journal of Comparative and International Education* 37, no. 1 (January): 37–51. https://doi.org/10.1080/03057920601061745

Lomsky-Feder, Edna. 2011. 'Competing Models of Nationalism: An Analysis of Memorial Ceremonies in Schools'. *Nations and Nationalism* 17, no. 3 (May): 581–603. https://doi.org/10.1111/j.1469-8129.2011.00492.x

Louie, Kam. 2002. *Theorising Chinese Masculinity*. Cambridge: Cambridge University Press.

Louie, Kam, and Louise Edwards. 1994. 'Chinese Masculinity: Theorizing Wen and Wu'. *East Asian History* 8 (Decemebr): 135–48.

Lu, Gaofeng. 2006. 'Xuesheng junxun neng fou gaobie yeman caolian' ['Can Students Say Goodbye to Barbaric Drills in Military Training']. *Jichu jiaoyu [Basic Education]* 8: 40.

Lu, Hongling, and Shuzhen Tan. 2011. 'Lun putong gaodeng xuexiao junxun zhong de hexie guanli' ['On Harmonious Management of Military Training in Colleges and Universities']. *Zhongguo waijiao jiaoyu [Extramural Education in China]* 3: 41–2.

Lu, Hua. 2005. 'Mao Zedong guofang jiaoyu sixiang yu di ci xuesheng junxun gongzuo gaochao' ['Mao Zedong's Thinking about National Defense Education and the First Climax of Students' Military Training']. *Nanjing hangkong hangtian daxue (shehui kexue ban) [Journal of Nanjing University of Aeronautics &Astronautics (Social Sciences)]* 7, no. 1: 10–14.

Lu, Sheldon H. 2004. 'Beautiful Violence: War, Peace, Globalization'. *Positions* 12, no. 3 (Winter): 759–71. muse.jhu.edu/article/175599

Luo, Ji. 2014. 'Junxun, rencai peiyang de zhanlüe jucuo' ['Military Training: Strategic Measures for Personnel Training']. *Jiefang ribao [Liberation Army Daily]*, 11 September 2014.

Lutz, Catherine. 2009. 'The Military Normal: Feeling at Home with Counterinsurgency in the United States'. In *The Counter-Counterinsurgency Manual*, edited by Network of Concerned Anthropologists. Chicago: Prickly Paradigm Press.

Lutz, Catherine. 2018. 'Militarization'. In *The International Encyclopedia of Anthropology*, edited by Hilary Callan, 318–31. Wiley Online Library.

Lyu, Zhaojin, and Haiyan Zhou. 2023. 'Contesting Master Narratives: Renderings of National History by Mainland China and Taiwan'. *The China Quarterly* 255 (February): 768–84. https://doi.org/10.1017/S030574102300019X

Ma, Weijun. 2014. 'Chinese Main Melody TV Drama: Hollywoodization and Ideological Persuasion'. *Television & New Media* 15, no. 6 (January): 523–37. https://doi.org/10.1177/1527476412471436

Ma, Zhenqing, and Xiu Li. 2015. 'Zhong xiaoxue guojia anquan yishi jiaoyu de wenti yu duice' ['The Problems and Countermeasures of National Security Awareness Education in Primary and Secondary Schools']. *Zhongguo deyu [Chinese Moral Education]* 4: 23–7.

Maartens, Brendan. 2021. 'Narratives of Service, Sacrifice, and Security: Reflecting on the Legacy of Military Recruitmenr'. In *Propaganda and Public Relations in Military Recruitment: Promoting Military Service in the Twentieth and Twenty-First Centuries*, edited by Brendan Maartens and Thomas Bivins, 209–22. London and New York: Routledge.

MacFarquhar, Roderick, and Michael Schoenhals. 2006. *Mao's Last Revolution*. Cambridge, MA: Harvard University Press.

Macmillan, Lorraine. 2011. 'Militarized Children and Sovereign Power'. In *The Militarization of Childhood: Thinking beyond the Global South*, edited by J. Marshall Beier, 61–76. New York: Palgrave Macmillan.

Mao, Tse-tung. [1961] 1936. 'Problems of Strategy in China's Revolutionary War'. In *Selected Works of Mao Zedong*. Peking: Foreign Languages Press.

Martin, Peter. 2021. *China's Civilian Army: The Making of Wolf Warrior Diplomacy*. New York: Oxford University Press.

Martin, Roberta. 1975. 'The Socialization of Children in China and Taiwan: An Analysis of Elementary School Textbooks'. *The China Quarterly* 62 (February): 242–62. https://doi.org/10.1017/S0305741000007013

Masuda, Hajimu. 2016. *Cold War Crucible: The Korean Conflict and the Postwar World*. Cambridge, MA: Harvard University Press.

Mazzocco, Ilaria, and Scott Kennedy. 2022. 'Public Opinion in China: A Liberal Silent Majority?' CSIS Report, February 9, 2022. https://www.csis.org/features/public-opinion-china-liberal-silent-majority

McSorley, Kevin. 2013. 'War and the Body'. In *War and the Body: Militarisation, Practice and Experience*, edited by Kevin McSorley, 1–31. London: Routledge.

McSorley, Kevin. 2016. 'Doing Military Fitness: Physical Culture, Civilian Leisure, and Militarism.' *Critical Military Studies* 2, nos. 1–2 (February): 103–19. https://doi.org/10.1080/23337486.2016.1148292

Meyskens, Covell F. 2020. *Mao's Third Front: The Militarization of Cold War China*. Cambridge: Cambridge University Press.

Miao, Song, and Wen-cui Song. 2021. 'Zheng ticai tuhua duwu de xushi bijiao ji dui dangdai ertong jiaoyu de sikao' ['Narrative Comparison of War-Themed Picture Books and a Reflection on Contemporary Children's Education']. *Shandong qingnian zhengzhi xueyuan xuebao [Journal of Shandong Youth University of Political Science]* 37, no. S1: 61–5.

Ministry of Education of the PRC. 2008. 'Zhong xiaoxue jiaoshi zhiye daode guifan' ['Code of Professional Ethics for Primary and Secondary School Teachers']. *Ministry of Education of the PRC*. 1 September 2008. http://www.moe.gov.cn/srcsite/A10/s7002/200809/t20080901_145824.html

Ministry of Education of the PRC. 2016. 'Zhonggong jiaoyu bu dangzu guanyu jiaoyu xitong shenru kaizhan aiguo zhuyi jiaoyu de shishi yijian' ('Opinions of the CPC Party Group of the Ministry of Education on Strengthening and Improving the Implementation of Patriotic Education in the Education System'), January 26, 2016. http://www.moe.gov.cn/srcsite/A13/s7061/201601/t20160129_229131.html

Ministry of Education of the PRC. 2020 [2017]. *Putong gaozhong lishi kecheng biaozhun [Regular High School History Curriculum Standards]*. Beijing: Renmin jiaoyu chuban she [People's Education Press].

Mitter, Rana. 2020. *China's Good War: How World War II Is Shaping a New Nationalism*. Cambridge, MA: Harvard University Press.

Montgomery, Ken. 2006. 'Racialized Hegemony and Nationalist Mythologies: Representations of War And Peace in High School History Textbooks, 1945–2005'. *Journal of Peace Education* 3, no. 1 (August): 19–37. https://doi.org:10.1080/17400200500532094

Moore, Gregory J., and Christopher B. Primiano. 2020. 'Audience Costs and China's South China Sea Policy'. *Journal of Asian Security and International Affairs* 7, no. 3 (November): 325–48. https://doi.org/10.1177/2347797020962635

Morris, Andrew. 2000. '"To Make the Four Hundred Million Move": The Late Qing Dynasty Origins of Modern Chinese Sport and Physical Culture'. *Comparative Studies in Society and History* 42, no. 4 (December): 876–906. https://doi.org/10.1017/S0010417500003340

Müller, Gotelind. 2011. 'Teaching "the Others' History" in Chinese Schools'. In *Designing History in East Asian Textbooks: Identity Politics and Transnational Aspirations*, edited by Gotelind Müller, 32–59. London: Routledge.

Murphy, Rachel. 2004. 'Turning Peasants into Modern Chinese Citizens: "Population Quality" Discourse, Demographic Transition and Primary Education'. *The China Quarterly* 177 (May): 1–20. https://doi.org/10.1017/S0305741004000025

Myers, Steven Lee, and Amy Chang Chien. 2021. 'For China's Holidays, a Big-Budget Blockbuster Relives an American Defeat'. *The New York Times*, 5 October 2021. https://www.nytimes.com/2021/10/05/world/asia/battle-lake-changjin.html

Naftali, Orna. 2014a. 'Chinese Childhood in Conflict: Children, Gender, and Violence in China of the Cultural Revolution Period (1966–76)'. *Oriens Extremus* 53: 85–110. https://www.jstor.org/stable/26372425

Naftali, Orna. 2014b. 'Marketing War and the Military to Children and Youth in China: Little Red Soldiers in the Digital Age'. *China Information* 28, no. 1 (March): 25–3. https://doi.org/10.1177/0920203X13513101

Naftali, Orna. 2016. *Children in China* (China Today Series). Cambridge: Polity Press.

Naftali, Orna. 2018. '"These War Dramas Are Like Cartoons": Education, Media Consumption, and Chinese Youth Attitudes towards Japan'. *Journal of Contemporary China* 27, no. 113 (April): 703–18. https://doi.org/10.1080/10670564.2018.1458058

Naftali, Orna. 2019. 'Rights of Children and Youth in China: Protection, Provision, and Participation'. In *Handbook on Human Rights in China*, edited by Sarah Biddulph and Joshua Rosenzweig, 273–99. Cheltenham, UK and Northampton, MA, USA: Edward Elgar.

Naftali, Orna. 2020. '"Life Is Wonderful because of the Military": PLA Recruitment Campaigns in Contemporary China'. In *Propaganda and Public Relations in Military Recruitment: Promoting Military Service in the Twentieth and Twenty-First Centuries*, edited by Brendan Maartens and Tom Bivins, 178–91. London: Routledge.

Naftali, Orna. 2021a. '"Being Chinese Means Becoming Cheap Labour": Education, National Belonging, and Social Positionality among Youth in Contemporary China'. *The China Quarterly* 245 (February): 51–71. https://doi.org/10.1017/S0305741020000120

Naftali, Orna. 2021b. 'Celebrating Violence? Children, Youth, and War Education in Maoist China (1949–76)'. *Journal of the History of Childhood and Youth* 14, no. 2 (Spring): 254–73. https://doi.org/10.1353/hcy.2021.0022

Naftali, Orna. 2021c. 'Youth Military Training in China: Learning to "Love the Army"'. *Journal of Youth Studies* 24, no. 10 (October): 1340–57. https://doi.org/10.1080/13676261.2020.1828847

Naftali, Orna. 2024 'Schooling "Soft-Spoken Boys" and "Masculine Girls": Morality, Equality, and Difference in China's Gender Education'. *Nan Nü* 26: 85–113.

Nagel, Joane. 1998. 'Masculinity and Nationalism: Gender and Sexuality in the Making of Nations'. *Ethnic and Racial Studies* 21, no. 2 (December): 242–69. https://doi.org/10.1080/014198798330007

Nagel, Joane. 2003. *Race, Ethnicity, and Sexuality: Intimate Intersections, Forbidden Frontiers*. New York: Oxford University Press.

Nagel, Joane. 2017. 'The Continuing Significance of Masculinity'. *Ethnic and Racial Studies* 40, no. 9 (June): 145–1459. https://doi.org/10.1080/01419870.2017.1308530

Nathan, Andrew J., and Boshu Zhang. 2022. '"A Shared Future for Mankind": Rhetoric and Reality in Chinese Foreign Policy under Xi Jinping'. *Journal of Contemporary China* 31, no. 133 (May): 57–71. https://doi.org/10.1080/10670564.2021.1926091

National People's Congress of the PRC. 2020a. *National Defense Law of the People's Republic of China [Zhonghua renmin gongheguo guofang fa]*. https://npcobserver.com/wp-content/uploads/2023/09/2020-National-Defense-Law-Revision_Gazette.pdf

National People's Congress of the PRC. 2020b. *Veterans Law of the People's Republic of China [Tuiyi junren baozhang fa]*. https://www.chinajusticeobserver.com/law/x/veterans-protection-law-20201111/enchn

National People's Congress of the PRC. 2023. Patriotic Education Law of the People's Republic of China [Zhonghua renmin gongheguo aiguozhuyi jiaoyu fa]. https://www.gov.cn/yaowen/liebiao/202310/content_6911481.htm

Ng, Naomi. 2015. 'Chinese Teens Complain Compulsory Military Training Too Difficult, but Teachers Say Toughen Up'. *South China Morning Post*, 17 August 2015. https://www.scmp.com/news/china/society/article/1850182/chinese-teens-complain-compulsory-military-training-too-difficult

Ni, Dandan. 2023. 'In China, Military Boot Camps for Kids Are Wildly Popular – and Unsafe'. *Sixth Tone*, Jun 29, 2023, https://www.sixthtone.com/news/1013175

Nie, Hongping Annie. 2013. 'Gaming, Nationalism, and Ideological Work in Contemporary China: Online Games Based on the War of Resistance against Japan'. *Journal of Contemporary China* 22, no. 81 (January): 499–517. https://doi.org/10.1080/10670564.2012.748968

Ning, Xinchun. 2014. 'Junxun cheng "shizhan" beihou de gong jiaolü' ['Public Anxiety Behind Military Training Becomes "Actual Combat"']. Commentary. *Dongguan ribao* (*Dongguan Daily*). 27 August: 2.

Norma, Caroline. 2015. *The Japanese Comfort Women and Sexual Slavery during the China and Pacific Wars*. New York: Bloomsbury Academic.

Noth, Juliane. 2021. 'Militiawomen, Red Guards, and Images of Female Militancy in Maoist China'. *Twentieth-Century China* 46, 2 (May): 153–80. https://doi.org/10.1353/tcc.2021.0013

Nyíri, Pál. 2009. 'From Starbucks to Carrefour: Consumer Boycotts, Nationalism and Taste in Contemporary China'. *PORTAL Journal of Multidisciplinary International Studies* 6, no. 2 (December): 1–25. https://doi.org/10.5130/portal.v6i2.936

O'Brien, Kevin, and Neil Diamant. 2015. 'Contentious Veterans: China's Retired Officers Speak Out'. *Armed Forces & Society* 41, no. 3 (July): 563–81. https://doi.org/10.1177/0095327X14542176

Operation Red Sea (*Honghai Xingdong*), Dante Lam (Lin Chaoxian), 2018, 142 min.

Pan, Jennifer, and Yiqing Xu. 2017. 'China's Ideological Spectrum'. *The Journal of Politics* 80, no. 1 (November): 254–73. http://dx.doi.org/10.1086/694255

Pan, Jennifer, and Yiqing Xu. 2020. 'Gauging Preference Stability and Ideological Constraint under Authoritarian Rule'. *21st Century China Center Research Paper*, 24 August 2020. DOI: 10.2139/ssrn.3679076

Pang, Qin, Junhao Pan, and Lingzhen Lin. 2022. 'China's Growing Power Makes Its Youth Hawkish? Evidence from the Chinese Youth's Attitudes toward the US and Japan'. *Journal of Contemporary China* 31, no. 137 (December): 776–92. https://doi.org/10.1080/10670564.2021.2010881

Peacock, Margaret. 2015. *Innocent Weapons: The Soviet and American Politics of Childhood in the Cold War.* Chapel Hill: University of North Carolina Press.

Peng, Altman Yuzhu. 2022. 'Gender Essentialism in Chinese Reality TV: A Case Study of You Are So Beautiful'. *Television & New Media* 23, no. 7 (June): 743–60. https://doi.org/10.1177/15274764211027234

Pennell, Catriona. 2020. '"Remembrance Isn't Working": First World War Battlefield Tours and the Militarization of British Youth during the Centenary'. *Childhood* 27, no. 3 (February): 383–98. https://doi.org/10.1177/0907568220908307

People's Education Press. 2007. *Putong gaozhong kecheng biaozhun shiyan jiaokeshu lishi bixiu 1 [Standard Senior High School Experimental Textbook: History Compulsory 1].* Beijing: Renmin jiaoyu chubanshe.

People's Education Press. 2009. *Putong gaozhong kecheng biaozhun shiyan jiaokeshu lishi xuanxiu: Ershi shiji de zhanzheng yu heping [Standard Senior High School Experimental Textbook: History Elective 3: War and Peace in the 20th Century].* Beijing: Renmin jiaoyu chubanshe.

People's Education Press. 2017. *Daode yu fazhi ba nianji shangce [Morality and Legal Rule, Grade Eight, Volume One].* Beijing: Renmin jiaoyu chubanshe.

People's Education Press. 2019a. *Daode yu fazhi liu nianji xiace, jiaoshi jiaoxue yongshu [Morality and Legal Rule, Grade Six, Volume Two, Teacher's Handbook].* Beijing: Renmin jiaoyu chubanshe.

People's Education Press. 2019b. *Putong gaozhong jiaokeshu lishi bixiu zhongwai lishi gangyao (shang) [Standard Senior High School History Compulsory Textbook: Outline of Chinese and Foreign History, Part 1].* Beijing: Renmin jiaoyu chubanshe.

People's Education Press. 2019c. *Putong gaozhong jiaokeshu lishi bixiu zhongwai lishi gangyao (xia) [Standard Senior High School History Compulsory Textbook: Outline of Chinese and Foreign History, Part 2]*. Beijing: Renmin jiaoyu chubanshe.

Pérez, Gina. 2006. 'How a Scholarship Girl Becomes a Soldier: The Militarization of Latina/o Youth in Chicago Public Schools'. *Identities: Global Studies in Culture and Power* 13, no. 1 (August): 53–72. https://doi.org/10.1080/10702890500534346

Perry, Elizabeth J. 2006. *Patrolling the Revolution: Worker Militias, Citizenship, and the Modern Chinese State*. Lanham, MD: Rowman and Littlefield.

Pissin, Annika. 2021. 'The Social Construction of Internet Addiction in China: Youth between Reality and Temporal Autonomy in the Documentary Web Junkie'. *Journal of Current Chinese Affairs* 50, no. 1 (February): 86–105. https://doi.org/10.1177/1868102621993134

Plum, Colette M. 2012. 'Lost Childhoods in a New China: Child-Citizen-Workers at War, 1937–1945'. *European Journal of East Asian Studies* 11, no. 2 (January): 237–58. https://doi.org/10.1163/15700615-20121106

Pomfret, John, and Matt Pottinger. 2023. 'Xi Jinping Says He Is Preparing China for War: The World Should Take Him Seriously'. *Foreign Affairs*. 29 March 2023. https://senaldealerta.pe/wp-content/uploads/2023/06/xi-jinping-says-he-is-preparing-china-for-war-2023-03-30-09-59.pdf

Ponzio, Alessio. 2015. *Shaping the New Man: Youth Training Regimes in Fascist Italy and Nazi Germany*. Madison, WI: University of Wisconsin Press.

Power, Marcus. 2007. 'Digitized Virtuosity: Video War Games and Post 9/11 Cyber-Deterrence'. *Security Dialogue* 38, no. 2 (June): 271–88. https://doi.org/10.1177/0967010607078552

PRC State Council. 2021. *Military Service Law of the People's Republic of China* (Zhonghua renmin gongheguo bingyi fa). http://www.gov.cn/xinwen/2021-08/21/content_5632513.htm

Pu, Xiaoyu. 2022. 'National Security and Chinese Foreign Policy'. In *CPC Futures: The New Era of Socialism with Chinese Characteristics*, edited by Frank N. Pieke and Bert Hofman, 181–7. Singapore: National University of Singapore University Press.

Pun, Ngai, and Anita Koo. 2019. 'Double Contradiction of Schooling: Class Reproduction and Working-Class Agency at Vocational Schools in China'. *British Journal of Sociology of*

Education 40, no. 1 (November): 50–64. https://doi.org/10.1080/01425692.2018.1507818

Pun, Ngai, and Jack Qiu. 2020. '"Emotional Authoritarianism": State, Education and the Mobile Working-Class Subjects'. *Mobilities* 15, no. 4 (May): 620–34. https://doi.org/10.1080/17450101.2020.1764264

Qi, Dongtao, Suixin Zhang, and Shengqiao Lin. 2022. 'Urban Chinese Support for Armed Unification with Taiwan: Social Status, National Pride and Understanding of Taiwan'. *Journal of Contemporary China* 32, no. 143 (August): 727–44. https://doi.org/10.1080/10670564.2022.2107390

Qian, Licheng, Bin Xu, and Dingding Chen. 2017. 'Does History Education Promote Nationalism in China? A "Limited Effect" Explanation'. *Journal of Contemporary China* 26, no. 104 (September): 199–212. https://doi.org/10.1080/10670564.2016.1223103

Qiu, Peipei, with Su Zhiliang and Chen Lifei. 2013. *Chinese Comfort Women: Testimonies from Imperial Japan's Sex Slaves*. Vancouver: UBC Press.

Rao, Yichan. 2019. 'From Confucianism to Psychology: Rebooting Internet Addicts in China'. *History of Psychology* 22, no. 4 (November): 328–50. https://doi.org/10.1037/hop0000111

Rawnsley, Gary D. 2009. '"The Great Movement to Resist America and Assist Korea": How Beijing Sold the Korean War'. *Media, War & Conflict* 3, no. 2 (November): 285–315. https://doi.org/10.1177/1750635209345186

Regan, Patrick M. 1994. 'War Toys, War Movies, and the Militarization of the United States, 1900–85'. *Journal of Peace Research* 31, no. 1 (February): 45–58. https://doi.org/10.1177/0022343394031001005

Reilly, James. 2011. 'Remember History, Not Hatred: Collective Remembrance of China's War of Resistance to Japan'. *Modern Asian Studies* 45, no. 2 (March): 463–90. https://doi.org/10.1017/S0026749X11000151

Ren, Shuang. 2018. '"Honghai xingdong" zhenshi ma? Qing kan Zhongguo jun wang dujia caifang zhuchuang tuandui' ['How Real is "Operation Red Sea"? See China Military Network's Exclusive Interview with the Main Creative Team]. *China Military Network [Zhongguo jun wang]*, 25 February 2018. http://www.81.cn/jwgz/2018-02/25/content_7951221.htm

Renmin ribao [People's Daily]. 1967. 'Shanghai Wuhan ge xiaoxue luxu kaixue' ['Primary Schools Opening in Shanghai and Wuhan']. *Renmin ribao [People's Daily]* 22 October 1967: 3.

Renmin ribao [People's Daily]. 2021. 'Niandu quanmin guofang jiaoyu wan ying jihua kaiqi' ['The 2022 National Defense Education Ten Thousand Screening Project kicks off']. 29 October 2023. http://military.people.com.cn/n1/2021/1029/c1011-32268394.html

Reuters. 2023. 'As China's Birth Rate Slumps, Political Advisor Urges Egg Freezing for Single Women'. 1 March 2023. https://www.reuters.com/world/china/chinas-birth-rate-slumps-political-advisor-urges-egg-freezing-single-women-2023-02-28./

Riggan, Jennifer. 2016. *The Struggling State: Nationalism, Mass Militarization, and the Eduation of Eritrea*. Philadelphia: Temple University Press.

Robb, David L. 2019. 'Operation Hollywood'. In *Militarization: A Reader*, 230–4. Edited by Catherine Besteman and Daniel M. Goldstein. Durham: Duke University Press.

Roberts, Rosemary. 2004. 'Positive Women Characters in the Revolutionary Model Works of the Chinese Cultural Revolution: An Argument against the Theory of Erasure of Gender and Sexuality'. *Asian Studies Review* 28, no. 4 (August): 407–22. https://doi.org/10.1080/10357820500032487

Robinson, Luke. 2011. 'Animating the Chinese Child Consumer: Remaking Sparkling Red Star for the Market'. *Journal of Children and Media* 4, no. 5 (October): 426–41. https://doi.org/10.1080/17482798.2011.587293

Rofel, Lisa. 2018. 'The Said and Unsaid of the New Worlding of China-Africa-U.S. Relations'. In *Wolf Warrior II: The Rise of China and Gender/Sexual Politics*, edited by Petrus Liu and Lisa Rofel. Columbus, Ohio: MCLC Resource Center, The Ohio State University. http://u.osu.edu/mclc/online-series/liu-rofel/

Rose, Caroline. 2013. 'Changing Views of the Anti-Japanese War in Chinese High-School History Textbooks'. In *Imagining Japan in Post-war East Asia: Identity Politics, Schooling and Popular Culture*, edited by Paul Morris, Naoko Shimazu, and Edward Vickers, 129–48. London: Routledge.

Saunders, Phillip C. 2020. 'China's Global Military-Security Interactions'. In *China and the World*, edited by David Shambaugh, 181–207. Oxford: Oxford University Press.

Schillinger, Nicolas. 2016. *The Body and Military Masculinity in Late Qing and Early Republican China: The Art Of Governing Soldiers*. Lanham, MD: Lexington Books.

Schubart, Rikke. 2009. 'Introduction'. In *War Isn't Hell, It's Entertainment: Essays on Visual Media and the Representation of Conflict*, edited by Rikke Schubart et al., 1–10. Jefferson, NC, and London: McFarland.

Scobell, Andrew. 1992. 'Why the People's Army Fired on the People: The Chinese Military and Tiananmen'. *Armed Forces & Society* 18, no. 2 (Winter): 193–213. https://doi.org/10.1177/0095327X9201800203

Scobell, Andrew. 2022. 'The Party in Uniform: The Institutional Irony of Chinese Gun Control'. In *The Party Leads All: The Evolving Role of the Chinese Communist Party*, edited by Guobin Yang and Jacques deLisle, 347–70. Washington, DC: Brookings Institution Press.

Sen, Abdulkerim, and Hugh Starkey. 2019. *Citizenship Education in Turkey: From Militant-Secular to Islamic Nationalism*. Lanham, MD: Lexington Books.

Shambaugh, David. 1991. 'The Soldier and the State in China: The Political Work System in the People's Liberation Army'. *The China Quarterly* 127 (February): 527–68. https://doi.org/10.1017/S0305741000031052

Shambaugh, David. 2020. 'China's Long March to Global Power'. In *China and the World*, edited by David Shambaugh, 3–21. Oxford: Oxford University Press.

Sheehan, Mark, and Martyn Davison. 2017. '"We Need to Remember They Died for Us": How Young People in New Zealand Make Meaning of War Remembrance and Commemoration of the First World War'. *London Review of Education* 15, no. 2 (July): 251–71. https://doi.org/10.18546/LRE.15.2.09

Shen, Yuxi. 2008. 'Huajie xuesheng junxun zhong de xiaoji qingxu' ['Resolving Negative Emotions in Students' Military Training']. *Zhongguo deyu [Chinese Moral Education]* 2: 50–2.

Shepherd, Laura J. 2018. 'Militarisation'. In *Visual Global Politics*, edited by Roland Bleiker, 209–14. Abingdon, UK: Routledge.

Shih, Gerry. 2020. 'China, and Xi, Commemorate the Korean War as Victory over United States'. *The Washington Post*, 23 October 2020. https://www.washingtonpost.com/world/china-and-xi-commemorate-the-korean-war-as-a-victory-over-america/2020/10/23/122a403e-144e-11eb-a258-614acf2b906d_story.html

Sichuan waiyu xueyuan wuzhuang bu [Armed Forces Department of Sichuan University of Foreign Languages]. 1991. 'Qian tan ruhe xiaochu xuesheng junxun Zhong de nifan xinli' ['Talking about How to Eliminate the Rebellious Psychology of Students in Military Training']. *Sichuan waiyu xueyuan bao [Journal of Sichuan University of Foreign Languages]* 4: 84–7.

Sinkkonen, Elina. 2013. 'Nationalism, Patriotism and Foreign Policy Attitudes among Chinese University Students'. *The China Quarterly* 216 (November): 1045–63. https://doi.org/10.1017/S0305741013001094

Sinkkonen, Elina, and Marko Elovainio. 2020. 'Chinese Perceptions of Threats from the United States and Japan'. *Political Psychology* 41, no. 2 (April): 265–82. https://doi.org/10.1111/pops.12630

Smith, Anthony D. 1981. 'War and Ethnicity: The Role of Warfare in the Formation, Self-Images, and Cohesion of Ethnic Communities'. *Ethnic and Racial Studies* 4, no. 4 (October): 375–97. https://doi.org/10.1080/01419870.1981.9993347

Soh, C. Sarah. 2008. *The Comfort Women: Sexual Violence and Postcolonial Memory in Korea and Japan*. Chicago: The University of Chicago Press.

Sohu. 2016. '"Zhenzheng nanzihan 2" diaocha: zenyang xuanze jiabin zhenrong & zhenren xiu you duo zhen?' ['"Real Men 2" Survey: How to Choose a Guest Lineup and How Real is the Reality Show?']. 9 November 2016. https://www.sohu.com/a/118550090_161796

Solomon, Inbal, and Myriam Denov. 2010. 'Militarised Bodies: The Global Militarisation of Children's Lives'. In *Contested Bodies of Childhood and Youth*, edited by Kathrinand Hörschelmann and Rachel Kolls, 163–77. Houndmills, UK: Palgrave Macmillan.

Song, Geng. 2022. '"Little Fresh Meat": The Politics of Sissiness and Sissyphobia in Contemporary China'. *Men and Masculinities* 25, no. 1 (April): 68–86. https://doi.org/10.1177/1097184X211014939

Song, Geng, and Derek Hird. 2014. *Men and Masculinities in Contemporary China*. Boston: Brill.

Song, Wei. 2012. '"90 Hou" daxuesheng junxun gongzuo cunzai de wenti ji duice yanjiu' ['Problems in Military Training for College Students Born after the 1990s: Research and Countermeasures']. *Henan gongye daxue xuebao [Journal of Henan University of Technology]* 8, no. 3: 150–3.

Stephens, Sharon. 1997. 'Nationalism, Nuclear Policy and Children in Cold War America'. *Childhood* 4, no. 1 (February): 103–23. https://doi.org/10.1177/0907568297004001006

Strand, Sanna, and Joakim Berndtsson. 2015. 'Recruiting the "Enterprising Soldier": Military Recruitment Discourses in Sweden and the United Kingdom'. *Critical Military Studies* 1, no. 3 (October): 233-48. https://doi.org/10.1080/23337486.2015.1090676

Sun, Jiaming, and Xun Wang. 2010. 'Value Differences between Generations in China: A Study in Shanghai'. *Journal of Youth Studies* 13, no. 1 (February): 65-81. https://doi.org/10.1080/13676260903173462

Sun, Jing. 2021. *Red Chamber, World Dream: Actors, Audience, and Agendas in Chinese Foreign Policy and Beyond*. Ann Arbor: University of Michigan Press.

Svensson, Marina. 2023. 'Chinese Youth and the Communist Party of China: Cultivating a Loyal Generation through Ideological and Political Education'. *China: An International Journal* 21, no. 2 (May): 72-91. https://doi.org/10.1353/chn.2023.a898342

Szablewicz, Marcella. 2010. 'The Ill Effects of "Opium for the Spirit": A Critical Cultural Analysis of China's Internet Addiction Moral Panic'. *Chinese Journal of Communication* 3, no. 4 (November): 453-70. https://doi.org/10.1080/17544750.2010.516579

Tajima, Yukio. 2023. 'China Revises Conscription Law, Eyeing Taiwan Conflict'. *Nikkei Asia*. 1 May 2023. https://asia.nikkei.com/Politics/China-revises-conscription-law-eyeing-Taiwan-conflict

Takes a Real Man (*Zhenzheng nanzihan*), Hunan Television, 2015-2017, 26 episodes, 90 min.

Tanaka, Yuki. 2002. *Japan's Comfort Women: Sexual Slavery and Prostitution during World War II and the US Occupation*. London: Routledge.

Tang, Wenfang, and Benjamin Darr. 2012. 'Chinese Nationalism and Its Political and Social Origins'. *Journal of Contemporary China* 21, no. 77 (May): 811-26. https://doi.org/10.1080/10670564.2012.684965

Tang, Yuxiang. 1990. 'Xuesheng junxun ying zhuzhong zengqiang guofang yishi' ['Students' Military Training Should Focus on Enhancing National Defense Awareness']. *Guo fang* [*National Defense*] 25.

The Economist. 2023a. 'China's New "Top Gun" Normalises War with America'. Chaguan. 4 May 2023. https://www.economist.com/china/2023/05/04/chinas-new-top-gun-normalises-war-with-america

The Economist. 2023b. 'China Is Struggling to Recruit Enough Highly Skilled Troops'. Special Report. November 6, https://www.economist.com/special-report/2023/11/06/china-is-struggling-to-recruit-enough-highly-skilled-troops

Thomas, Tanja. 2009. 'Gender Management, Popular Culture and the Military'. In *War Isn't Hell, It's Entertainment: Essays on Visual Media and the Representation of Conflict*, edited by Rikke Schubart, Fabian Virchow, and Debra White-Stanley, 97–114. Jefferson, NC, and London: McFarland.

Thornton, Patricia M. 2023. 'Who's Afraid of Chizuko Ueno? The Party's Ongoing Counteroffensive against Feminism in the Xi Era'. China Leadership Monitor, Issue 78, https://www.prcleader.org/post/who-s-afraid-of-chizuko-ueno-the-party-s-ongoing-counteroffensive-against-feminism-in-the-xi-era?ref=neican.org

Tiezzi, Shannon. 2020. 'In Korean War Commemoration, Xi Warns That China Will "Use War to prevent War"'. *The Diplomat*, 24 October 2020. https://thediplomat.com/2020/10/in-korean-war-commemoration-xi-warns-that-china-will-use-war-to-prevent-war/

Tillman, Margaret Mih. 2018. *Raising China's Revolutionaries: Modernizing Childhood for Cosmopolitan Nationalists and Liberated Comrades, 1920s–1950s*. New York: Columbia University Press.

Trejo, Jose Enrique Coutiño, and Alejandro Madrazo. 2023. 'Militarized High Schools in Mexico: From Militarization to Militarism in a Context of Violence (2006–2022)'. *Alternatives: Global, Local, Political*, published Online First (July): 1–16. https://doi.org/10.1177/03043754231183561

Tu, Ying, and Xin Cui. 2021. 'Hudong tiyan, rang guofang jiaoyu "wendu"' ['Interactive Experience Makes National Defense Education "Hotter"']. *Taizhou ribao [Taizhou Daily]*. 18 January 2021.

Twum-Danso Imoh, Afua, Lucia Rabello de Castro, and Orna Naftali. 2022. 'Studies of Childhoods in the Global South: Towards an Epistemic Turn in Transnational Childhood Research?' *Third World Thematics: A TWQ Journal*, 7, nos. 1–3: 1–16, https://doi.org/10.1080/23802014.2022.2161619

Udochi, Aisha Chioma. 2018. 'Wolf Warrior II: "China's Great Restoration"'. In *Wolf Warrior II: The Rise of China and Gender/Sexual Politics*, edited by Petrus Liu and Lisa Rofel. Columbus, Ohio: MCLC Resource Center, The Ohio State University. http://u.osu.edu/mclc/online-series/liu-rofel/

Unger, Jonathan. 1982. *Education under Mao: Class and Competition in Canton Schools, 1960–1980*. NYC: Columbia University Press.

US Department of Defense. 2022. *Military and Security Developments Involving the People's Republic of China 2022: Annual Report to Congress*. United States Government.

van de Ven, Hans. 1997. 'The Military in the Republic'. *The China Quarterly* 150 (June): 352–74. https://doi.org/10.1017/S0305741000052516

Van Oudenaren, John S. 2023. 'Party Pushes National Defense Education for All'. *China Brief*, 17 February 2023. https://jamestown.org/program/party-pushes-national-defense-education-for-all/

Vickers, Edward. 2007. 'Museums and Nationalism in Contemporary China'. *Compare: A Journal of Comparative Education* 37, no. 3 (July): 368–82. https://doi.org/10.1080/03057920701330255

Vickers, Edward. 2009. 'Selling "Socialism with Chinese Characteristics": "Thought and Politics" and the Legitimisation of China's Developmental Strategy'. *International Journal of Educational Development* 29, no. 5 (September): 523–31. https://doi.org/10.1016/j.ijedudev.2009.04.012

Vickers, Edward. 2022. 'Smothering Diversity: Patriotism in China's School Curriculum Under Xi Jinping'. *Journal of Genocide Research* 24, no. 2 (September): 158–70. https://doi.org/10.1080/14623528.2021.1968142

Vickers, Edward, and Zeng Xiaodong. 2017. *Education and Society in Post-Mao China*. London: Routledge.

Wakeman, Fredric, Jr. 1997. 'A Revisionist view of the Nanjing Decade: Confucian Fascism'. *The China Quarterly* 105 (June): 395–432. https://doi.org/10.1017/S030574100005253X

Walder, Andrew, G. 2016. 'Rebellion of the Cadres: The 1967 Implosion of the Chinese Party-State'. *The China Journal* 75, no. 1 (January): 102–20. https://www.journals.uchicago.edu/doi/abs/10.1086/683125

Waley-Cohen, Joanna. 2006a. 'On the Militarization of Culture in the Eighteenth-Century Qing Empire'. *Common Knowledge* 12, no. 1 (Winter): 96– 106. muse.jhu.edu/article/191692

Waley-Cohen, Joanna. 2006b. *The Culture of War in China: Empire and the Military under the Qing Dynasty*. London: IB Tauris.

Wallace, Jeremy L, and Jessica Chen Weiss. 2015. 'The Political Geography of Nationalist Protest in China: Cities and the 2012 Anti-Japanese Protests'. *The China Quarterly* 222 (June): 403–29. https://doi.org/10.1017/S0305741015000417

Wan wei du zhi wang. 2021. 'Zhongguo qian gaoguan shou tan "shei shi zui ke'ai de ren" bei shan zhenzheng yuanyin' ['Former Senior Official Explains the Real Reason for the Deletion of "Who Are the Most Beloved People"']. CReaders.net, 28 January 2021. https://m.creader.com/news/page/1058038

Wan, Zhengru, and Hongjun Zhou. 1987. 'Xuesheng canjia junxun shouhuo da' ['Students Benefit from Military Training']. *Renmin jiaoyu [People's Education]* 12: 13.

Wang, Chih-Ming. 2018. 'New China in New Times'. In *Wolf Warrior II: The Rise of China and Gender/Sexual Politics*, edited by Petrus Liu and Lisa Rofel. Columbus, Ohio: MCLC Resource Center, The Ohio State University. http://u.osu.edu/mclc/online-series/liu-rofel/

Wang, Howard. 2023. '"Security Is a Prerequisite for Development": Consensus-Building toward a New Top Priority in the Chinese Communist Party'. *Journal of Contemporary China* 32, no. 142 (August): 525–39. https://doi.org/10.1080/10670564.2022.2108681

Wang, Jingyao. 1998. 'Qian tan gaoxiao junxun gongzuo de shenru fazhan' ['A Discussion on the In-Depth Development of Military Training in Colleges and Universities']. *Shenyang daxue xuebao zhexue shehui kexue ban [Journal of Shenyang University Philosophy and Social Sciences edition]* 3: 76–7.

Wang, Juntao, and Anne-Marie Brady. 2012. 'Sword and Pen: The Propaganda System of the People's Liberation Army'. In *China's Thought Management*, edited by Anne-Marie Brady, 122–45. London: Routledge.

Wang, Junyang. 2022. 'Behind Veterans' Protests: Passive and Piecemeal Policy-Making in China'. *Modern China* 48, no. 2 (November): 253–88. https://doi.org/10.1177/0097700420967667

Wang, Lianzhang. 2017. 'People's Liberation Army Warns of Rise in Dropouts'. *Sixth Tone*, 26 January 2017. https://www.sixthtone.com/news/1876

Wang, Long. 2015. 'Wu Jing wei "Zhan Lang" xunlian 1 nian ban chengji zai tezhongbing minglie qianmao' ['Wu Jing Trained for "Wolf Warrior" for a Year and a Half, and His Performance Was among the Best in the Special Forces']. *Renmin ribao [People's Daily]*, 17 April 2015. http://military.people.com.cn/n/2015/0417/c1011-26861006.html

Wang, Mei, and Liguo Yang. 1987. 'Lai zi Fudan Daxue xuesheng junxun yingdi de baogao' ['Report from Fudan University Student

Military Training Camp']. *Zhongguo gaodeng jiaoyu [Higher Education in China]* 11: 10, 35–6.
Wang, Peng. 2016. 'Military Corruption in China: The Role of Guanxi in the Buying and Selling of Military Positions'. *The China Quarterly* 228 (November): 970–991. https://doi.org/10.1017/S0305741016001144
Wang, Shaofang, and Kaiyi Li. 2022. 'Military Skills and War Readiness: Students' Summer Military Drill in China in 1934'. In *War and Education*, edited by Engelmann, Sebastian, Bernhard Hemetsberger, and Frank Jacob, 349–71. Leiden, The Netherlands: Brill.
Wang, Shumei. 2015. *The PLA and Student Recruits: Reforming China's Conscription System*. Asia Paper, January 2015. Stockholm-Nacka: Institute for Security and Development Policy. https://isdp.eu/content/uploads/publications/2015-wang-the-PLA-and-student-recruits.pdf
Wang, Xian. 2023. 'Contested Memories: An Imaginary Museum for a Chinese Female Revolutionary Martyr, Liu Hulan'. *Modern China*, published OnlineFirst (May): 1–33. https://doi.org/10.1177/00977004231170267
Wang, Xiaohui, and Xiang Li. 2018. 'Yi junren yanggang zhi qi yinling shehui fengshang' ('Leading Social Trends with Military Masculinity'). *Zhongguo jun wang* (*China Military Network*) 2, September 18: 3. http://www.81.cn/gfbmap/content/2018-09-18/content_216093.htm
Wang, Yi, and Matthew M. Chew. 2021. 'State, Market, and the Manufacturing of War Memory: China's Television Dramas on the War of Resistance against Japan'. *Memory Studies* 14, no. 4 (June): 877–91. https://doi.org/10.1177/17506980211024319
Wang, Yingzi, and Thoralf Klein. 2022. 'Representing the Victorious Past: Chinese Revolutionary TV Drama between Propaganda and Marketization'. *Media, Culture & Society* 44, no. 1 (July): 105–20. https://doi.org/10.1177/01634437211022721
Wang, Yuan. 1998. 'Xuesheng junxun cong xiaoxue bu hao' ['Student Military Training Should Start from Elementary School']. *Guofang [National Defense]* 2: 22–3.
Wang, Yuhua. 2019. 'The Political Legacy of Violence during China's Cultural Revolution'. *British Journal of Political Science* 51, no. 2 (December): 463–87. https://doi.org/10.1017/S0007123419000255
Wang, Yuxiang, and Wenhan Zhang. 1994. 'Zongjie junxun jingyan: tansuo zi xun zhi lu' ['Summary of Military Training Experience:

Explore the Path of Self-Training']. *Gaodeng jiaoyu yanjiu [Higher Education Research]* 3: 24–26.

Wang, Zheng. 2012. *Never Forget National Humiliation: Historical Memory in Chinese Politics and Foreign Relations.* New York: Columbia University Press.

Weatherley, Robert, and Qiang Zhang. 2017. *History and Nationalist Legitimacy in Contemporary China.* London: Palgrave Macmillan.

Weiss, Jessica Chen. 2014. *Powerful Patriots: Nationalist Protest in China's Foreign Relations.* Oxford: Oxford University Press.

Weiss, Jessica Chen. 2019. 'How Hawkish Is the Chinese Public? Another Look at "Rising Nationalism" and Chinese Foreign Policy'. *Journal of Contemporary China* 28, no. 119 (March): 679–695. https://doi.org/10.1080/10670564.2019.1580427

Welty, Emily.2014. '76 Cups of Tea: Ethnography in Peace and Conflict Research'. In *Peace and Conflict Studies Research: A Qualitative Perspective*, edited by Robin Cooper and Laura Finley, 111–36. Charlotte, NC: IAP Publishing.

Wen, Hua. 2021. 'Gentle yet Manly: Xiaoxianrou, Male Cosmetic Surgery and Neoliberal Consumer Culture in China'. *Asian Studies Review* 45, no. 2 (April): 253–71. https://doi.org/10.1080/10357823.2021.1896676

West, Michael J., and Aurelio Insisa. 2023. 'Reunifying Taiwan with China through Cross-Strait Lawfare'. *The China Quarterly*, published online first (May): 1–16. https://doi.org/10.1017/S0305741023000735

West, Philip, Steven I. Levine, and Jackie Hiltz. 1997. *America's Wars in Asia: A Cultural Approach to History and Memory.* Armonk, NY: M. E. Sharpe.

White, Lynn T. III. 1989. *The Policies of Chaos: The Organizational Causes of Violence in China's Cultural Revolution.* Princeton, NJ: Princeton University Press.

Wolf Warrior (*Zhan Lang*), Wu Jing, 2015, 90 min.

Wolf Warrior II (*Zhan Lang II*), Wu Jing, 2017, 123 min.

Wood, Peter. 2013. 'The Spirit of Xu Sanduo: The Influence of China's Favorite Soldier'. *China Brief*, 26 July 2013, 15–18. https://jamestown.org/program/the-spirit-of-xu-sanduo-the-influence-of-chinas-favorite-soldier/

Wood, Peter. 2017. 'PLA Attempts to Attract Higher-Quality Recruits'. *China Brief*, 21 September 2017, 1–4. https://jamestown.org/program/pla-attempts-to-attract-higher-quality-recruits/

World Bank Group. 2021. 'Fertility Rate, Total (Births Per Woman)'. https://data.worldbank.org/indicator/sp.dyn.tfrt.in?year_high_desc=false

Wuthnow, Joel. 2023. 'Why Xi Jinping Doesn't Trust His Own Military: The Real Meaning of China's Disappearing Generals'. *Foreign Affairs*, 26 September 2023. https://www.foreignaffairs.com/china/why-xi-jinping-doesnt-trust-his-own-military

Wuthnow, Joel, and M. Taylor Fravel. 2023. 'China's Military Strategy for a "New Era": Some Change, More Continuity, and Tantalizing Hints'. *Journal of Strategic Studies* 46, nos. 6–7 (March): 1149–1184. https://doi.org/10.1080/01402390.2022.2043850

Xia, Lei. 1951. 'Zhuo fei te' ['Catch the Bandits']. *Xiao pengyou [Little Friends]* 1013, 25 June 1951: 12–13.

Xiang, Zairong. 2018. 'Toxic Masculinity with Chinese Characteristics'. In *Wolf Warrior II: The Rise of China and Gender/Sexual Politics*, edited by Petrus Liu and Lisa Rofel. Columbus, Ohio: MCLC Resource Center, The Ohio State University. http://u.osu.edu/mclc/online-series/liu-rofel/

Xiao, Xiangzi. 1951. 'Chaoxian Haizi da di ji' ['North Korean Children Fight Enemy Planes']. *Xiao pengyou [Little Friends]* 1017, 25 August 1951: 5.

Xie, Lingu. 1989. 'Shi lun xuesheng junxun zuoyong ji shishi' ['On the Role and Implementation of Military Training for Students']. *Qinghai shifan daxue xuebao (zhexue shehui kexue ban) [Journal of Qinghai Normal University (Philosophy and Social Sciences Edition)]* 4: 48–51.

Xin Jing bao [The Beijing News]. 2016. '"Zhenzheng nanzihan" "juedui bu shi xiu"' ['"Take a Real Man" Is "Definitely Not a Show"']. 2 November 2016. http://epaper.bjnews.com.cn/html/2016-11/02/content_657937.htm?div=1

Xin, Li. 2022. 'More Chinese Minors Are Online but Fewer Addicted, Report Says'. *Sixth Tone*. 30 November 2022. https://www.sixthtone.com/news/1011784

Xinhua News Agency. 2006. 'Quan min guofang qiaoyu dagang' ['Outline of National Defense Education for All Citizens']. https://www.gov.cn/jrzg/2006-12/05/content_461862.htm

Xinhua News Agency. 2016a. 'Dianshi zongyi jiemu "Zhenzheng nanzihan" wei sha neng huo?' ['Why is the TV Variety Show "Takes a Real Man" So Popular?'. 5 December 2016. http://www.xinhuanet.com//mil/2016-12/05/c_129390718.htm

Xinhua News Agency. 2016b. '"Langya shan wu zhuangzhi" hou ren qisu Hong Zhenkuai qinhai mingyu an xuanpan ['Descendants of

"Five Heroes of Langya Mountain" Prosecute Hong Zhenkuai for Infringement of Honor']. 27 June 2016.

Xinhua News Agency. 2017. 'Zhenxi! Ni meiyou chusheng zai heping de niandai, er shi yi ge heping de guojia' ['Cherish It! You Were Not Born in a Peaceful Era, but in a Peaceful Country']. 10 April 2017.

Xinhua News Agency. 2019a. 'Woguo quanmian zhankai daxuesheng zhengbing gongzuo shi zhounian zongshu' ['A Summary of the 10th Anniversary of the Country's Comprehensive Recruitment of College Students']. 23 September 2019. http://www.xinhuanet.com/mil/2019-09/23/c_1210288894.htm

Xinhua News Agency. 2019b. 'Zhonggong zhongyang guowuyuan yinfa "xin shidai aiguo zhuyi jiaoyu shisi gangyao"' ['The Central Committee of the Communist Party of China and the State Council Issue the "Outline for the Implementation of Patriotic Education in the New Era"']. 12 November 2019.

Xinhua News Agency. 2020. 'Xi Jinping: Zai jinian Zhongguo renmin zhiyuajun Kang Mei Yuan Chao chuguo zuozhan 70 zhounian dahui shang de jianghua' ['Xi Jinping: Speech at the Meeting to Commemorate the 70th Anniversary of the CPV's Mission to Resist America and Aid Korea']. 23 October 2020. http://www.xinhuanet.com/politics/leaders/2020-10/23/c_1126649916.htm.

Xinhua News Agency. 2021. 'China Passes Law Banning Defamation of Military Personnel'. 11 June 2021. https://www.xinhuanet.com/english/2021-06/10/c_1310000865.htm

Xinhua News Agency. 2022. 'Zhonggong zhongyang: Guanyu jiaqiang he gaijin xin shidai quanmin guofang jiaoyu gongzuo de yijian' ['Central Committee of the Communist Party of China: Opinion on Strengthening and Improving National Defense Education for All in the New Era']. 1 September 2022. https://www.gov.cn/zhengce/2022-09/01/content_5707818.htm

Xu, Haozhe. 2016. 'Yangmi Tongliya huashen nü bing "zhenzheng nanzihan 2" jiaru nü zhanshi geng haokanle' ['"Take a Real Man 2" Is Even Better with the Addition of Women Warriors Yang Mi and Tong Liya']. *Renmin ribao [People's Daily]*, 25 October 2016.

Xu, Lanjun. 2015. *Ertong yu Zhanzheng: Guozu, jiaoyu, ji dazhong wenhua [Children and War: Nation, Education, and Popular Culture]*. Beijing: Beijing daxue chubanshe.

Xu, Wei. 2016. 'Reality Show Script Claims Stir Controversy'. *Shanghai Daily*, 5 November 2016: A11. https://archive.shine.cn/feature/art-and-culture/Reality-show-script-claims-stir-controversy/shdaily.shtml

Xu, Xu. 2011. '"Chairman Mao's Child": Sparkling Red Star and the Construction of Children in the Chinese Cultural Revolution'. *Children's Literature Association Quarterly* 36, no. 4 (Winter): 381–409. https://doi.org/10.1353/chq.2011.0046.

Xu, Yan. 2019. *The Soldier Image and State-Building in Modern China, 1924–1945*. Lexington, Kentucky: University Press of Kentucky.

Yan, Fei, Zhou Zhong, Haoning Wang, and Qiao Wen. 2021. 'Grafting Identity: History Textbook Reform and Identity-Building in Contemporary China'. *Journal of Educational Change* 22 (December): 175–190. https://doi.org/10.1007/s10833-019-09365-z

Yan, Hairong. 2013. 'What If Your Client/Employer Treats Her Dog Better Than She Treats You? Market Militarism and Market Humanism in Postsocialist Beijing'. In *Global Futures in East Asia: Youth, Nation, and the New Economy in Uncertain Times*, edited by Hai Ren, Andrea Arai, and Ann Anagnost, 85–97. Stanford: Stanford University Press.

Yan, Yunxiang. 2009. *The Individualization of Chinese Society*. Oxford: Berg Publishers.

Yan, Yunxiang. 2021a. 'Introduction: The Inverted Family, Post-Patriarchal Intergenerationality and Neo- Familism'. In *Chinese Families Upside Down: Intergenerational Dynamics and Neo-Familism in the Early 21st Century*, edited by Yunxiang Yan, 1–30. Leiden, The Netherlands: Brill.

Yan, Yunxiang. 2021b. 'Three Discourses on Neo-Familism'. In *Chinese Families Upside Down: Intergenerational Dynamics and Neo-Familism in the Early 21st Century*, edited by Yunxiang Yan, 253–74. Leiden, The Netherlands: Brill.

Yang, Huzhi. 2006. 'Dangqian daxuesheng junxun cunzai de wenti ji qi duice' ['Current Problems and Countermeasures in College Students' Military Drilling']. *Hunan diyi shifan xuebao [Journal of Hunan First Normal College]* 6, no. 3: 77–8, 85.

Yang, Jian. 1985. 'Jianchi ba junshi xunlian zuowei daxuesheng de bixiu ke' ['Insist on Making Military Training a Compulsory Course for College Students']. *Gaojiao zhanxian [Higher Education Front]* 10: 40–2.

Yang, Lijun, and Yongnian Zheng. 2012. 'Fen Qings (Angry Youth) in Contemporary China'. *Journal of Contemporary China* 21, no. 76 (May): 637–53. https://doi.org/10.1080/10670564.2012.666834

Yang, Mayfair Mei-hui. 1999. 'From Gender Erasure to Gender Difference: State Feminism, Consumer Sexuality, and Women's Public Sphere in China'. In *Spaces of Their Own: Women's Public Sphere in Transnational China*, edited by Mayfair Mei-hui Yang. Minneapolis: University of Minnesota Press.

Yang, Wen. 2016. '"Zhenzheng nanzihan" di er ji: Ba guofang jiaoyu "yinggutou" zuo cheng "xiang bo bo"' ['The Second Season of "Takes a Real Man": Making the "Hard Bone" of National Defense Education into a "Delicious Cake"']. *Renmin ribao [People's Daily]*, 7 December 2016.

Yang, Wenqi, and Fei Yan. 2017. 'The Annihilation of Femininity in Mao's China: Gender Inequality of Sent-Down Youth during the Cultural Revolution'. *China Information* 31, no. 1 (February): 63–83. https://doi.org/10.1177/0920203X17691743

Yang, Xiao. 2023. 'The "Wolf Warrior Cycle": Chinese Blockbusters in the Age of the Belt and Road Initiative'. *The China Quarterly*, published OnlineFirst (May): 1–15. https://doi.org/10.1017/S0305741023000693

Yang, Xiaoyu. 1989. 'Zhengque renshi xuesheng junxun de biyaoxing' ['Correctly Understand the Necessity of Military Training for Students']. *Guofang [National Defense]* 11: 40–1

Yang, Zhihua, and Jixiang Li. 1986. 'Xuesheng junxun yu "wenge" zhong "xue jun" jieran butong' ['Student Military Training Is Completely Different from the "Learning from the Army" of the "Cultural Revolution"']. *Zhongguo minbing [Chinese Militia]* 8: 5.

Yau, Kinnia Shuk-ting. 2014. 'Meanings of the Imagined Friends: Good Japanese in Chinese War Films', in *Imagining Japan in Postwar East Asia: Identity Politics, Schooling and Popular Culture*, edited by Paul Morris, Naoko Shimazu and Edward Vickers, 68–84. London and New York: Routledge.

Ye, Zhanhang. 2023. 'China's Comedy Powerhouse in Hot Water after Comic's Military Joke'. *Sixth Tone*, 16 May 2023.

Yiu, Lisa, and Min Yu. 2022. 'Empowerment from What? Teacher "Citizenship Talk" Practices for Migrant Children in China'. *Comparative Education* 58, no. 4: 526–41. https://doi.org/10.1080/03050068.2022.2088691

Yuval-Davis, Nira. 1993. 'Gender and Nation'. *Ethnic & Racial Studies* 16, no. 3 (September): 621–31. https://doi.org/10.1080/01419870.1993.9993800

Zarrow, Peter. 2015. *Educating China: Knowledge, Society and Textbooks in a Modernizing World, 1902–1937*. Cambridge: Cambridge University Press.

Zeng, Wenna, and Colin Sparks. 2019. 'Production and Politics in Chinese Television'. *Media, Culture & Society* 41, no. 1 (April): 54–69. https://doi.org/10.1177/0163443718764785

Zhang, Chi, and Yiben Ma. 2023. 'Invented Borders: The Tension between Grassroots Patriotism and State-Led Patriotic Campaigns in China'. *Journal of Contemporary China* 32, no. 144 (January): 897–913. https://doi.org/10.1080/10670564.2023.2167054

Zhang, Chong, and Catherine Fagan. 2016. 'Examining the Role of Ideological and Political Education on University Students' Civic Perceptions and Civic Participation in Mainland China: Some Hints from Contemporary Citizenship Theory'. *Citizenship, Social and Economics Education* 15, no. 2 (December): 117–142. https://doi.org/10.1177/2047173416681170

Zhang, Chunni. 2014. *Military Service and Life Chances in Contemporary China, Population Studies Center Research Report 14–829*. September 2014. Institute for Social Research, University of Michigan.

Zhang, Donghua, and Guoshun Liu. 2019. 'China Launches Preparation for 2019 Conscription Campaign'. *China Military Online*. 9 January 2019. http://eng.chinamil.com.cn/CHINA_209163/TopStories_209189/9400648.html

Zhang, Fengpo. 2017. 'Xuesheng junxun qi rong mohei – Guifan guanli pozai meijie' ['How Can We Discredit Students' Military Training? Standardized Management Is Urgently Required']. Commentary. *Zhongguo wang* [*China Network*]. September 11. http://military.china.com.cn/2017-09/11/content_41565984.htm

Zhang, Ge. 2004. 'Gaoxiao guofang jiaoyu yu daxuesheng suzhi yang cheng' ['National Defense Education in Colleges and Universities and the Cultivation of College Students' Quality']. *Shanxi shifan daxue xuebao (zhexue shehui kexue ban) [Journal of Shanxi Normal University Philosophy and Social Sciences Edition])* 33 Supplement (October): 285–86.

Zhang, Guangquan, and Qingyun Ma. 2009. 'Xuesheng junxun ying zhongshi guofang jiaoyu' ('Student Military Training Should Attach Importance to National Defence Education'). *Zhongguo minbing* (*Chinese Militia*) 8: 38–39.

Zhang, Jingbo. 2022. 'Zai "bajie yunsui qi" mai hao qingchun zhengbu' ['Take a Good Step Forward in the "Jointing and Booting Period"']. *Zhongguo jun wang [China Military Network]*. 29 Augsust 2022. http://www.81.cn/dy_208579/jdt_208580/10181170.html

Zhang, Miaofang. 1988. 'Jianguo hou xuesheng junxun de xingqi he fazhan' ['The Rise and Development of Military Training for Students after the Founding of the People's Republic of China']. *Guofang [National Defense]* 4: 16–17.

Zhang, Qian, and Keith Nagus. 2020. 'East Asian Pop Music Idol Production and the Emergence of Data Fandom in China'. *International Journal of Cultural Studies* 23, no. 4 (February): 493–511. https://doi.org/10.1177/1367877920904064

Zhang, Xiaoxiao. 2019. 'Narrated Oppressive Mechanisms: Chinese Audiences' Receptions of Effeminate Masculinity'. *Global Media and China* 4, no. 2 (April): 254–71. https://doi.org/10.1177/2059436419842667

Zhang, Yinxian, Jiajun Liu, and Ji-Rong Wen. 2018. 'Nationalism on Weibo: Towards a Multifaceted Understanding of Chinese Nationalism'. *The China Quarterly* 235 (September): 758–83. https://doi.org/10.1017/S0305741018000863

Zhang, Zhang. 2015. 'Junxun lei dao yao baojing buquan shi xuesheng de wenti' ['Calling the Police due to Military Training Fatigue: The Students Are Not Entirely to Blame']. *Guangzhou ribao [Guangzhou daily]*. 26 August 2015.

Zhang, Zhiwu. 1987. 'Gaoxiao jiaoyu gaige de zhongyao neirong: xuesheng canjia junshi xunlian' ['Important Content of Educational Reform in Colleges and Universities: Student Participation in Military Training']. *Tiyu Jiaoxue [Physical Education]* 2: 26.

Zhao, Jingru. 1997. 'Qian lun xuesheng junxun shi dangqian qingshaonian guofang jiaoyu de yi xiang youxiao shouduan' ['A Brief Discussion on Student Military Training as an Effective Means of National Defense Education for Young People']. *Zhongguo qingnian zhengzhi xueyuan bao [China Youth Institute of Political Science Journal]* 2: 23–7.

Zhao, Kiki. 2016. 'Chinese Court Upholds Ruling against Historian Who Questioned Tale of Wartime Heroes'. *The New York Times*, 15 August 2016. https://www.nytimes.com/2016/08/16/world/asia/china-hong-zhenkuai-langya.html

Zhao, Lei. 2020. 'China Passes Law to Enhance Veterans' Benefits'. *China Daily*. 11 November 2020. https://global.chinadaily.com.cn/a/202011/11/WS5fab7d12a31024ad0ba93717.html

Zhao, Siwei. 2021. 'Zhe shi er: Re yi "yanggang qi": Xuezhe guanzhu nanhai bian wenruo, you xuexue kai nansheng ban' ['Fact: Hot Discussion on "Masculinity": Scholars are Concerned about Boys Becoming Weak, and Some Schools Open Boys' Classes']. *Pengpai Xinwen* [*ThePaper*]. 30 January 2021. https://www.thepaper.cn/newsDetail_forward_10999144

Zhao, Suisheng. 2013. 'Foreign Policy Implications of Chinese Nationalism Revisited: The Strident Turn'. *Journal of Contemporary China* 22, no. 82 (March): 535–53. https://doi.org/10.1080/10670564.2013.766379

Zhao, Suisheng. 2021. 'From Affirmative to Assertive Patriots: Nationalism in Xi Jinping's China'. *The Washington Quarterly* 44, no. 4 (February): 141–61. https://doi.org/10.1080/0163660X.2021.2018795

Zhao, Suisheng. 2022. 'Is Beijing's Long Game on Taiwan about to End? Peaceful Unification, Brinkmanship, and Military Takeover'. *Journal of Contemporary China* 32, no. 143 (September): 705–26. https://doi.org/10.1080/10670564.2022.2124349

Zhao, Suisheng. 2023. 'The Patriotic Education Campaign in Xi Jinping's China: The Emergence of a New Generation of Nationalists'. *China Leadership Monitor* 1 March 2023, 1–13. https://www.prcleader.org/zhao-spring-2023

Zhao, Yao. 2018. 'Yong dianying jiangshou guofang jiaoyu ke' ['Teaching National Defense Education Classes with Movies']. *Zhongguo Xizang wang* [*China Tibet Net*]. 17 July 2018. http://www.tibet.cn/cn/news/yc/201807/t20180717_6099366.html.

Zhao, Zhongxin. 2003. *Zhongguo jiating jiaoyu wuqiannian* [*Five Thousand Years of Family Education in China*]. Beijing: Zhongguo fazhi.

Zheng, Fudong. 1993. 'Gaodeng xuexiao guofang jiaoyu zhi wo jian' ['My Views on National Defense Education in Institutions of Higher Learning']. *Huazhong li gong daxue xuebao (shehui kexuebao)* [*Journal of Huazhong University of Science and Technology (Social Science Edition)*] 3, no. 16: 89–91.

Zheng, Hao, and Hua-Yu Sebastian Cherng. 2020. 'State-led Chinese Nationalism: An Analysis of Primary School Textbooks'. *China: An International Journal* 18, no. 4 (November): 27–48. https://doi.org/10.1353/chn.2020.0040

Zheng, Haolan. 2021. 'Childhood, Education, and Everyday Militarism in China before and after 1949'. In *Childhoods in Peace and Conflict*, edited by J. Marshall Beier and Jana Tabak, 103–22. Cham: Palgrave Macmillan.

Zheng, Tiantian. 2015. 'Masculinity in Crisis: Effeminate Men, Loss of Manhood, and the Nation-State in Postsocialist China'. *Etnográfica* 19, no. 2: 347–65. https://doi.org/10.4000/etnografica.4026

Zhengzhi yanjiu. 'Ruhe zuo hao xinsheng junxun gongzuo' ('How to Do a Good Job in Military Training for New Students'). 1988. *Zhengzhi yanjiu (Political Studies)* 1: 75–78.

Zhong, Yang, and Wonjae Hwang. 2020. 'Why Do Chinese Democrats Tend to Be More Nationalistic? Explaining Popular Nationalism in Urban China'. *Journal of Contemporary China* 29, no. 121 (June): 61–74. https://doi.org/10.1080/10670564.2019.1621530

Zhonghua renmin gongheguo jiaoyu bu [PRC Ministry of Education]. 2020. 'Guanyu zhengxie shisan jie quanguo weiyuanhui di san ci huiyi di 4404 hao (jiao lei 4210 hao) ti'an dafu de han' ['Reply to Proposal No. 4404 (No. 410 for Education) of the Third Meeting of the 13th National Committee of the Chinese People']. 8 December 2020. http://www.moe.gov.cn/jyb_xxgk/xxgk_jyta/jyta_jiaoshisi/202101/t20210128_511584.html.

Zhonghua renmin gongheguo jiaoyu bu [PRC Ministry of Education]. 2021. 'Gaozhong jieduan xuexiao xuesheng junshi xunlian jiaoxue dagang' ['Syllabus of Military Training for High School Students']. 18 April 2021. http://www.dffyw.com/faguixiazai/xzf/202104/49199.html

Zhongguo guofang bao [China National Defense News]. 2006. 'Quanmin guofang jiaoyu dagang' ['National Defense Education Outline']. 7 December 2006. http://jczs.news.sina.com.cn/2006-12-07/0838417877.html

Zhou, Junlai, and Aichun Li. 2008. 'Junshi tiyu duanlian dui butong jiating beijing daxuesheng xinli zhuangkuang de yingxian' ['Influence of Military Physical Exercise on College Students' Mental Status in Different Family Backgrounds']. *Wuhan tiyu xueyuan xuebao (Journal of Wuhan Institute of Physical Education)* 42, no. 5: 69–73.

Zhou, Viola. 2022. 'An Anti-War Protester in China Got Hugs on the Street. But the Authorities Weren't Impressed'. VICE. 28 February 2022. https://www.vice.com/en/article/88gkkz/china-ukraine-war-protester-russia

Zhu, Pingchao. 2014. 'Mao's Martyrs: Revolutionary Heroism, Sacrifice, and China's Tragic Romance of the Korean War'. *Library of Social Science Newsletter: Ideologies of War* 16, May 2014. https://www.libraryofsocialscience.com/essays/zhu-maos-martyrs/

Zou, Qiang. 2015. 'Zhongxiao xuesheng junxun yu ren gongneng toushi' ['A Functional Perspective on Military Training for Primary and Junior and Senior High School Students']. *Zhongguo deyu [Chinese Moral Education]* 14: 29–33.

Zurndorfer, Harriet. 2018. 'Escape from the Country: The Gender Politics of Chinese Women in Pursuit of Transnational Romance'. *Gender, Place & Culture* 25, no. 4 (March): 489–506. https://doi.org/10.1080/0966369X.2018.1453488

INDEX

Africa
  Belt and Road Initiative (BRI), 3
  In PRC history textbooks, 77
  in the *Wolf Warrior* films, 131, 134, 135, 140
  wars in, 159

Basham, Victoria M., 93, 118
Bax, Trent, 105, 106
Belt and Road Initiative (BRI), 3–4, 82
Blanchette, Jude, 86
body, the
  bio-politics of youth military training, 10, 93, 114–15
  bodily discipline, 10, 41
  'effeminate' bodies of Confucian scholars, 32, 41
  youth military training to strengthen, 41, 55–6, 107–10
  see also youth military training; boys; girls
boys
  bodies, 92–3, 107–10, 112, 115, 178, 182, 202
  'effeminate boys', 107–10, 118, 125–7, 139
  as heroes of war stories, 47, 60
  internet addiction in, 106
  military service as rite of passage for, 9, 182–3, 188, 191
  military education of, 35–7, 40, 42, 55, 92–3, 11–213, 200
  see also gender; masculinity; One-Child policy; youth military training
Brady, Ann-Marie, 119
Büttner, Clemens, 34

Cai E, 35
Callahan, William, 12
'Century of humiliation', 66, 69, 142
Chang, Vincent K. L., 72, 73
Chen Danqing, 113
Chen Tang, 134
Chen, Tina Mai, 60
Chew, Matthew M., 122, 123, 155

Chiang Kai-shek, 39–41, 53–4
child soldiers, 10, 79
childhood
  ideologies of, 9, 39, 47, 58–9, 60, 87–8
  militarisation of, 9–11, 16–17, 29, 61, 197
children
  bodies of, 10, 107, 114
  as 'incomplete' human beings, 39
  internet addiction, 105–6
  in media and culture, 4–23, 46, 119, 129
  as militants, 9, 43, 46, 58–9, 88
  military-style camps for, 104, 120, 200
  as objects of military-style therapy, 92–3, 97, 113, 200
  as political actors, 11, 31, 39, 42–3, 46–7, 56–7, 58–9, 60–2, 79, 87, 198
  propaganda aimed at, 43, 46–7
  rights of, 88, 102, 112–13
  as victims of war, 10, 43, 46–7, 79, 87, 88, 133, 139–41, 154, 168
  see also boys; girls; One-Child policy; youth; youth military training
'China Dream', 3, 14, 73, 75, 77, 83, 88, 99, 121
Chinese Nationalist Party (*Kuomintang* [KMT])
  Civil war with CPC, 43–4, 49, 57, 61, 204
  gender norms, 42, 61
  militarisation strategies, 38, 40–2, 44

New Life Movement (NLF), 40–1
  wartime coalition with the CPC, 72–3
  youth military education, 38–40, 41–2, 44
Chinese Civil War, 43–4, 49, 57, 61, 204
Chinese People's Political Consultative Conference (CPPCC), 109
Chu, Stephen Yiu-Wai, 122
Chubb, Andrew, 148–9
class
  gender ideologies and, 125
  Maoist-era class struggle ideologies, 47, 51, 58, 64, 66, 72–3, 76
  middle classes, 144, 200
  People's Militia training, 52, 61
  socio-economic status of PLA recruits, 101–2, 173, 175–7, 179, 187–9, 194, 202
  youth military training, 27, 94, 100, 101–2
Cliff, Roger, 178
Cold War, 45, 61, 65–6, 71, 76, 82, 84, 198
Communist Party of China (CPC)
  Civil war with KMT, 43–4, 49, 57, 61, 204
  formation, 39
  fostering of citizen love for, 2
  gender norms, 43, 59–60, 108–9, 115, 125–6
  100th anniversary celebrations, 70
  public legitimacy concerns, 6
  use of militias, 43, 50–1

Communist Party of China (CPC) *(cont.)*
  wartime coalition with the KMT, 72–3
  youth military education, 43, 44
'comprehensive national security' concept, 4–7, 86
Communist Youth League, 65, 89 n.1, 96, 105
Compulsory History 1 (CH) textbook
  the costs of war, 79–80
  overview of textbook, 73–4
  on peaceful conflict resolution, 81
  on reunification with Taiwan, 83
  the USA as an obstacle to China's peaceful policies, 84–5
  War of Resistance against Japan, 79–80
Confucianism
  alleged pacifism of, 32
  children in, 39, 42, 56, 58
  education, 36, 39
  gender norms, 42, 126
  masculinity ideals, 32, 41, 125
  morality, 40–1, 56
  scholar-officials, 32–3, 41, 198
  textual tradition, 33
conscription *see* military service
Critical Military Studies, 7–8, 17, 29
Cultural Revolution (CR)
  children as political actors in, 56–7, 58–9, 198
  cultural works, 58, 59, 119

  female militancy, 59, 60, 124
  Mao Zedong's role in, 54–7, 59
  militarisation of youth education, 57–60
  Red Guards, 56–7
  Revolutionary Committees (RCs), 57
  youth's role in, 56–7
culture
  cultural works of the Cultural Revolution, 58, 59, 119
  culture (*wen*)/military (*wu*) masculinity ideal, 32–4, 108, 143
  dissemination of patriotic content, 6
  diverse gender representations in, 125
  see also media; popular culture; propaganda

Dai, Jinhua, 60
Darr, Benjamin, 148
Defence White Paper (2019), 4
'Defend the Homeland and Protect Our Country' slogan, 45
Deng Xiaoping
  crackdown against the Tiananmen protesters, 68
  and Mikhail Gorbachev's state visit, 67–8
  peaceful reunification policy for Taiwan, 82
Deng Xiaoping era
  education reforms, 25–6, 62
  gender ideologies, 125
  ideological and political education under, 97

Index / 257

'reform and opening-up'
    policy, 25, 62, 64–5, 125
    see also Open Door policy
Der Derian, James, 118
Diamant, Neil J., 175
    Diaoyu/Senkaku Islands
        dispute, 85, 147, 149,
        151–2, 156, 163–4, 166

East China Sea, 148, 149, 150,
    163–4
education
    abolition of the civil service
        examination, 35–6
    China's scouting programme,
        38–9
    college enrolment rates, 176
    concerns over masculinity,
        109
    CPC ideological control, 6
    during the Cultural
        Revolution, 57–8, 59–60
    curriculum control during Xi
        era, 72, 74, 75, 83
    during the Deng Xiaoping era,
        25–6, 62
    girls' education, late imperial
        era, 36–7
    during the Maoist era, 25,
        44–9, 54, 55, 57–8,
        59–60
    militarisation of, 10–11, 25,
        29, 31, 145–6, 197–9
    notions of war and peace, 10,
        15–16, 162–3, 165–7
    role of a strong army for
        national security, 55, 61,
        85–6
    state school education system,
        35–7
    see also history teaching;

history textbooks; National
    Defence Education (NDE)
    programme; Patriotic
    Education (PE) campaign;
    youth military training
Edwards, Louise, 61, 88
Enloe, Cynthia, 7–8, 145
ethnic conflicts
    as causes of wars, 76–7
    youth military training
        programme and, 99
ethnic minorities, 19–20, 24,
    69, 99

fascism
    definition in PRC history
        textbooks, 76
    proto-fascism of the KMT,
        40–1
    the War of Resistance against
        Japan as a fight against,
        72

film
    Back to 1942, 154–5
    Black Hawk Down, 169
    The Battle at Lake Changjin, 70,
        124
    Born to Fly, 117, 124, 137–8,
        142
    foreign blockbuster films,
        122
    gender-essentialist
        representations, 126–7
    Hacksaw Ridge, 155, 169 n.2
    Hollywood films, 117, 122–3,
        137–8
    impact on youth belligerence,
        164, 165
    importance of a strong
        military, 133, 142

film (cont.)
  military masculinity, 118, 124–5, 127, 138–9, 143
  military-action genre, 123–4, 127, 163
  'National Defence Education Ten Thousand Screenings Programme', 120–1
  Operation Mekong, 123
  PLA-backed commercial productions, 120, 124, 141–2, 164
  propaganda function, 124
  state-mandated films in schools, 120
  Sparkling Red Star, 129
  The Taking of Tiger Mountain 3D, 123
  War of Resistance against Japan in, 122, 154–5
  see also Operation Red Sea; Wolf Warrior films
First Sino-Japanese War, 32, 34, 76, 79
Fong, Vanessa, 42
Foucault, Michel, 10, 11, 66
Frühstück, Sabine, 118
Fu Qiutao, 52

gender
  'effeminised' men discourses, 32, 41, 108–9, 118, 125, 126, 138–9, 143
  expectations of military service, 27, 192–3
  female militancy during the Cultural Revolution, 59, 60, 124
  gender-essentialism in the media, 27, 126–7
  Maoist era gender ideologies, 59, 60, 124–5
  masculinity discourses, 93, 107–10, 199–200
  military masculinity, 8–9, 16, 27, 200
  military masculinity in films, 118, 124–5, 127, 138–9, 143
  nationalist masculinities, 125–6
  norms of the KMT, 42, 61
  in *Operation Red Sea* (film), 139
  within Patriotic Education (PE), 16
  promotion of youth military training, 92–3
  during 'Reform and Opening Up' era, 125
  in *Takes a Real Man* (TV show), 140–1, 143
  in *Wolf Warrior* films, 138–40
  and youth desire to enlist, 192–3
  youth military training, 92, 107–10
  see also boys; girls
Genevaz, Juliette, 15
girls
  attitudes towards military service, 192–3
  bodies, 93, 112, 200
  'boyish girls', 125
  education in Mao era, 48, 55, 59
  education in Qing era, 36–7
  education in Republican era, 42
  militarisation during Mao era, 59, 60, 198

Index / 259

military training, 111–12
role in war stories, 42, 47, 60–1
Gor, Haggith, 10
Gorbachev, Mikhail, 67–8
Great Leap Forward (GLF)
 failure of, 53, 54
 national defence, 51–2
 use of militias, 51–3
Gries, Peter, 12
Gulf of Tonkin Incident, 54

Harris, Ian, 146
'heroes and martyrs', term, 70
Hird, Derek, 125–6
historical nihilism, 70, 71
History Curriculum Standard (2003), 73
History Curriculum Standard (2017), 74
History Elective 3 (HE) textbook
 costs of war, 78–9, 80
 focus on war and peace, 74
 overview of, 73, 74
 on peaceful conflict resolution, 64, 81
 representation of military conflict, 74
 on reunification with Taiwan, 83
history teaching
 class struggle theory, 72–3, 76
 on the costs of war, 154–5, 168
 Five Heroes of Langya Mountain, 157
 historical materialism, 47
 during the Hu Jintao era, 65–7, 71–3, 79–82, 88
 during the Jiang Zemin era, 69, 71–3

 in the Maoist era, 47–8, 58
 revised historical narratives, 15–16
 state control over, 69–70
 during the Xi Jinping era, 69–70, 74
 and youth perceptions of warfare, 157–9
history textbooks
 children's role in violent conflict, 79, 87, 88
 China's commitment to peace, 67, 81–6, 87, 88–9, 157, 158–9, 199
 costs of war, 78–81, 154, 168
 Five Principles of Peaceful Coexistence, 81, 82, 85, 158–9
 justification for past military interventions, 26, 67
 Korean War, 77–8
 the Opium Wars, 77
 pacifism of the PRC, 67
 primacy of war accounts, 64, 65, 67
 publishers, 75
 reasons wars are fought, 66, 75–8, 87
 on reunification with Taiwan, 82–4
 role of a strong army, 26, 67, 85–6
 struggles against foreign aggression, 77–8, 84
 War of Resistance against Japan in, 15, 47–8, 72, 76, 77, 79–80, 183
 'Who are the most beloved people?' essay, 45, 72
 see also Compulsory History 1 (CH); History Elective 3

history textbooks (*cont.*)
  (HE); Outline of Chinese and Foreign History: Volume One and Volume Two
Hong Kong, 5–6, 24, 32, 122–3, 129–30, 148
Hong Zhenkuai, 157–8
Hu Jintao era, 3, 73–4, 76, 81–2, 89, 120, 159
Hua Mulan, 36
Hughes, Christopher, 15, 95, 96
hukou system, 21, 30 n.4
human rights, 84, 113
Hundman, Eric, 176
Hwang, Wonjae, 149

ideology
  of childhood, 9, 39, 47, 58–9, 60, 87–8
  of class struggle, 47, 51, 56, 58, 64, 72–3, 76
  state ideological control over education institutions, 6
  CPC concerns over ideological security, 6, 14, 54
  individualism as a challenge to CPC ideology, 14, 104
  Maoist era gender ideologies, 59, 60, 124–5
  the media's ideological function, 119, 122
  militarisation, 7–8
  threat of the Tiananmen protest movement, 68
  Xi Jinping thought, 14, 75
  youth support for official ideologies, 11–12
India, 5, 6, 54, 147
Inner Mongolia, 99

international relations
  border conflicts with India, 5, 6, 54, 147
  China as the 'sick man of Asia', 34, 143
  China-Japan relations, 5, 32, 34, 37, 41, 43–4, 47, 55, 61, 72–3, 77, 79
  China-Korea relations, 5–6, 12, 34, 45–9, 63 n.2, 70, 72, 77–8, 84–5, 145, 160–1, 170 n.5
  China-Latin America relations, 3, 204
  China-Russia relations, 5, 32, 65, 205
  China-US relations, 5–6, 45, 62, 72, 78, 84, 148, 152, 204
  Sino-Soviet (USSR) relations, 6, 43, 48, 53–6, 67–8, 73, 83–4, 98, 166
  territorial disputes, 5–6, 54, 147–8, 163–4
  see also Taiwan
Iran, 79, 85
Iraq, 74, 79, 84, 156

Japan
  'comfort women' system, 80, 89 n.5
  cultural products from, 108, 126, 139
  Diaoyu/Senkaku Islands dispute, 85, 147, 149, 151–2, 156, 163–4, 166
  the Japanese Army in Chinese history textbooks, 79–80
  the Japanese Army in PRC cultural products, 122–3
  Meiji era, 35

promotion of the military to youth, 92
see also War of Resistance against Japan
Jiang Zemin era, 82, 119
Jiao Lin, 125

Kao, Ying-Chao, 8
Kauffman, Andrew, 55
Klein, Thoralf, 122
Korean War ('Resist American Aggression and Aid [North] Korea')
  China's role in, 6, 45–6, 49, 63n2, 70, 77–8, 84
  The Battle at Lake Changjin (film), 70, 124
  commemoration of, 1, 70, 72, 145
  in history textbooks, 77–8
  in PRC film, 1, 120
  People's Volunteer Army (PVA), 45, 183
  propaganda during, 45–8, 61
  US involvement in, 45–6, 48–9
  'Who are the most beloved people?' essay, 45, 72, 183

Lam, Dante (Lin Chaoxian), 123, 124, 129
Lanza, Fabio, 55
Law on the Protection of Heroes and Martyrs, 29 n.1, 70–1, 158, 179–80
Lei Feng, 55
Li Haoshi (House) incident, 1–2, 70
Li, Nan, 14

Li, Xiaojun, 150
Lian, Hongping, 13
Liang Qichao, 31, 35
Lin, Jacqueline Zhenru, 175
Lin, Liza, 103, 121
Lin Biao, 51, 57
Lin, Shengqiao, 149–50
'little fresh meat', term, 109, 126, 143 n.1
Liu, Adam, 150
Liu, Fengshu, 13
Liu Hulan, 52, 88, 90 n.9
Liu, Petrus, 118, 135, 138, 140, 143
Luo Changping, 70–1
Lutz, Catherine, 7, 9
Lyu, Zhaojin, 69, 73, 76, 83

Maartens, Brendan, 174
MacFarquhar, Roderick, 56
MacMillan, Lorraine, 9, 201
Main Melody initiative, 119–20, 123
Manchu, 19, 34, 36
Mao Zedong
  ambivalence about children's political role, 59
  and civilian militias, 43, 51, 53
  notion of armed conflict, 43, 47, 49
  the 'People's War', 43, 49, 51, 54
  socialist education campaign, 54, 55
  and Taiwan, 49, 63 n.3
  the Third Front project, 54
  view of female combatants, 59
  see also Cultural Revolution (CR)

Maoist era
  children as political actors, 56–7, 58–9, 61–2, 79, 87
  education, 25, 44–9, 54, 55, 57–8, 59–60
  gender ideologies, 59, 60, 124–5
  history teaching, 47–8, 58
  ideology of class struggle, 47, 51, 56, 58, 64, 72–3, 76
  industrial production, 52, 54
  National Defence Education (NDE), 49–50
  national security threats, 53–4
  the PLA as military models, 45–6, 55, 61, 174, 198
  Sino-Soviet split, 53–4
  Taiwan during, 49, 53–4
  children's media and culture, 45–7, 58, 59, 119
  youth military training, 49–50, 93, 198
martial therapy
  concerns over, 91, 113, 201
  for internet addiction, 104, 106–7
  spread of in care facilities, 26–7, 93, 200
Martin, Roberta, 55
masculinity
  crisis of, 108–9, 125, 127, 199
  culture (*wen*)/military (*wu*) ideal of, 32–4, 108, 143
  'little fresh meat', term, 109, 126, 143 n.1
  military masculinity, 8–9, 16, 27, 29, 34, 61, 93, 109–10, 115, 117–18, 124, 138–41, 143, 182–3, 192–3, 195
  see also boys; gender; youth military training

May Fourth Movement, 37, 39
McSorley, Kevin, 92
media
  commercialisation and globalisation of, 119, 121
  dissemination of patriotic content, 6
  gender-essentialism in, 27, 126–7
  impact on youth belligerence, 164, 165
  influences on youth perceptions of military service, 180–1, 182, 185–6, 190, 194, 195, 202–3
  Main Melody initiative, 119–20, 123
  PLA-backed commercial productions, 27, 117–18, 124, 141–2, 164
  state censorship, 126–7
  state-led initiatives of the Xi Jinping era, 120–1
  state-owned media, 121–2
  war-themed materials during the Korean War, 46–7
  see also popular culture; film; propaganda; television
The Middle East, 77, 85, 183
migrant workers, 15, 20–1, 176
militarisation
  of childhood, 9–11, 16–17, 29, 197
  in contemporary China, 11, 197–8
  definition, 7–8
  of education, 25, 29, 145–6, 197–9
  in Late imperial China, 32–7
  during the Mao era, 44–61

martial masculinity, 9, 16, 200
militarised ethos creation,
 7–8, 10–11, 25
 during the Republican era,
 37–44
militarism
 to counteract China as the
 'sick man of Asia,' 34–5,
 143
 definition, 7
military
 culture (*wen*)/military (*wu*)
 ideal, 32–4, 108, 143
 hegemonic masculinity
 model, 8–9, 183
 popular culture engagement,
 118, 120
 reforms under Deng Xiaoping,
 62
 reforms under Xi Jinping, 4
 strength of in national
 discourses, 3, 26, 55, 61,
 67, 85–6
 students' sources of
 knowledge on, 181–3
 terminology, 24–5
 see also People's Liberation
 Army (PLA)
military entertainment
 (militainment), 9, 117; *see
 also* film; television
military service
 as character building, 182–3,
 191
 conscription challenges, 172,
 173–81, 199, 202
 education level of recruits,
 101–2, 176–8, 179, 180,
 194–5, 202
 enlistment rates, 173–4,
 176–7, 180

gender expectations, 27,
 192–3
 individualism as a challenge
 to, 172, 191–3
 marriage prospects for
 personnel, 175, 177–8
 masculinity ideals and,
 182–3, 188, 191, 192,
 199–200
 media influences on youth
 perceptions of, 180–1,
 182, 185–6, 190, 194, 195,
 202–3
 One-Child policy's impact on,
 172, 177, 189
 Open Door policy's impact
 on, 172, 174
 pre-college military training
 course, 15
 recruitment system, 173, 176
 refusal to serve, 176, 178–9
 socio-economic status of
 recruits, 101–2, 173, 175–7,
 179, 187–9, 194, 202
 voluntary propaganda drives,
 171–2
 youth desire to enlist, 174–5,
 187–8, 194–5, 202
 youth perceptions of, 16, 180,
 183–6, 193–5
Military Service Law, 50, 94,
 173, 179
militias
 CPC's use of, 43, 50–1, 54, 56
 Everyone a Soldier campaign,
 51–3
 People's Militia, 24, 50–1, 54
 reforms under Deng Xiaoping,
 62
Ministry of Education (MOE),
 72, 75, 109

Mitter, Rana, 73
Mongol rule, 34–5

Nagel, Joane, 8
Nathan, Andrew, 71, 72
National Defence Education Law (NDEL), 95
National Defence Education (NDE) programme
  aims of, 2, 26, 97, 148
  curriculum, 12, 26, 29, 65, 148
  demonstration and training bases, 95–6, 120
  in the Deng Xiaoping era, 93–5
  in the Hu Jintao era, 95
  historical overview, 31–2
  in the Jiang Zemin era, 94–5
  during the Maoist era, 49–50
  militarised ethos function, 10, 12, 15
  in propaganda and culture, 119
  in the Xi Jinping era, 95–6
  youth military training, 92, 93, 95–6, 199
  and youth perceptions of the military, 186
  youth-focus of, 2, 26
'National Defence Education Ten Thousand Screenings Programme,' 120–1, 182
National Defence Law (NDL), 95
National Defence Mobilisation Law (NDML), 95
nationalism
  in academic circles, 7
  within the CPC's ideology, 11
  dissemination of patriotic content, 6
  in Maoist era education, 47
  militant nationalism, 8
  nationalist masculinities, 125–6
  nation-building and narratives of warfare, 64, 65, 88
  patriotic education, 6–7
  popular, 11, 12, 71
  role of the PLA, 2
  state-led, 11–12, 14, 68–9, 71, 148
  and support for military intervention, 148–50
  threat perception, 8, 9, 12
  of the Xi Jinping era, 4–7, 11–12, 148
  youth nationalism, 12–15, 16
  see also patriotism
New Life Movement (NLF), 40–1
Ni Dandan, 104
North Korea, 45–6, 78, 85, 113, 160, 185

One-Child policy
  generational impact, 13–14
  impact on gender balance, 178
  impact on military service, 172, 177, 189
  impact on youth values and psychology, 102, 107, 109, 172, 178
  urban male singletons, 14, 107, 109–10, 178
Open Door policy
  education during, 62
  impact on conscription, 172, 174

impact on youth ideals, 97–9
national ideology risks, 4, 11
overview of, 25–6
Operation Red Sea (film)
  box office success, 123–4, 130
  depiction of 'terrorists' in, 129, 133
  entertainment elements, 137
  female characters, 139
  importance of a strong military, 133, 142
  marketisation of the military, 27, 137, 142
  military masculinity, 139, 143
  narrative arc, 129–30
  as a PLA Navy-backed production, 27, 129, 132–3
  righteousness of China's overseas military action, 133, 141–2, 164, 199
  US's portrayal in, 133
  war-action genre, 118, 130
  youth perceptions of the military and, 182
Opium Wars, 32, 68, 76, 77, 105
Outline of Chinese and Foreign History: Volume One (OCFH1) (textbook)
  on China's commitment for peace, 81–2
  on China's military strength, 85
  on the Japanese army, 80
  Korean War, 78
  overview of, 74
  the War of Resistance against Japan, 77
Outline of Chinese and Foreign History: Volume Two (OCFH2) (textbook)
  on China's commitment for peace, 81–2
  costs of war, 79
  on the Japanese army, 80
  overview of, 74–5

Patriotic Education law, 6–7
Patriotic Education (PE) campaign
  aims of, 2, 26, 65, 148
  gendered nature, 16
  during the Hu Jintao era, 71–2
  during the Jiang Zemin era, 65, 68–9, 71–2
  launch of, 26, 65, 67, 68
  militarised ethos function, 12
  military training in, 94
  in propaganda and culture, 119
  representation of war history, 65, 67
  reunification with Taiwan, 82
  school curriculum, 65, 69, 72–4, 83, 89, 90 n.8, 148, 196 n.11, 199, 203
  during the Xi Jinping era, 69, 71–2
  youth military training in, 92, 93, 94
  and youth perceptions of the military, 186
  youth-focus of, 2, 26, 65, 69
patriotism
  cultivation through military training, 49, 99, 102, 114–15
  in Maoist era education, 48–50, 54
  in contemporary Chinese education, 12, 201

patriotism (*cont.*)
  in the media, 9, 27, 119–22, 131, 133, 136, 138–40, 164
  in the Xi Jinping era, 6
  and willingness to enlist, 174
  among Chinese youth, 12, 194
peace
  China's commitment to in history textbooks, 67, 81–6, 87, 88–9, 157, 158–9, 199
  'China's Peaceful Development' (White Paper), 88–9
  commitment to peaceful cooperation of Xi's leadership, 71–2
  and Confucian ideology, 32
  in educational curriculum, 146, 162–3
  Five Principles of Peaceful Coexistence, 81, 82, 85, 158–9
  the 'peaceful rise' of China, 71, 88
  the USA as an obstacle to China's peaceful policies, 84
Pelosi, Nancy, 5
Peng, Altman Yuzhu, 125
Peng Dehuai, 51, 63 n.4, 78
Pennell, Catriona, 7–8
People Armed Police (PAP), 68
People's Education Press (PEP), 75
People's Liberation Army (PLA)
  Bayi Film Studio, 128
  corruption scandals, 184
  crackdown on the Tiananmen pro-democracy movement, 68, 100, 198
  counterterrorism role, 85
  disaster relief efforts, 85
  dissimulation tactics, 118
  fighting capacity, 6
  'Forge exemplary conduct, fight to win' motto, 1
  Gulf of Aden mission, 85
  lack of warfare experience, 6
  during the Maoist era, 45–6, 55, 61, 174, 198
  marketisation of in films, 27, 117, 137–8, 199
  as the 'most beloved people,' 45–6, 183–4
  'never taking any property from the masses' slogan, 183–4
  offence of defamation of military personnel, 1–2, 29 n.1, 70–1, 158, 179–80
  peacekeeping role, 81, 85, 90 n.7, 136, 183
  PLA-backed commercial productions, 27, 117–18, 124, 141–2, 164
  possible preparations for an attack on Taiwan, 5–6, 83
  reforms during the Deng Xiaoping era, 62
  reforms during the Xi Jinping era, 4
  role in civilian society, 54, 57
  role of a strong army in history textbooks, 26, 67, 85–6
  soldiers as social models, 55, 59–61, 93, 136, 174, 198
  socio-economic status of recruits, 101–2, 173, 175–7, 179

technological capacity, 4, 54, 177
uniform, 59–60
veterans' rights and status, 175, 179–80
youth perceptions of, 172, 180, 181–2, 183–6, 193–5
see also military service; military training (youth)
People's Militia, 24, 50–1, 54; *see also* militias
People's Volunteer Army (PVA), 45, 124, 183
popular culture
  global influences in, 119, 121
  Hollywood films, 117, 122–3, 13–78
  from Japan, 108, 126, 139
  Korean wave, 121
  the military in, 9, 10
  the military's engagement with, 27, 118
  New F4 incident, 126
  reproduction of gender hierarchies, 118
  restrictions on South Korean cultural works, 160–1
  see also film; media; military entertainment (militainment); South Korea; television
propaganda
  The Battle at Lake Changjin (film), 70
  and gender norms, 126–7
  during the Korean War, 45–8
  Mao's socialist education campaign, 54, 55
  in Maoist-era children's magazines, 46–7
  PLA-backed commercial productions, 27, 117–18, 124
  in state-owned media, 119, 122
  'Who are the most beloved people?' essay, 45, 72
Putin, Vladimir, 108

Qi, Dongtao, 149–50
Qing Dynasty, 32, 34–7

Rao Yichan, 105, 106, 107
Red Army, 43
Red Guards, 56, 57, 59–60
Republican period, 37–44
'Resist America and Aid [North] Korea' slogan, 45
Revolutionary Committees (RCs), 57
Rofel, Lisa, 135
Russo-Japanese War, 34

Saunders, Philip C., 148
Schillinger, Nicolas, 32, 33
Schoenhals, Michael, 56
Second Sino-Japanese War (War of Resistance against Japan) *see* War of Resistance against Japan (Second Sino-Japanese War)
sexuality, 8–9, 89 n.5, 90. n.6, 110, 118, 138, 143 n.1
South China Sea, 3, 147, 148, 149, 150, 163–4
South Korea
  cultural products from, 108, 121, 126–8, 137, 139, 143n.1, 160–1
  economic sanctions against, 5

South Korea (*cont.*)
  popular protest against, 12
  Terminal High Altitude Area Defence (or THAAD) system, 160–1, 170n.5
Soviet Union (USSR)
  Mikhail Gorbachev's state visit to China, 67–8
  Sino-Soviet split, 53–4, 56
Strand, Sanna, 174

Sun Jiaming, 13
Sun Jing, 122, 146
Sun Yat-sen, 37
Svensson, Marina, 14
Syria, 79, 154, 157
Szablewicz, Marcella, 105

Taiwan
  American support for, 6, 49
  Chinese support for armed unification with, 149–50
  during the Maoist era, 49, 53–4
  possible military preparations for an attack on, 5–6, 83
  reunification in Chinese history textbooks, 82–4
  reunification rhetoric under Xi Jinping, 5, 83, 84, 147
  surrender to Japan, 34
  Taiwanese identity, 83
  2016 election, 83
Taiwan Straits crisis, 51
Takes a Real Man (TV show)
  entertainment elements, 137
  gendered dynamic, 140–1, 143
  marketisation of the military, 27, 136–7, 142
  as a military-themed reality show, 118, 121, 127–9, 135–6
  PLA propaganda work of, 27, 132, 136
  youth as the target audience, 136, 140
  youth perceptions of the military and, 182
Tao Ran, 106
television
  commercialisation of, 121, 122
  Drawing Sword 3, 123
  gender-essentialist representations, 27, 126–7
  Main Melody genre, 123
  political vs entertainment functions, 122–3
  reality TV, 27, 121, 128
  state censorship and propaganda, 126–7
  state-owned media, 121–2
  war dramas, 122–3, 155, 182
  see also *Takes a Real Man* (TV show)
Thomas, Tanja, 8, 118
Tiananmen pro-democracy movement
  events of, 67–8
  the Patriotic Education (PE) campaign and, 65, 67
  PLA's crackdown on, 68, 100, 119, 198
  state censorship over, 185
  youth military training following, 62, 94, 97
  and youth perceptions of the PLA, 184–5
Tibet, 83, 99

Udochi, Aisha Chioma, 135
Ukraine, 5, 205
Unger, Jonathan, 55
United Kingdom (UK), 32, 36, 38–9, 92, 118, 121
United Nations (UN), 45, 63 n.2, 78, 81, 84–5, 90 n.7, 134–5, 169 n.4
United States of America (USA)
  aggressive interventionism, 77–8, 84, 134, 155
  China-US relations, 5–6, 45, 62, 72, 78, 84, 148, 152, 204
  Hollywood films in China, 117, 122–3, 137–8
  in Afghanistan, 84
  in PRC films, 124, 130, 132–5, 144 n.2
  in PRC history textbooks, 84–5
  in Iraq, 84, 156
  JROTC, 92
  Korean War, 45
  Kosovo War, 84
  military recruitment strategies, 174
  promotion of youth military training, 92
  support for Taiwan, 6, 49
  Vietnam War, 54, 84

Van Oudenaren, John, 95, 96, 120
Veterans Law, 179
Vickers, Edward, 69, 75, 86, 111
Vietnam, 6, 54, 62, 84, 147

Wang, Lianzhang, 177
Wang, Xian, 88
Wang, Xuming, 72

Wang, Xun, 13
Wang Yingzi, 122, 123, 155
Wang, Zheng, 69, 73
War of Resistance against Japan (Second Sino-Japanese War)
  Drawing Sword 3, 123
  in film, 122, 154–5
  in history textbooks, 15, 47–8, 76, 77, 79–80, 183
  nationalist ideology and, 43, 61, 72
  war dramas, 122–3
warfare
  children as victims of, 79, 87, 88
  in China's imperial culture, 32–3
  demonstrations against, 84, 205
  economic costs, 151, 161–2
  ethical opposition to, 150–1, 153–5, 159–60
  government presentation of, 2
  'just' and 'unjust' wars, 45, 77, 78, 87, 199
  legitimisation of through education, 10
  nation-building and narratives of, 64, 65, 88
  pragmatic opposition to, 151, 156, 159–60
  revised historical narratives, 15–16
  Terminal High Altitude Area Defence (or THAAD) system, 160
  youth support for use of military force by China, 2, 28, 148–50, 151–2, 153, 163–7, 202

Warlord Era, 37–40
Weatherley, Robert, 69
Weber, Max, 32
Wei, Wei, 45
Weiss, Jessica Chen, 149
Wen Hua, 108, 127
'wolf warrior' diplomacy, 124, 134–5
Wolf Warrior films
  Africa in, 131, 134, 135, 140
  box office success, 123–4, 131, 132
  entertainment elements, 137
  female characters, 139–40
  marketisation of the military, 27, 137, 142, 164, 165
  military masculinity, 138–9, 143
  PLA propaganda work of, 27, 132, 135
  as a PLA-backed commercial productions, 130
  righteousness of China's overseas military action, 133–5, 141–2, 164, 199
  the UN's portrayal in, 134, 135
  the US's portrayal in, 134, 135
  war-action genre, 118
  Wolf Warrior I narrative, 130–1
  Wolf Warrior II narrative, 131–2
  youth perceptions of the military and, 182, 190
women
  under the CCP, 43
  exemption from military service, 173
  girls' education, pre-Republican era, 36–7
  military nursing courses for girls, 42
  see also gender; girls
World War I, 37–8, 74, 157
World War II, 60, 72–3, 76–7, 79, 155, 157, 169 n.2
Wu, Jing, 123, 130–1, 139
Wuthnow, Joel, 83

Xi Jinping
  'Forge exemplary conduct, fight to win' phrase, 1
  intellectual agenda, 70
  on the Korean War, 145
  'Shared Future for Mankind' vision, 159, 169 n.4
Xi Jinping Thought, 14, 75
Xi Jinping era
  anti-corruption campaigns in the PLA, 184
  'China Dream', 3, 75, 77
  China's national rejuvenation, 14, 73, 83, 88, 99, 108, 121
  commitment to peaceful cooperation, 71–2
  'comprehensive national security' concept, 4–7, 86
  foreign policy, 2–6, 147–8, 156
  history teaching, 69–70, 74, 85
  ideological control, 6, 12, 23, 75
  military policy, 4
  National Defence Education (NDE) programme, 95–6
  Patriotic Education (PE) campaign, 71–2
  reunification rhetoric, 5, 83, 84, 147
  role of a strong army, 3, 85–6

state-led nationalism, 4–7, 11–12, 148
use of media initiatives, 120–1
'win–win' phrase, 156
Xiang, Zairong, 138

Xinjiang, 83, 99, 148

Yan, Fei, 60
Yan, Hairong, 104
Yan, Yunxiang, 14
Yang, Mayfair Mei-hui, 60
Yang, Xiao, 60, 135
Yemen, 129, 182
Young Pioneers, 65, 89 n.1
youth
  desire to enlist, 174–5, 187–8, 194–5, 202
  deviant, 27, 107, 115
  individualisation in, 14, 104
  influences on youth perceptions of military service, 180–1, 182, 185–6, 190, 194, 195, 202–3
  internet addiction, 105–6
  militarisation of childhood, 9–11, 16–17
  nationalism trends, 12–15, 16
  notions of war and peace, 146–7, 151–2, 162–3, 165–8
  objections to the use of military force by China, 151, 153–63
  patriotism and party-loyalty, 6, 12–13
  perceptions of military service, 16, 180, 183–6, 193–5
  perceptions of the PLA, 2, 172, 180, 181–2, 183–6, 193–5
  support for use of military force by China, 2, 28, 148–50, 151–2, 153, 163–7, 202
youth military training
  as an antidote to complacent youth, 97–9
  bio-politics of, 10, 93, 114–15
  as character building, 102–4, 114
  under Chinese law, 95
  for civilian-military awareness, 100–2, 110
  class aspects, 27, 94, 100, 101–2
  concerns over, 91, 93, 110, 112–14, 186–7, 201
  contents and goals, 26, 91–2, 95–6
  gendered nature, 27, 92–3
  incidents during, 112–15
  incompatibility with contemporary socio-economic aspirations, 110–12
  under the KMT, 38–40, 41–2, 44
  in the late Qing era, 36–7, 107
  during the Maoist era, 49–50, 93, 198
  martial pedagogies and, 26–7, 92
  masculinity discourses, 93, 107–10, 199–200
  military drills, 95, 96, 97, 102, 110
  national security threat awareness, 98–100

youth military training (*cont.*)
  as part of NDE and PE, 15, 26, 92, 93, 95–6, 199
  patriotic education through, 99, 102, 114
  within the People's Militia, 50–1
  physical fitness and strength, 41, 55–6, 107–10
  post-1978 era, 93–7
  in pre-Republican China, 35, 36
  for primary school children, 103–4
  during the Republican era, 38–40
  scholarship on, 15, 92
  at summer camps, 104
  war education of the Maoist era, 44–9, 57–8, 59–60, 198
  and youth perceptions of the military, 15, 186–7, 201–2
  see also martial therapy
Yuan Shikai, 37

Zarrow, Peter, 32
Zeng, Xiaodong, 69, 111
Zhang, Boshu, 71, 72
Zhang, Qiang, 69
Zhang, Suixin, 149–50
Zhao, Kiki, 157
Zhao, Suisheng, 12, 82
Zheng, Haolan, 10, 61
Zhong, Yang, 149
Zhou Enlai
  Five Principles of Peaceful Coexistence, 81
  on the Korean War, 77–8
Zhou, Haiyan, 69, 73, 76, 83
Zhou Zhengtian, 139
Zurndorfer, Harriet, 125, 126

EU Authorised Representative:
Easy Access System Europe Mustamäe tee 50, 10621 Tallinn, Estonia
gpsr.requests@easproject.com

Printed and bound by CPI Group (UK) Ltd, Croydon, CR0 4YY